COLLAPSE
and
RECOVERY

COLLAPSE
and
RECOVERY

How the COVID-19 Pandemic Eroded Human Capital and What to Do about It

Norbert Schady, Alaka Holla,
Shwetlena Sabarwal,
Joana Silva, and Andres Yi Chang

 WORLD BANK GROUP

ISBN (paper): 978-1-4648-1901-8
ISBN (electronic): 978-1-4648-1934-6
DOI: 10.1596/978-1-4648-1901-8

Cover and interior design: Nicole Hamam, Hamam Design

Library of Congress Control Number: 2023931863

CONTENTS

Boxes

Figures

Tables

FOREWORD

We are living at a time when multiple crises compete for our attention. The world just experienced a global pandemic that triggered a global recession and a reversal of decades of progress in reducing extreme poverty. Meanwhile, war and conflict, new and old, are affecting many countries, and the hazards associated with a warming climate are building up into yet another crisis.

Today, a focus on human capital is more important than ever. Human capital—the health, knowledge, skills, and experience that people accumulate over their lifetime—is a key driver of productivity and economic growth. In addition, it helps individuals cope with shocks. But shocks also interrupt human capital accumulation. Moreover, shocks frequently affect poor people the most, and so they tend to exacerbate inequality. Because the acquisition of human capital is cumulative and sequential, losses sustained early in individuals' lives, if not addressed, can haunt them into adulthood—and can even limit the human capital accumulation of their children. Setbacks in human capital can therefore jeopardize the welfare of multiple generations.

As part of the World Bank's role in supporting low- and middle-income countries seeking to build human capital, it is important that we take stock of what happens to human capital during a large, global shock such as the COVID-19 pandemic. How large was the setback, and how far are we still from a recovery? It is clear, however, that we need to focus on new ways to protect human capital and recover from systemwide shocks, as well as build resilience for the future.

This report is the first comprehensive analysis of what happened to human capital during the pandemic. It focuses on individuals who were 25 years or younger at the outset of the pandemic. These cohorts will make up 90 percent of prime-age adults in 2050. They are the workforce of tomorrow.

Data available today suggest that there were serious declines in many dimensions of human capital during the pandemic. Young children missed vaccinations and other critical services, and their cognitive and social-emotional development declined. One billion school-age children missed at least a year of schooling, and they learned little, if anything, while schools were shuttered. Meanwhile, young workers could not find a job or entered the labor market with fewer skills. As the report shows, the pandemic truly resulted in a collapse in human capital accumulation, especially among the poor.

In addition to quantifying the magnitude of the losses from the pandemic and proposing a menu of evidence-based policies capable of recovering these losses, this report takes a step back to review governments' responses to the crisis, assessing *why* there was a collapse in human capital accumulation, *what* was missing in the policy architecture to protect human capital during the crisis, and *how* governments can better prepare to withstand future shocks.

Just as a swift and strong macroeconomic policy response helped many countries climb out of the pandemic recession, a similarly rapid and robust effort can help societies recover from the less visible collapse in human capital. Unaddressed, this collapse will have long-lasting harmful effects on individual and aggregate welfare. Charting a new course for human capital should start now. The quality of life and economic opportunities of billions of people depend on it.

Mamta Murthi
Vice President, Human Development Practice Group
The World Bank

ACKNOWLEDGMENTS

This report would not have been possible without the generous support of a team of colleagues and collaborators. Special thanks are due to Mamta Murthi, Vice President for Human Development (HD), World Bank, for her leadership. Margarita Isaacs and Diego Parra in the HD Chief Economist Office provided outstanding research assistance.

This effort greatly benefited from the many contributions of Noam Angrist, Laura Becerra, Sharnic Djaker, Ritika D'Souza, Aart Kraay, and Shrihari Ramachandra. The authors are also very grateful to Chris Andersen, Ugo Gentilini, Yuko Okamura, Owen Smith, and Michael Weber for their many valuable inputs to chapter 5 and the publication as a whole. Important examples of country responses to the COVID-19 pandemic were provided by Luis Benveniste, Amit Dar, Daniel Dulitzky, Halil Dundar, Melis Guven, Huma Kidwai, Toby Linden, Keiko Miwa, Jamele Rigolini, Dena Ringold, and Fadia Saadah.

This report benefited considerably from the comments and suggestions of its peer reviewers, including Francisco Ferreira, Amartya Sen Professor of Inequality Studies, and Director, International Inequalities Institute, London School of Economics; Deon P. Filmer, Director, Development Research Group (DECRG), World Bank; Jesko Hentschel, Country Director for Maghreb and Malta, World Bank; Ana María Ibañez, Principal Economics Adviser, Inter-American Development Bank; William Maloney, Chief Economist, Latin America and the Caribbean, World Bank; and Carolina Sanchez, Director, Strategy and Operations for the Europe and Central Asia Vice Presidency, World Bank.

The authors are also very grateful for the insightful comments from World Bank colleagues Rythia Afkar, Salman Asim, Kathleen Beegle, Christian Bodewig, Fadila Caillaud, Eliana Carranza, Daisy Demirag, Amanda Devercelli, Lelys Dinarte, Maria Marta Ferreyra, Emanuela Galasso, Koen Geven, Salina Giri, Melis Guven, Maddalena Honorati, Sachiko Kataoka, Victoria Levin, David McKenzie, Shinsaku Nomura, Berk Ozler, Iamele Rigolini, Halsey Rogers, Michal Rutkowski, Iffath Sharif, Meera Shekar, Lars Sondergaard, Victoria Strokova, Diego Ubfal, Ian Walker, Michael Weber, and Emily Weedon as well as from David Evans at the Center for Global Development.

Participants in several regional presentations provided helpful comments. At the World Bank, the HD Regional Directors—Luis Benveniste, Amit Dar, Daniel Dulitzky, Keiko Miwa, Dena Ringold, Fadia Saadah, and Lynne Sherburne-Benz—as well as the HD Global Directors—Hana Brixi, Michal Rutkowski, Jaime Saavedra Chanduvi, and Juan Pablo Uribe—and other members of the HD leadership also provided valuable feedback.

Nicole Hamam designed the volume, including the cover art. Nancy Morrison skillfully edited the report, which was copyedited by Sabra Ledent and Elizabeth Forsyth. Gwenda Larsen proofread the typeset pages, and Stephen Pazdan in the World Bank's formal publishing program coordinated production of the volume.

ABOUT THE AUTHORS

LEAD AUTHORS

Alaka Holla is a Senior Economist in the Human Development Chief Economist Office of the World Bank and Program Manager of the World Bank's Strategic Impact Evaluation Fund, a multidonor trust fund that promotes the use of randomized controlled trials and quasi-experimental methods to inform policies in education, health, water and sanitation, and early childhood development in low- and middle-income countries. Since joining the World Bank as a Young Professional, she has worked in both research and operational settings in a diverse set of country contexts and on multilateral initiatives to promote the measurement of child development and the costing of programs. Holla has published in peer-reviewed publications such as the *American Economic Review, Health Affairs,* and *Journal of Public Economics.* She also has been a coauthor of World Bank reports such as the flagship *World Development Report 2015: Mind, Society, and Behavior* and *Citizens and Service Delivery: Assessing the Use of Social Accountability Approaches in the Human Development Sectors.* Her research has focused on the quality of health care, discrimination, early childhood development and education, and cost analysis. Holla received her PhD in economics from Brown University and completed postdoctoral work at Harvard University and Innovations for Poverty Action.

Shwetlena Sabarwal is a Senior Economist in the World Bank's Education Global Practice. She was a coauthor of *World Development Report 2018: Learning to Realize Education's Promise, World Development Report 2019: The Changing Nature of Work,* and *The COVID-19 Pandemic: Shocks to Education and Policy Responses.* Her research, which focuses on education service delivery, teacher effectiveness, and teacher and student mindsets, has been published in leading journals. Sabarwal leads the World Bank's Education and Climate Change Global Solutions Group and has led the World Bank's education engagement in Bangladesh, Nepal, Saudi Arabia, Tanzania, and Uganda. She holds a PhD in applied economics from the University of Minnesota.

Norbert Schady is Chief Economist for Human Development at the World Bank Group. Previously, he was Principal Economic Adviser, Social Sector, at the Inter-American Development Bank (2010–21); at the World Bank he was Senior Economist in the Development Research Group (2003–10), Economist in the Poverty Group of the Latin America and the Caribbean region (2000–2003), and a Young Professional (1998–2000). He has also taught at Georgetown University and Princeton University. Schady has published extensively in academic journals, including in the *American Economic Journal: Applied Economics, American Economic Journal: Economic Policy, Journal of Development Economics, Journal of Human Resources, Quarterly Journal of Economics,* and *Review of Economics and Statistics,* among many others. He is also the author of numerous flagship reports, including *The Early Years: Child Well-Being and the Role of Public Policy, Conditional Cash Transfers: Reducing Present and Future Poverty,* and *Closing the Gap in Education and Technology.* Schady's main research areas are early childhood development, teacher quality, cash transfer programs, and the effects of economic contractions on the accumulation of human capital. He received a BA from Yale University and a PhD from Princeton University.

Joana Silva is a Senior Economist in the Human Development Chief Economist Office of the World Bank and an associate professor at Católica Lisbon School of Business and Economics. She has expertise in applied economics, labor economics, international economics, development economics, and public economics.

Silva has led several World Bank lending operations and has extensive experience advising governments—in particular, on the design, implementation, and evaluation of economic reforms, social programs, and monitoring and evaluation systems. Her research has been published in leading academic journals, including the *American Economic Review* and *Journal of International Economics*. She has coauthored five books, including three World Bank regional flagship reports: *Employment in Crisis: The Path to Better Jobs in a Post–COVID-19 Latin America*, *Wage Inequality in Latin America: Understanding the Past to Prepare for the Future*, and *Inclusion and Resilience: The Way Forward for Social Safety Nets in the Middle East and North Africa*. She holds a PhD in economics from the University of Nottingham.

Andres Yi Chang is an Economist in the Human Development Chief Economist Office of the World Bank. He began working at the World Bank in 2015, first in its Research Development Group and then in its Human Development Chief Economist Office in 2019. Before joining the World Bank, he worked at Yale University, the Organization of American States, the Pan American Health Organization, and Leibniz University Hannover. His research and operational experience are in the areas of education, health, and social development projects in low- and middle-income countries, particularly in Africa, Latin America, and Southeast Asia. Yi Chang has a BA in economics from the University of California–Berkeley, and an MA in international and development economics from Yale University.

CONTRIBUTING AUTHORS

Noam Angrist is a Senior Fellow at the University of Oxford and a cofounder of Youth Impact, one of the largest nongovernmental organizations dedicated to scaling up health and education programs backed by rigorous randomized trial evidence. Headquartered in Botswana, the organization has expanded evidence-based programs to over 100,000 youth across 10 countries. Angrist has published in leading academic journals, including the *Journal of Economic Perspectives*, *Nature*, and *Nature Human Behaviour*. He has consulted for the World Bank Chief Economist and the Chief Economist of the United Kingdom's Foreign, Commonwealth and Development Office, and he codeveloped the education pillar of the World Bank's Human Capital Index, which included developing a new global measure of education—Harmonized Learning Outcomes and Learning-Adjusted Years of Schooling. He also led the academic research underpinning the inaugural report of the Global Education Evidence Advisory Panel, which reviewed over 150 impact evaluations in education, providing recommendations on cost-effective approaches to improving learning outcomes in low- and middle-income countries. Angrist was a Fulbright and Rhodes scholar; he received a BS in mathematics and economics from the Massachusetts Institute of Technology and a PhD from the University of Oxford.

Ritika D'Souza is an Economist in the Human Development Chief Economist Office of the World Bank. She works on the Human Capital Index (HCI) and related analytics, including methodologies for the socioeconomic and spatial disaggregation of the HCI. She is also engaged in World Bank lending operations in Africa, with a focus on education in fragile contexts. Previously, D'Souza worked in the South Asia Chief Economist Office, where her research covered nutrition, education, gender, and jobs. She has also managed the field implementation of impact evaluations of agriculture, food security, and nutrition projects in Nepal and Rwanda with the World Bank's Development Impact Evaluation (DIME) group. D'Souza holds an MA in public administration from the School of International and Public Affairs at Columbia University.

MAIN MESSAGES

Worldwide, COVID-19 (coronavirus) was an enormous shock to health, economies, and daily life. But what has yet to be fully acknowledged is the pandemic's impact on young people's trajectories through life. Indeed, it is a ticking time bomb.

This report focuses on human capital—the health, knowledge, and skills that people accumulate over their lifetime. Often, it is the only asset poor people have and is what determines a person's productivity and earnings. Human capital trajectories are set during childhood, adolescence, and early adulthood. Shocks like the COVID-19 pandemic reduce both the levels of human capital and the subsequent rates of accumulation. If losses continue to be unaddressed, both lifetime earnings and economic growth will decline for decades to come. Losses will also increase inequality.

COVID-19 knocked individuals off course at critical moments in their lives. This report estimates the impacts of the pandemic on the human capital of young children (0–5), school-age children (6–14), and youth (15–24) and discusses the urgent actions needed to reverse the damage.

What was the pandemic's impact on people 24 years of age and younger? Early childhood is a critical period for brain development and lays the foundations for skills such as literacy and mathematics. Because of the pandemic, very young children missed essential vaccinations and stopped going to preschool. There was also unprecedented stress in families. The declines observed in cognitive and social-emotional development are alarming. In Bangladesh, for example, toddlers tested in 2022 lagged far behind toddlers tested in 2019. The observed declines, unless remedied, could translate into a 25 percent reduction in earnings when these children are adults.

The pandemic also resulted in school closures everywhere. Nearly 1 billion children in low- and middle-income countries missed at least one year of in-person schooling. And despite enormous efforts in remote learning, the data reveal that children did not learn during the closures. On average, each month of school closure led to one month of lost learning. For some students, losses were even greater because many forgot things they had already learned. The learning losses observed today could reduce future earnings around the world by US$21 trillion.

Youth is another crucial stage in the life cycle. At this stage, young people are making important decisions such as whether to stay in school, work, or raise a family. COVID-19 led to dramatic drops in employment and a worse transition for young people into the labor market. The number of youth neither employed nor enrolled in education or training increased substantially. In Pakistan alone, the pandemic created 1.6 million additional idle youth. Moreover, in several countries analyzed there was little sign of recovery after 18 months. Being unemployed or holding a low-paying job when one first enters the labor market can result in "scarring." Evidence suggests that scarring can last for up to 10 years.

In all these stages—early childhood, school age, and youth—the impacts of the pandemic were consistently worse for children from poorer backgrounds. The pandemic could therefore increase inequality between and within countries. All age groups also suffered marked declines in mental health.

These losses are a call for action. People who were under the age of 25 when the pandemic hit will make up 90 percent of the prime-age workforce of 2050. Faced with this true collapse in human capital, what can countries do? The good news is that there are evidence-proven strategies to recover these losses. Extending the coverage of pre-primary education and improving its content are good examples. Both would have short-term benefits, helping children become more prepared to learn. Over the long term, they have been shown to increase college attendance and earnings. They have even been shown to lower the propensity to commit crime.

For school-age children, simply having them back in school will not be enough. A child who stopped going to school in second grade and stayed home for a year will not be able to follow a fourth-grade curriculum. It will be important to match instruction to these students' levels of learning. Increasing instructional time and catch-up programs—such as tutoring—can also reverse learning losses.

Youth need help for a good start in the labor market. For countries in which youth employment has not yet recovered, training, entrepreneurship programs adapted for youth, and apprenticeships are particularly important.

All of these programs—across all three life stages—will not just address human capital losses. When higher individual earnings and tax revenue and a lower need for social assistance are factored in, most of these programs targeting children and youth end up paying for themselves and have higher returns than those targeting adults.

To address losses in human capital and better prepare for future shocks such as climate change, wars, and recessions, a new approach is needed, and it requires political will to act. In some cases, interventions in health will be most appropriate to address specific losses in human capital. In others, it may be that policies in education or social protection are the most effective. In the majority of cases, however, solutions that bring these sectors together into a human development system are needed. Evidence suggests that during the COVID-19 crisis very few countries responded with integrated approaches, and most lacked the capacity to collect and link data from programs in different sectors. This must change.

Faced with other global pressures and fiscal constraints, some countries may find the list of policy options too long. This report sets out an approach to help countries prioritize their options. It emphasizes the importance of targeting recovery policies to children who are about to transition or just transitioned to a subsequent stage in the life cycle. These defining moments can create skill deficits that interfere with the entire trajectory of human capital accumulation.

This report also provides estimates of the full cost of each proposed policy. This cost includes fiscal costs as well as costs stemming from implementation complexity and political commitment. It highlights that many of the proposed policies do not require important fiscal efforts. Rather, they require institutional capacity building and political will.

It is nearly impossible to overstate the severity of COVID-19's impact on young people. If countries fail to act now, the losses documented in this report will become permanent and last for multiple generations. Starting now is critical.

ABBREVIATIONS

ALMPs	active labor market policies
COVID-19	coronavirus disease 2019
CSO	civil society organization
DPT	diphtheria, pertussis, and tetanus
GDP	gross domestic product
HD	human development
HIV-AIDS	human immunodeficiency virus-acquired immune deficiency syndrome
HLO	Harmonized Learning Outcome
IQ	intelligence quotient
IRT	item response theory
ISAS	Integrated Social Assistance Information System (Türkiye)
LAYS	Learning-Adjusted Years of Schooling
MPL	minimum proficiency level
NEET	Not in Education, Employment, or Training
NGO	nongovernmental organization
OECD	Organisation for Economic Co-operation and Development
PFM	public financial management
PPR	pandemic preparedness and response
SMEs	small and medium enterprises
TARL	Teaching at the Right Level
TVET	technical and vocational education and training
UIS	UNESCO Institute for Statistics
UNESCO	United Nations Educational, Scientific, and Cultural Organization
WHO	World Health Organization

EXECUTIVE SUMMARY

Everybody is eager to return to normal ... but normal is not enough.

—Thomas Kane, Center for Education Policy Research, Harvard University
"All Things Considered," National Public Radio, June 22, 2022

❝

COVID-19 (coronavirus), first detected in Wuhan, China, in late December 2019, spread around the world, culminating in a global health emergency. It was quickly followed by a deep economic contraction in virtually every country. The world tumbled into recession, and the overall global gross domestic product (GDP) shrank by 4.3 percent in 2020.

These figures hide immense human suffering. By December 2021, there were 14.9 million excess deaths globally—deaths attributable to the pandemic.[1] Poverty increased dramatically. There were 70 million more people living in extreme poverty in 2020 than in 2019—an 11 percent increase. To put things in context, this increase in extreme poverty is roughly four times larger than the spike in poverty during the Asian financial crisis of 1997–98.[2]

The consequences of the pandemic, however, were not limited to its effects on mortality, economic growth, or poverty. Households were ridden with stress. Mental illness, domestic violence, teen pregnancy, and early marriage spiked in some settings. Millions of children lost a caregiver or were orphaned. Many more missed out on vital nutrition and health care and suffered declines in early childhood development. Nearly 1 billion children missed a year or more of schooling and learned little, if anything, while schools were closed. Tens of millions of young people were shut out of the job market or entered it with fewer skills and diminished prospects. Taken together, these effects represent a profound loss of human capital. Unless they are reversed, these losses will lead to declines in productivity and earnings as the children and youth of today become the labor force of tomorrow.

The erosion of human capital from the pandemic—and what to do about it—are the subjects of this report. Although many of the consequences of the pandemic may not fully emerge for years (or even decades), this report presents solid evidence of the impacts of the pandemic to date. It assesses the impact of the pandemic using new individual- and household-level data from low- and middle-income countries and reviews the existing literature. It extracts lessons from actions and policies implemented around the world in response to the pandemic, as well as past evidence on program effectiveness. Moreover, the report recommends concrete policies for the short and medium term that will help recover human capital losses from the pandemic and prepare for future shocks.

It is useful to start with a working definition of human capital. *Human capital* refers to the health, skills, knowledge, and experience that people accumulate over their lifetime. Not just of intrinsic value, these attributes also make people more productive. Or, put differently, human capital is wealth embodied in people. Indeed, for many poor people around the world, their human capital is the *only* important source of wealth they have.

Building human capital requires sustained investments along multiple dimensions. The process is *sequential* and *cumulative*: skills build on earlier skills, and current skills beget future skills.[3] Although human capital can be acquired over an entire lifetime, it is built most effectively when people are young. There are a variety of reasons for this, including greater brain plasticity at early ages and the fact that younger people are generally expected to engage in activities that deliberately build skills (such as formal schooling). Any disruption to the process of building human capital can have long-lasting effects. There is evidence from earlier crises that the effects of shocks to human capital can reverberate across multiple generations.

Human capital losses not only affect individuals through declines in their future earnings. They also can have negative economywide effects. Human capital is one of the main drivers of economic growth, and so, anything that erodes it, could result in lower growth rates for many years to come. Indeed, the long-term costs of the pandemic—working through the reductions in human capital caused by the pandemic—are likely to dwarf the short-term costs.[4]

The erosion of human capital from the pandemic was greatest among poorer households. This erosion could lead to a sharp increase in inequality in the future—an increase that would compound the rising inequality already observed in many countries in recent decades. Lower wages, more poverty, more inequality, and less growth are an explosive mix.

So what should be done? After quantifying the present collapse of human capital among young people under the age of 25, this report describes interventions that governments must put in place quickly to limit and reverse the damage. Concrete examples illustrate that recovery is possible if the right actions are taken. However, if countries fail to prioritize these efforts, they risk having multiple lost generations of children and young people—the workforce of tomorrow. The time to act is short.

And what should governments do now to better prepare for systemic shocks in the future? The report also discusses the kinds of agile, resilient, and adaptive human development systems that need to be in place for a country to respond to future shocks, whether an epidemic (or pandemic), a natural disaster, or an aggregate economic crisis. This is truly a case in which an ounce of prevention is worth a pound of cure, and where the costs of not preparing can be enormous.

THE PANDEMIC DESTROYED HUMAN CAPITAL AT CRITICAL MOMENTS IN THE LIFE CYCLE

The pandemic led to a sharp decline in human capital at critical stages of the life cycle. This report focuses on changes in human capital during early childhood (0–5 years), among school-age children (6–14 years), and in early adulthood (15–24 years). People younger than 25 today—those most affected by the erosion of human capital—will make up 90 percent of the prime-age workforce in 2050.[5]

Poor start: The impact of the COVID-19 pandemic on early childhood development

The first five years of life are a period of rapid brain development and physical growth. Early life experiences shape both the architecture and functions of the brain and can even modify which genes are expressed.[6]

Learning during these early years is the foundation for later learning, as children begin to learn about numbers, language, and social interactions and develop executive functions such as inhibition and working memory.[7] Early nutrition and health also determine physical and mental health and cognitive skills later in life.

The pandemic led to sharp reductions in critical inputs for child development. In many countries, as household incomes shrank and lockdowns made it difficult for households to access markets, food insecurity increased. Compared with 2019, the share of households reporting smaller food portions for children increased dramatically in 2020—by 68 percent in Sierra Leone, 69 percent in Kenya, and 100 percent in Bangladesh.[8]

Concurrently, lockdowns and restrictions on movement, fears of infection in the community, and shortages of frontline health care staff led to declines in the use of health services critical for children. Some of these declines occurred even before children were born. Relative to the levels observed in 2019, births in hospitals and clinics fell by more than 14 percent in Nigeria and 25 percent in Haiti. This is a concern because births not attended by health staff have a higher risk of complications and death for mothers and their children, and complications in birth can also result in disabilities in childhood and adulthood. In addition, millions of young children were not fully vaccinated against diphtheria, pertussis, and tetanus in 2020, thereby reversing approximately 10 years of global progress in combating preventable diseases.[9]

The quality of the home environment experienced by young children deteriorated sharply during the pandemic. One recent study estimates that by May 2022, at least 7.5 million children had been orphaned by the pandemic, with the largest numbers in Sub-Saharan Africa and South Asia.[10] Moreover, even in the absence of death, the pandemic led to a decline in the mental health of mothers and a rise in the proportion of young children subjected to harsh corporal punishment—both of which are predictive of worse child outcomes.[11]

Preschools closed almost universally at the beginning of the pandemic and remained closed for a year or longer in many countries. Even after they reopened, enrollment levels in preschool have continued to be below their pre-pandemic levels in many countries—by between 10 and 15 percentage points in Brazil, Pakistan, and South Africa. Moreover, in countries where the coverage of preschool was high (such as Brazil), the largest losses in preschool coverage occurred among households with low socioeconomic status. Children acquire many skills in preschool, and missing preschool can leave them ill-prepared for the beginning of elementary school and can even reduce their chances of completing high school and moving on to tertiary education.[12]

Data on child development (specifically, cognitive, language, motor, and social-emotional skills) are not collected regularly in most countries, and so little was known about these outcomes in the first months of the pandemic. Nevertheless, the declines in the various contributors to child health and development just discussed were clear cause for concern. Data from a few low- and middle-income countries have now become available, and they are worrisome.

Studies of toddlers in a lower-middle-income country, Bangladesh, and preschool-age children in an upper-middle-income country, Brazil, find large declines in child development and early learning (figure ES.1).[13] Pandemic-induced losses in cognitive, language, and motor skills in Bangladesh (figure ES.1, panel a) were concentrated among the most vulnerable children, thereby widening preexisting gaps. Nonetheless, effects did not vary by the gender of the child. A simple exercise that uses evidence from a well-known study in Jamaica to "translate" these declines in development into expected reductions in earnings suggests that, unless remediated, young children affected by the pandemic could have earnings in adulthood that, on average, are roughly 25 percent lower than they would have been in the absence of the pandemic.[14] In a sample of preschools from Sobral, Brazil (figure ES.1, panel b), the cohort starting preschool in 2020 learned only two-thirds of what the 2019 cohort had learned over an entire school year. The cohort starting preschool in 2021 could not be assessed at the start of the year (schools were closed), but their test scores at the end of the year (black dot) suggest they lost even more learning than the 2020 cohort.

FIGURE ES.I The pandemic led to steep losses in early childhood development and early learning in very young children in Bangladesh and Brazil

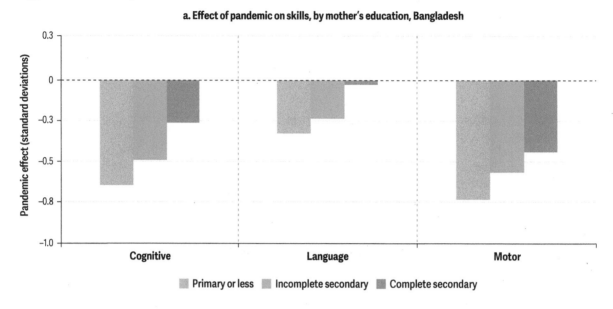

a. Effect of pandemic on skills, by mother's education, Bangladesh

■ Primary or less ■ Incomplete secondary ■ Complete secondary

b. Language learning during school year (2019, 2020, 2021 cohorts), Brazil

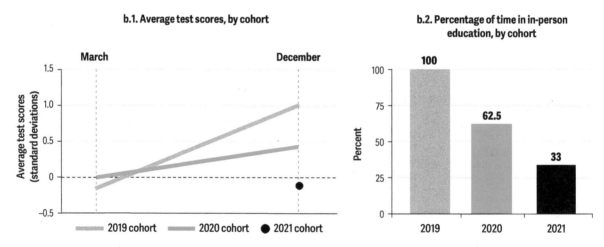

b.1. Average test scores, by cohort

2019 cohort — 2020 cohort ● 2021 cohort

b.2. Percentage of time in in-person education, by cohort

Sources: Panel a: Hamadani et al, forthcoming. Panel b: Maria Cecilia Souto Vidigal Foundation 2021.
Note: Panel a: Children are 20 months old. Panel b: Children are in preschool. See chapter 2 for additional figure details.

Learning losses and dropouts: The heavy cost of the COVID-19 pandemic on school-age children

A very large literature, spanning hundreds of studies, shows that schooling—both its quantity (as measured by years of schooling completed) and its quality (as measured by amount of learning)—is a robust predictor of labor market success. Indeed, for millions of people around the world schooling is the only pathway to a better, more prosperous life.

In March 2020, when the pandemic first hit, schools closed in 180 countries. One year later, in March 2021, schools were still partially or fully closed in 94 countries. Overall, 1.3 billion children in low- and middle-income countries missed at least half a year of school; 960 million missed at least a full year; and 711 million missed a year and a half or more.[15] Schools were closed for a particularly long time in Latin America and the Caribbean and South Asia, but within regions there was considerable variation in the length of school closures. For example, between April 2020 and March 2022, schools were closed for 61 days in Tanzania but 448 days in Uganda; 107 days in Morocco but 326 days in Saudi Arabia; and 47 days in Vietnam but 510 days in the Philippines.

Once school closures went into effect, nearly all education systems pivoted to remote learning. However, remote learning was not accessible to all. Globally, more than two-thirds of children ages 3–17 (1.3 billion children) lack internet access at home.[16] And parents, especially those who themselves have low levels of education, were ill-equipped to help their children. In Indonesia, for example, 29 percent of parents reported that they had insufficient time, and 25 percent reported lacking the capacity to support their children in learning from home.[17] In Bangladesh, 39 percent of students in the bottom socioeconomic quartile received support from a family member, compared with 62 percent in the top quartile.[18]

Lengthy school closures had two effects on human capital. First, they led to deep learning losses. In fact, this report shows that one month of school closures led to one month of learning lost, on average. Put differently, little learning occurred while schools were closed, despite widespread remote-learning efforts.

This pattern is evident in panel a of figure ES.2, which summarizes the results from dozens of studies and plots months of learning lost against months of school closures by country. Most countries fall somewhere near the 45-degree line, where months of learning lost are equal to the months of school closures. Overall, for every 30 days of school closures, students lost about 32 days of learning.[19] Across all these studies, the average learning loss was 6.2 months, and the average length of school closures was 5.9 months.

Learning losses seem to have been larger in countries with lower GDP per capita, after controlling for the length of school closures (see panel b of figure ES.2, which plots the ratio of learning loss to school closures against log GDP per capita). Although high-, middle-, and low-income countries all show steep learning losses, the ratio of learning losses to school closures is larger in lower-income countries.[20] Therefore, the pandemic exacerbated inequality in learning outcomes because lower-income countries had lower achievement to begin with.

For countries above the 45-degree line in panel a of figure ES.2, months of lost learning were larger than months of school closure. This finding implies that not only was there *forgone* learning—learning that would have occurred had schools remained open—but also *forgotten* learning—erosion of skills children had mastered before schools closed. In Bangladesh, for example, 14.5 months of school closures led to nearly 26 months of learning lost. For example, a 10-year-old girl who knew how to add and subtract at the beginning of the pandemic and was next meant to learn how to multiply and divide did not learn these new skills (forgone learning) but also forgot how to add and subtract (forgotten learning). This is the stark reality in many countries, especially lower-income ones, and it portends the magnitude of the challenge ahead.

In addition, some children did not return to school even after schools reopened. Student dropouts did not increase notably in upper-middle-income countries, but the picture is different in lower- and lower-middle-income countries. In Ethiopia and Pakistan, for example, school enrollment among children ages 6–14 dropped by 4 percentage points and 6 percentage points, respectively, once schools reopened. Declines in enrollment were similar for boys and girls, but they were substantially larger for children in households in which adults had lower levels of education.

Dropouts are a concern because children who acquire less schooling will have less human capital, be less productive, and earn lower wages. Moreover, it may take time for dropouts to materialize and could become a larger issue if policies are not put in place to limit learning losses. If children cannot keep up with the material taught in class, they will become unmotivated and may eventually leave school. This could occur in any grade, but especially in grades that correspond to the transition from one education level (for example, primary school) to the next (for example, lower-secondary school), when many students abandon school. This is a concern in both upper-middle-income and poorer countries.

FIGURE ES.2 During the pandemic, each month of school closures led to one month of learning losses, and more so in countries with lower GDP per capita

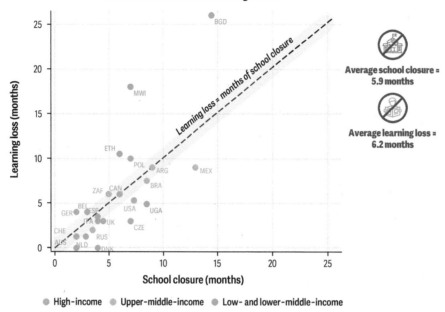

a. School closures versus learning losses

Learning loss = months of school closure

Average school closure = 5.9 months

Average learning loss = 6.2 months

● High-income ● Upper-middle-income ● Low- and lower-middle-income

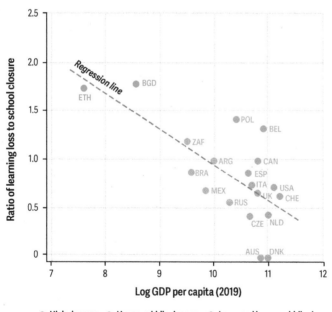

b. Ratio of learning losses to school closures versus GDP per capita

Regression line

● High-income ● Upper-middle-income ● Low- and lower-middle-income

Source: Original calculations for this publication.
Note: See chapter 3 for additional figure details. For country abbreviations, see International Organization for Standardization (ISO), https://www.iso.org/obp/ui/#search.

Lost opportunities: The protracted effect of the pandemic on youth and young adults

Youth (ages 15–24) is the period when people make the transition from mainly accumulating to utilizing human capital.[21] Young people may be in school, employed (whether formally or informally and in high- or low-wage jobs), or idle. They can also engage (or not) in behaviors such as unprotected sex, drug use, criminal activity, and gang membership.

The decisions made by young people have long-term consequences—and the pandemic affected them in critical ways. First, at the outset of the pandemic youth suffered deep employment losses (figure ES.3). In 10 of the 12 countries in figure ES.3, there was a decline in youth employment in the second quarter of 2020, ranging from 1 percentage point in Vietnam to 11 percentage points in the Philippines. The exceptions are the two lower-income countries in the sample, where youth employment increased—by 1 percentage point in Ethiopia (2021) and by 3 percentage points in Pakistan.

Figure ES.3 also reveals substantial differences in the pattern of recovery. By the end of 2021, youth employment had recovered fully and exceeded pre-pandemic levels in Brazil, Mexico, and Türkiye. On the other hand, there is no evidence of a recovery in South Africa, while in Bulgaria, Jordan, and—especially—Vietnam, youth employment continued to decline throughout 2021. These job losses were compounded by declines in wages for young people in many countries.

FIGURE ES.3 Youth employment fell in most countries during the pandemic
Percentage point change in youth employment (ages 15–24)

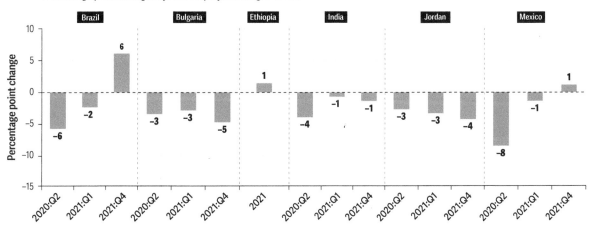

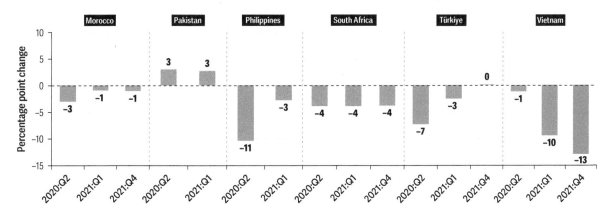

Source: Original calculations for this publication, based on data from labor force surveys.
Note: See chapter 4 for additional figure details. Q = quarter.

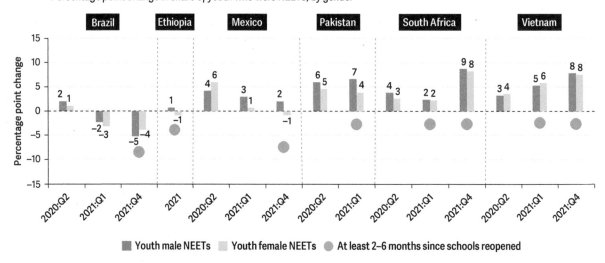

FIGURE ES.4 Declines in employment of young people during the pandemic were not offset by increases in schooling or training

Percentage point change in share of youth who were NEETS, by gender

Source: Original calculations for this publication, based on data from labor force surveys.
Note: See chapter 4 for additional figure details. NEET = Not in Education, Employment, or Training; Q = quarter.

The implications of job losses are very different if young people who, in normal times, would have been employed seek more schooling instead. To gauge whether this occurred in practice, figure ES.4 plots the effects of the pandemic on the proportion of young people, by gender, who are Not in Education, Employment, or Training (NEETs) in six countries that collected data on both employment and school enrollment. The share of NEETs increased in most countries, even after schools reopened. Although the results of the analysis suggest that the differences in pandemic effects across gender were modest, structural impediments to women's participation in the labor market are far higher in many countries than they are for men's participation.

Declines in employment not matched by increases in school enrollment are a grave concern for two reasons. First, time out of the labor force is time spent without acquiring on-the-job experience, and such experience is a key way to build human capital. Second, time spent out of work can lead to *scarring* in the labor market. In the United States, for example, individuals entering the labor market in a typical recession (associated with a 4–5 percentage point rise in unemployment rates) have initial earnings that are 10–15 percent lower than those of similar cohorts entering labor markets in "normal" times. These negative effects may not fade out for a decade.[22]

Finally, evidence suggests that beyond the labor market, the pandemic worsened a variety of outcomes for young people in some settings, including higher rates of teenage pregnancy, worse mental health, and declines in the development of key social-emotional skills and executive functions. However, fewer data are available on these outcomes than for schooling and employment.

POLICIES TO REVERSE HUMAN CAPITAL LOSSES

The pandemic eroded human capital at critical ages. Whether this erosion leads to a permanent reduction in future stocks of human capital depends on both the size of the initial drop in the *level* of human capital as well as the *rate* at which human capital accumulates thereafter. This point is illustrated in figure ES.5, which shows three possible paths for an individual.

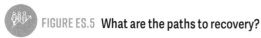 FIGURE ES.5 What are the paths to recovery?

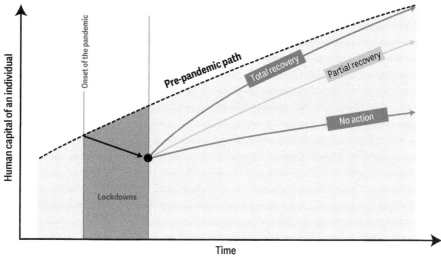

Source: Original figure for this publication.

Because human capital is built in a sequential, cumulative fashion, in the absence of remediation policies early deficits will increase over time. This is the worst-case scenario in figure ES.5 (red line), which shows an increasing divergence in human capital accumulation relative to the pre-pandemic path.

It is also possible that, after the initial drop, human capital grows along a trend exactly parallel to its pre-pandemic path (yellow line). Two points are important about this scenario. First, because the effect of shocks tends to compound over time, setting out on this recovery path implies substantial investments in human capital over and above those that would have been made in the absence of the pandemic. Second, this scenario only results in a partial recovery of human capital losses. Thus, in this scenario the stock of human capital would still be lower in the future.

Finally, as figure ES.5 illustrates, the only path that does not entail permanent losses in human capital is the one in which human capital grows at a higher rate after the initial shock (green line). Achieving this convergent path is a tall order. It would mean, for example, that children would have to learn more in every grade in school than they were learning before the pandemic. However, this is the only path by which individuals and countries can achieve the levels of human capital they would have had in the absence of the pandemic.

Figure ES.5 clearly indicates the magnitude of the task ahead. It is possible to recover human capital losses, but it will require a substantial sustained effort—including, but not only, additional expenditures. With this framework in mind, this section points out what actions should receive priority at each stage in the life cycle. Some of the most important ones are summarized in table ES.1.

Young children have missed critical investments in health and preschool, and their levels of cognition, vocabulary, and early learning in math and language have in many cases dropped dramatically. To prevent this poor start from amplifying into greater human capital losses as these children progress along the life cycle, policies should prioritize transfers for households whose income has not recovered, catch-up campaigns for vaccination and nutrition, parenting programs to encourage more cognitive and social-emotional stimulation in the home, restored and expanded coverage of pre-primary education, and mental health counseling programs for parents.

School-age children suffered from unprecedented school closures. They learned little if anything while schools were closed, and so their learning losses are massive. In addition, some children may be at risk of dropping out of school altogether, especially in lower-income countries. To reverse learning losses,

TABLE ES.1 There are evidence-proven policies that can reverse human capital losses

Life cycle phase	Challenge	Policy recommendations
Early childhood	*For infants and toddlers* • Declines in immunizations and possible declines in nutritional status • Deficits in cognitive, language, social-emotional, and motor skills *For children ages 3–5* • Deficits in cognitive, early literacy, early numeracy, social-emotional, and motor skills	• Support targeted campaigns for vaccinations and nutritional supplementation. • Expand coverage of cash transfers for households with young children. • Increase coverage of parenting programs. • Expand coverage of pre-primary education. • Insert social-emotional skills into curricula and plan transitions to primary school.
School-age children	Learning losses—in both low- and middle-income countries School dropouts—primarily in lower-income countries	• Keep schools open and increase instructional time. • Assess learning, match instruction to students' level, launch catch-up campaigns for students who have fallen furthest behind. • Focus on foundations and streamline the curriculum. • Create a political commitment for learning recovery. • Track students at risk of dropping out. • Alleviate financial constraints and provide incentives for students to attend school.
Youth	Employment losses among young people Declines in enrollment in upper-secondary school, university, TVET institutions More young people neither studying nor working Teenage pregnancy, impairments in mental health, and worse social-emotional skills in some contexts	*Policies will vary by country type:* • In countries where neither youth nor adult employment has recovered, focus policies primarily on the demand side, encouraging firms to start hiring again. • In countries where adult employment has recovered and youth employment has not, emphasize supply-side policies such as adapted training, job intermediation, entrepreneurship programs, and new workforce-oriented initiatives for youth. • In countries where both adult and youth employment have recovered, there is no emergency. *Policies also vary within country by age:* • For younger youth (ages 15–18), support conditional cash transfers and information campaigns. • For older youth (ages 19–24), make post-secondary education relevant and engaging and partner with service providers and the private sector to offer short-term practical credentials.
Human development systems	Sector-specific pandemic responses unable to protect all dimensions of human capital across the life cycle Existing systems unable to deliver support and services at the scale required during the crisis	• Invest in data collection and information systems to provide targeted support when required. • Leverage technology to deliver services (including developing cross-sectoral beneficiary registries, platforms, and payment systems). • Invest in coordination mechanisms (including joint committees with representation from all ministries involved in different aspects of human capital). • Invest in flexible payment systems and contractual mechanisms that allow for the rapid reallocation of resources in response to evolving crises (including agile cross-sectoral public finance management systems and contractual relationships with the private sector to meet surges in demand).

Source: Original table for this publication.
Note: TVET = technical and vocational education and training.

decision-makers should keep schools open and increase instructional time, assess learning and match instruction to students' learning level, implement targeted catch-up policies such as tutoring for children who have fallen the furthest behind, and streamline curricula to focus on foundational learning. To minimize dropouts, countries should track students at risk of dropping out, especially in transition years, and alleviate the financial constraints to school attendance.

Youth have suffered from sharp declines in their job prospects, and the extent to which employment has recovered varies a great deal across countries. Appropriate policies will therefore vary by country—in particular, by the extent to which there has been a recovery of both adult and youth employment. For countries where neither adult nor youth employment has recovered, policies should primarily be geared toward demand-side interventions that spur firms to start hiring again. For countries where adult employment has recovered but youth employment has not, support for supply-side policies such as adapted training, job intermediation, entrepreneurship programs, and new workforce-oriented initiatives for youth are all important. Countries where both adult and youth employment have recovered should monitor developments in the labor market to ensure that the recovery has been equal across groups. In all countries, policies should recognize that youth are a diverse group and that skills are the best insurance against a crisis.

BUILDING AGILE, RESILIENT, AND ADAPTIVE HUMAN DEVELOPMENT SYSTEMS FOR FUTURE SHOCKS

The COVID-19 pandemic has arguably been the largest global shock to human capital in the past century. Moreover, countries will continue to face shocks in the future—health and climate emergencies, natural disasters, and macroeconomic crises—that, like the pandemic, can erode human capital across the life cycle. In addition to impeding human capital accumulation at each stage of the life cycle, the pandemic has revealed systemic weaknesses in how governments integrate efforts across sectors to address the multidimensional nature of human capital deficits. In some cases, interventions in health will be most appropriate to address specific losses in human capital; in others, it may be that education or social protection policies are most effective. But in most cases, countries need solutions that bring these sectors together into a holistic human development system. Evidence suggests that during the COVID-19 crisis, very few countries responded with integrated approaches, and most countries lacked the capacity to collect and link data from programs in different sectors.

Such a human development system should build on existing sector-specific systems and individual programs to take a broader look at how investments in human capital could be coordinated and how complementarities could be exploited. In a crisis, human development systems can help policy makers resolve trade-offs across many competing needs in a constrained fiscal environment. To be effective, such systems should have three key characteristics:

1. They should be agile, resilient, and adaptive and able to expand and contract quickly during crises to reach vulnerable groups.
2. They should have a mandate and authority to coordinate across sectors, identify interventions that are complementary, and resolve trade-offs.
3. They should be data-driven, effectively use technology, and identify problems and "pain points" as a crisis unfolds.

To build these systems, countries need to invest in data collection and information systems to provide targeted support when required. They also need to leverage technology to deliver services (including cross-sectoral beneficiary registries, platforms, and payment systems) and to invest in coordination mechanisms (including joint committees with representation from all ministries involved in aspects of human capital). Finally, countries should invest in flexible payment systems and contractual mechanisms that allow for the rapid reallocation of resources in response to an evolving crisis.

During the pandemic, most countries were able to expand existing programs in all sectors, but especially in health and social protection. For example, Argentina relied on expansions of Programa Sumar to ensure access to health care for the unemployed. Social protection programs grew rapidly during the pandemic, reaching nearly 1.4 billion people (17 percent of the world's population) over 2020–21. Notably, countries that had made earlier investments in technology, such as in interoperable beneficiary identification and payment systems, were able to expand social assistance coverage faster.

Some countries were also able to retool, redirect, or reactivate programs built in response to earlier shocks. Sierra Leone adapted the social safety net systems set up to respond to Ebola, flooding, and landslides for use in rolling out cash transfers and providing additional types of support during the pandemic. Some countries were able to engage service providers beyond the traditional public sector to deliver services. For example, in 2020 and 2021 the Indian state of Kerala contracted with more than 300 private hospitals so it could add them to the publicly funded insurance scheme for the poor and vulnerable to help sustain service delivery during the pandemic. This expansion—effectively more than doubling the number of private hospitals in the scheme—built on years of previous engagement of the private sector by the state government. Uruguay was able to move from in-person instruction to remote learning during the pandemic thanks to Plan Ceibal, a functional remote-learning program launched in 2007 that has helped ensure access to free laptops for students and teachers, has provided them with internet connections, and, critically, has trained teachers in remote instruction over the last decade.

By contrast, truly cross-sectoral approaches were rare. By and large, countries failed to assess the costs and benefits of specific sectoral policies *jointly*. The timing and length of lockdowns and mobility restrictions generally did not take into account the coverage of social protection, which made it difficult for households to comply with the restrictions. Keeping schools closed for as long as many countries did, even after restrictions on the use of public transportation had been lifted, and markets, stores, movie theaters, and restaurants had opened, reflected a failure to balance competing risks—the risk of infection in schools (low) relative to the risk of learning losses (high)—and to update policy choices as new information became available.

A HUMAN CAPITAL RECOVERY: WHAT WILL IT TAKE?

Table ES.1 lists, for each phase of the life cycle, policy recommendations for recovering from pandemic-induced human capital losses and building resilience for the next shock. The list is long, particularly in the context of competing crises and tight fiscal space.

Which policies should countries put at the top of their human capital recovery list? First, an emphasis on transition periods in the life cycle—from early childhood to school age, from one level of education to another, from school to work, and from youth to adulthood—can help stem the accumulation of losses. Transitions are defining moments: what happens during these stages may generate deficits that interfere with the entire trajectory of human capital accumulation in subsequent stages of the life cycle.

Second, the report also provides evidence on the full cost of each proposed policy. This full cost includes fiscal costs, as well as costs stemming from implementation complexity and political commitment required. It highlights that many of the proposed policies do not require important fiscal efforts. Rather, they require institutional capacity building and political will.

Recovery is possible, and many countries have already made progress in recovering losses in human capital that arose from the pandemic. In Pakistan, for example, more than 1.2 million children missed immunizations during the first year of the pandemic, but intensive outreach efforts, in part enabled by an electronic immunization registry, contributed to successful catch-up efforts that had immunized 76 percent of these children by March 2021.[23] In Tamil Nadu, India, school-age children exhibited severe deficits in reading and math when they returned to in-person learning after pandemic-induced school closures. After six months, two-thirds of the losses had been recovered, with 24 percent of the recovery attributable to government-run after-school catch-up programs.[24]

The pandemic may have led to a clear-cut collapse in human capital, but what is needed to get on a path of recovery is equally clear. Transforming the collapse into a recovery should begin now.

NOTES

1. Msemburi et al. (2022).
2. World Bank (2022).
3. Heckman (2006).
4. World Bank (2022).
5. Original calculations for this publication. The International Labour Organization (ILO) defines prime-age adults as those between the ages of 25 and 55.
6. Fox, Levitt, and Nelson (2010); Johnson (2001); Mukherjee (2016).
7. Spelke and Schutts (2022).
8. Egger et al. (2021); Miguel and Mobarak (2021).
9. WHO and UNICEF (2021).
10. Hillis et al. (2022).
11. Bau et al. (2022); Bullinger et al. (2021); Moya et al. (2021).
12. Bailey, Sun, and Timpe (2021).
13. For Bangladesh, Hamadani et al. (forthcoming); for Brazil, Maria Cecilia Souto Vidigal Foundation (2021).
14. Gertler et al. (2021); Grantham-McGregor et al. (1991).
15. These estimates include school-age children from pre-primary to upper-secondary education (ages 5–17) from 140 countries with a school-age population of 500,000 or more. For simplicity, it is assumed that one school year is equal to 32 academic weeks across all countries. World Bank estimations are based on data from the United Nations Educational, Scientific, and Cultural Organization (UNESCO) Institute for Statistics (UIS).
16. UNICEF and ITU (2020).
17. UNICEF, UNDP, and SMERU (2021).
18. Biswas et al. (2020).
19. This estimate is derived from a simple linear regression of learning losses on school closures with no constant.
20. This relationship is robust to a number of specifications, such as including all countries, excluding high-income countries, limiting the sample to the highest-quality studies, or excluding data points that disproportionately influence the regression results. Resulting coefficients are all significant and in the range of −0.28 to −0.42.
21. The chapter uses the terms *youth* and *young people* interchangeably.
22. Von Wachter (2020).
23. Chandir et al. (2021).
24. Singh, Romero, and Muralidharan (2022).

REFERENCES

Bailey, M. J., S. Sun, and B. Timpe. 2021. "Prep School for Poor Kids: The Long-Run Impacts of Head Start on Human Capital and Economic Self-Sufficiency." *American Economic Review* 111 (12): 3963–4001.

Bau, N., G. Khanna, C. Low, M. Shah, S. Sharmin, and A. Voena. 2022. "Women's Well-Being during a Pandemic and Its Containment." *Journal of Development Economics* 156: 102839.

Biswas, K., T. M. Asaduzzaman, D. K. Evans, S. Fehrler, D. Ramachandran, and S. Sabarwal. 2020. "TV-Based Learning in Bangladesh." World Bank, Washington, DC.

Bullinger, L. R., A. Boy, S. Messner, and S. Self-Brown. 2021. "Pediatric Emergency Department Visits Due to Child Abuse and Neglect following COVID-19 Public Health Emergency Declaration in the Southeastern United States." *BMC Pediatrics* 21 (401): 1–9.

Chandir, S., D. A. Siddiqi, M. Mehmood, S. Iftikhar, M. Siddique, S. Jai, V. K. Dharma, et al. 2021. "1-Year Impact of COVID-19 on Childhood Immunizations in Pakistan: Analysis of >3.7 Million Children." *European Journal of Public Health* 31 (Suppl. 3): ckab164.538.

Egger, D., E. Miguel, S. S. Warren, A. Shenoy, E. Collins, D. Karlan, D. Parkerson, et al. 2021. "Falling Living Standards during the COVID-19 Crisis: Quantitative Evidence from Nine Developing Countries." *Science Advances* 7 (6): eabe0997.

Fox, S. E., P. Levitt, and C. A. Nelson, III. 2010. "How the Timing and Quality of Early Experiences Influence the Development of Brain Architecture." *Child Development* 81 (1): 28–40.

Gertler, P., J. J. Heckman, R. Pinto, S. M. Chang, S. Grantham-McGregor, C. Vermeersch, S. Walker, et al. 2021. "Effect of the Jamaica Early Childhood Stimulation Intervention on Labor Market Outcomes at Age 31." NBER Working Paper 29292, National Bureau of Economic Research, Cambridge, MA.

Grantham-McGregor, S. M., C. A. Powell, S. P. Walker, and J. H. Himes. 1991. "Nutritional Supplementation, Psychosocial Stimulation, and Mental Development of Stunted Children: The Jamaican Study." *The Lancet* 338 (8758): 1–5.

Hamadani, J., M. Imrul, S. Grantham-McGregor, S. Alam, M. Tipu, D. Parra Alvarez, S. Shiraji, et al. Forthcoming. "The Effect of the COVID-19 Pandemic on Children's Development and Nutritional Status at Age 20 Months in Rural Bangladesh."

Heckman, J. J. 2006. "Skill Formation and the Economics of Investing in Disadvantaged Children." *Science* 312 (5782): 1900–02.

Hillis, S., J. P. N. N'konzi, W. Msemburi, L. Cluver, A. Villaveces, S. Flaxman, and H. J. T. Unwin. 2022. "Orphanhood and Caregiver Loss among Children Based on New Global Excess COVID-19 Death Estimates." *JAMA Pediatrics* 176 (11): 1145–48.

Johnson, M. H. 2001. "Functional Brain Development in Humans." *Nature Reviews Neuroscience* 2 (7): 475–83.

Maria Cecilia Souto Vidigal Foundation. 2021. "Learning in Early Childhood Education and the Pandemic: A Study in Sobral/CE." https://www.fmcsv.org.br/en-US/biblioteca/impacto-aprendizadem-covid-sobral/.

Miguel, E., and A. M. Mobarak. 2021. "The Economics of the COVID-19 Pandemic in Poor Countries." NBER Working Paper 29339, National Bureau of Economic Research, Cambridge, MA.

Moya, A., P. Serneels, A. Desrosiers, V. Reyes, M. J. Torres, and A. Lieberman. 2021. "The COVID-19 Pandemic and Maternal Mental Health in a Fragile and Conflict-Affected Setting in Tumaco, Colombia: A Cohort Study." *The Lancet Global Health* 9 (8): e1068–e1076.

Msemburi, W., A. Karlinsky, V. Knutson, S. Aleshin-Ghendel, S. Chatterji, and J. Wakefield. 2022. "The WHO Estimates of Excess Mortality Associated with the COVID-19 Pandemic." *Nature* 613: 130–37.

Mukherjee, S. 2016. *The Gene: An Intimate History*. New York: Scribner.

Singh, A., M. Romero, and K. Muralidharan. 2022. "COVID-19 Learning Loss and Recovery: Panel Data Evidence from India." NBER Working Paper 30552, National Bureau of Economic Research, Cambridge, MA.

Spelke, E., and K. Schutts. 2022. "Learning in the Early Years." In *Quality Early Learning: Nurturing Children's Potential*, edited by M. Bendini and A. E. Devercelli. Washington, DC: World Bank.

UNICEF (United Nations Children's Fund) and ITU (International Telecommunication Union). 2020. "How Many Children and Young People Have Internet Access at Home? Estimating Digital Connectivity during the COVID-19 Pandemic." New York: UNICEF and ITU.

UNICEF (United Nations Children's Fund), UNDP (United Nations Development Programme), Prospera, and SMERU (SMERU Research Institute). 2021. "Analysis of the Social and Economic Impacts of COVID-19 on Households and Strategic Policy Recommendations for Indonesia." Jakarta.

Von Wachter, T. 2020. "The Persistent Effects of Initial Labor Market Conditions for Young Adults and Their Sources." *Journal of Economic Perspectives* 34 (4): 168–94.

WHO (World Health Organization) and UNICEF (United Nations Children's Fund). 2021. "Progress and Challenges with Sustaining and Advancing Immunization Coverage during the COVID-19 Pandemic: 2021 WHO/UNICEF Estimates of National Immunization Coverage (WUENIC)." WHO and UNICEF, Geneva and New York.

World Bank. 2022. *Poverty and Shared Prosperity 2022: Correcting Course*. Washington, DC: World Bank.

1

A HUMAN CAPITAL CAPITAL COLLAPSE

The Impact of the COVID-19 Pandemic on Early Childhood, School-Age Children, and Young Adults

Alaka Holla

ABSTRACT

The future of 90 percent of the prime working-age population in 2050 has been jeopardized by the COVID-19 pandemic. An individual's human capital grows in a cumulative fashion, building on earlier investments. Human capital accumulates unevenly across the life cycle, with the most rapid growth in the early childhood, school-age, and adolescent periods. Shocks during these sensitive periods reduce both the level of subsequent human capital and the future rate of accumulation so that, without remediation, the impacts of shocks amplify over time. Countries therefore have three potential post-pandemic pathways: permanently lower trajectories, partial recovery, or complete recovery. A complete recovery is possible but would require governments to act immediately.

A PENDING CRISIS IN PRODUCTIVITY COULD LAST FOR MULTIPLE GENERATIONS

The COVID-19 pandemic not only led to death; it also triggered the first increase in extreme poverty in more than two decades and deepened global inequality.[1] Less visible but potentially longer lasting have been its effects on human capital—the wealth embodied in people's health, knowledge, skills, and emotional and mental well-being. Long after the pandemic has been declared over, these effects will work their way through economies and societies around the world.

Setbacks in human capital among individuals under the age of 25 today threaten not only individual prosperity and welfare but also future economic growth.

The lockdowns associated with the pandemic and the resulting economic slowdowns have jeopardized the ability of current cohorts of children and youth to accumulate the skills, knowledge, health, and experience that are essential for them to be productive workers as adults and to invest in their own children's human capital.[2] These setbacks, in turn, threaten both individual prosperity and welfare as well as aggregate economic growth for coming generations. Indeed, evidence suggests that differences in human capital across countries can account for half to three-quarters of cross-country differences in income.[3]

Unlike the case of physical capital, when it would be apparent if a machine were malfunctioning or equipment was held up along a supply chain, setbacks in human capital are less visible. It is empirically challenging to estimate how much variance in human capital can be attributed to single causes, such as the pandemic. Moreover, without relatively sophisticated and regular measurement, it is difficult to observe declines in people's cognitive skills or mental health unless they lead to obvious functional impairments. School systems in many low-income countries struggle to implement and reach all children with a common assessment that can help to diagnose proficiency levels for even basic skills such as reading and math. Shortfalls in social-emotional skills—or "soft skills," as they are sometimes called—are not always noticeable and are even more difficult to measure,[4] although evidence to date suggests that these skills determine much of an individual's success in school and the labor market.[5] Unlike a person in immediate need of oxygen, a mother in need of mental health care is unlikely to attract the same sense of urgency, although the implications of her crisis for her children's and her own future productivity can be quite dire.[6]

Without an ambitious agenda to identify, quantify, and reverse the impacts of the COVID-19 pandemic on human capital, governments, donors, and multilateral organizations will fail to stem a pending crisis in productivity that could last for multiple generations. This report gathers the latest evidence on the impacts of the pandemic on human capital and identifies the unique attributes of human capital that should be considered when designing policies and systems to recover losses and dampen the effects of future shocks.

Public investments to improve children's human capital generally pay for themselves and have much higher returns than those targeting adults.

Many studies to date have carefully predicted or documented the effects of the pandemic for single dimensions of human capital, such as learning,[7] nutrition,[8] and mental health,[9] and for single age groups, such as children in primary school or prime working-age adults. None, however, has addressed the pandemic's impacts on the total stock of human capital expected in the future or the multisectoral policy agenda needed to recover the losses in human capital observed today; none has restricted its attention to studies that estimate the impacts of the pandemic relative to what would have prevailed in its absence (that is, relative to a valid counterfactual situation). Using new individual- and household-level data from low- and middle-income countries and reviews of the existing literature to assess impacts, this report examines all dimensions of human capital together—physical and mental health, skills, employment, and experience—and concentrates on the three stages of the life cycle when human capital accumulates most rapidly: early childhood (gestation to age 5), school age (ages 6 to 14), and youth (ages 15 to 24). Together these cohorts will make up approximately 90 percent of the prime-age workforce in 2050.[10]

Examining the impacts of the COVID-19 pandemic on multiple dimensions of human capital for multiple segments of the life cycle highlights both the depth of setbacks caused by the pandemic and the implications for what is needed to recover future productivity. These multiage and multidimensional setbacks, along with the variation in choices that governments made during the height of the pandemic, also make evident the need for a policy agenda that actively engages and coordinates the sectors typically responsible for promoting human capital—such as education, health, and social protection—and that creates systems able to respond to future threats to human capital accumulation.

BUILDING HUMAN CAPITAL REQUIRES SUSTAINED INVESTMENTS ALONG MANY DIMENSIONS FROM MANY SOURCES

Human capital refers to the health, skills, knowledge, and experience that people accumulate over their lifetime and that translate into productivity when they enter the labor market and invest in their own children. It is not something that can be purchased as a whole; instead, building human capital requires sustained investments along multiple dimensions from multiple sources.

Human capital increases when parents or other caregivers in the home invest material and time in their children. A child's health, for example, depends on both the food she eats and the cleanliness of her home environment. When her parents regularly play, sing, and read with her, they are helping to advance her language, motor, and social-emotional skills and set her up for success once she enters formal schooling. Lack of wealth and disposable income constrain the extent to which parents can purchase inputs that promote human capital, such as a diet with adequate nutrients or after-school tutoring. Parents' capacity to make these investments also depends on their own human capital. An illiterate parent may not be able to read to his child or fully understand a treatment protocol recommended by a doctor, which in turn could inhibit the child's acquisition of literacy skills or deepen the impacts of illness. Likewise, a parent suffering from anxiety or depression may find it difficult to play with her children or assist in the regulation of their emotions, making it more difficult for them to acquire the social-emotional skills, such as focus and perseverance, that foster learning in a formal classroom setting.

Governments also invest in human capital through the provision, financing, or monitoring of services, such as health care, childcare, education, employment programs, and social assistance. Evidence indicates that public investments in children's health and education yield such high returns—higher wage earnings, less criminal activity, and less reliance on social assistance in adulthood—that government programs aiming to improve children's human capital generally pay for themselves. Notably, these returns are much higher than returns to investments in human capital or income support for adults.[11]

In many countries, the non-state sector—for-profit firms, non-profit organizations, and religious groups—also provides these services, sometimes serving as the dominant service provider in some areas. For example, nearly 50 percent of total health care expenditure in low- and middle-income countries is private, and in some countries such as India, private health care providers account for nearly 75 percent of primary care providers,[12] while globally private organizations provide more than 40 percent of pre-primary education.[13]

Due to its multidimensional nature and the role of both caregivers in the home and public and private services in promoting human capital accumulation, effective investments need not fit neatly into specific sectors. For example, cash transfers to households can improve the mental health of children and adolescents.[14] Similarly, home visits in which nurses counsel parents on best practices to promote the nutrition and cognitive stimulation of their children can partially substitute for pre-primary education.[15]

HUMAN CAPITAL TRAJECTORIES ARE SET DURING CHILDHOOD, ADOLESCENCE, AND EARLY ADULTHOOD

> *Life cycle skill formation is a dynamic process in which early inputs strongly affect the productivity of later inputs.*
>
> —James Heckman, Nobel Laureate in Economics (Heckman 2006)

Human capital, like physical capital, works like an investment. Spending on it today generates returns in the future. Unlike physical capital, however, returns to investments may not be immediately apparent, as tangible returns to human capital investments—such as protection from chronic diseases, improvements in earnings, more innovation and better adoption of technology, and reduction in criminal activities—accrue with a very long lag.[16] A preschool program in the United States, for example, generated no contemporaneous effects on IQ but 20 years later increased school completion, salaries, and home ownership and decreased criminal activity and reliance on social assistance.[17]

Because multiple decades can pass before investments yield monetary value, there may be underinvestment in human capital, as pressing policy concerns with more immediate payoffs (such as increasing the employment of prime-age adults today) compete for attention. Moreover, human capital accumulates unevenly over the life cycle, and what happens in earlier periods of an individual's life cycle greatly determines his or her future trajectory.

The process of human capital accumulation starts as early as the time of conception.[18] Short-lived fasting during gestation, for example, decreases a child's birthweight and test scores in primary school and increases the likelihood of disability in adulthood.[19]

During the *early childhood* period (from gestation through age 5), children physically grow, acquire immunity to debilitating and fatal diseases, and develop the cognitive, language, social-emotional, and motor skills that not only prepare them for formal schooling but also directly translate into health and labor market success in adulthood.[20]

School-age children (approximately between the ages of 6 and 14) receive much more explicit instruction through schooling and continue to acquire skills and gain knowledge in subjects that have been deemed essential for individuals to contribute productively to society. During both the early childhood and school-age periods, the quality and conditions of children's social and physical environments can either increase or decrease their propensity to experience chronic disease as adults, including mental health disorders.[21]

During late adolescence and early adulthood, a period often described as *youth*, skill acquisition continues, as individuals learn on the job and gain experience.[22]

Prime-age adults can continue to acquire skills on the job, but for the most part, this age group is translating their human capital into labor productivity and investing some of it back into their children. Depreciation of human capital starts in *old age*, as an individual's health declines and productive tasks become more challenging to perform than at earlier stages of the life cycle.

The curve in figure 1.1 depicts this process of human capital accumulation across an individual's life cycle. This report focuses on the life-cycle stages that correspond to the steepest part of the curve—early childhood, school age, and youth. Evidence from the fields of neuroscience, developmental psychology, education, and economics indicates that the curve is steeper at earlier ages and flatter later in life: that is, the rate of human capital accumulation is higher for younger individuals, and gains happen more slowly as individuals age.[23] This pattern of development is biologically determined but also reinforced by the timing of investments made by households and governments, as the bulk of time that individuals spend learning in school and that parents spend caring for their children occurs in the early childhood, school-age, and youth periods.

As suggested by the term, human capital accumulation is *cumulative*. One hypothesis of human capital accumulation, well supported by empirical evidence, posits that human capital exhibits "self-productivity."[24] Put simply, self-productivity means that "skills beget skills"—that is, later levels build on foundations set earlier. Thus, a school-age child's skills—such as the mathematical concepts he can grasp as well as his ability to focus and process new information in a classroom setting—are strongly affected by his experiences during early childhood. Likewise, the human capital he acquires during his school age will directly shape his acquisition of skills during his youth and prime working age.

Evidence suggests that, for some dimensions of human capital, higher investments in one period increase the effectiveness of investments in another period, in a process that has been called "dynamic complementarity." For instance, higher investments in early childhood programs increase the future gains from higher investments in primary education, just as higher investments in primary education increase the returns to investments in early childhood programs.[25]

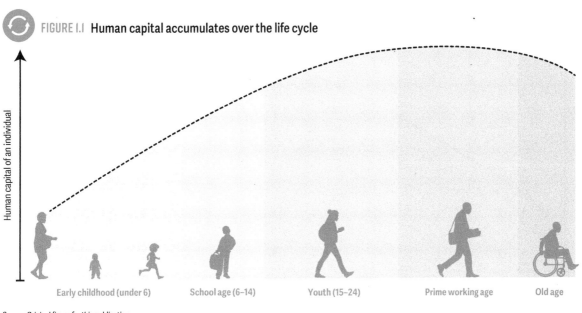

FIGURE I.I **Human capital accumulates over the life cycle**

Human capital of an individual (vertical axis)

Early childhood (under 6)   School age (6–14)   Youth (15–24)   Prime working age   Old age

Source: Original figure for this publication.

SHOCKS LIKE THE COVID-19 PANDEMIC DECREASE BOTH LEVELS OF HUMAN CAPITAL AND SUBSEQUENT RATES OF ACCUMULATION

One implication of the early steepness in how human capital accumulates is that early declines in human capital have larger impacts on an individual's ultimate stock of human capital than setbacks that occur later in life because early declines affect an individual's entire trajectory of human capital accumulation (figure 1.2). Shocks affect human capital accumulation in two ways. First, they can shift down the *levels* of human capital accumulated at any point in the life cycle. For example, a bout of diarrheal disease can immediately decrease a child's weight and his cognitive skills. Likewise, a spell of unemployment reduces work experience—and therefore limits on-the-job training. In figure 1.2, the downward shift in the level of human capital is shown as an immediate drop in the curve at the time of a shock.

Second, shocks can also change the *rate* at which human capital accumulates. An early setback in nutrition in the womb, for example, can affect a child's ability to learn in the future.[26] Lack of access to pre-primary education can hinder the development of skills that enable learning, such as perseverance and attention, making it more difficult for children to learn more traditional skills, such as language and math, when they transition to primary school.[27] A shaky foundation in literacy when young will impede a student's progress and success in later stages of education where literacy will be assumed. This change in the rate of human capital accumulation is shown by a flattening of the curve after the shock. This well-documented persistence and amplification of early adversity runs counter to the often-expressed notion that children are resilient and have plenty of time to make up for early setbacks.[28]

The lockdowns and economic slowdowns triggered by the pandemic decreased households' and governments' investments in human capital, causing an immediate drop in the level of an individual's human capital observed today. As chapters 2 through 4 show, these downward shifts in current stocks of human capital occurred at every stage of the life cycle when human capital is meant to accumulate the most rapidly: that is, during the early childhood period, spanning a child's gestation through age 5 (chapter 2); during the period

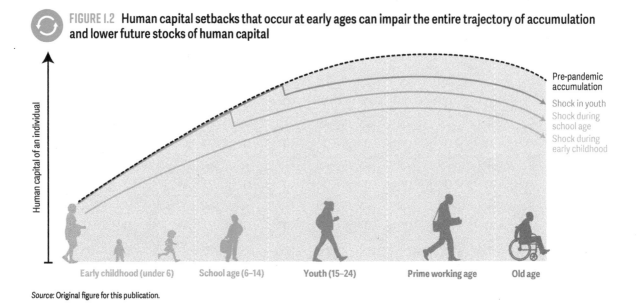

FIGURE I.2 Human capital setbacks that occur at early ages can impair the entire trajectory of accumulation and lower future stocks of human capital

Source: Original figure for this publication.

when children are meant to be in school, approximately between the ages of 6 and 14 (chapter 3); and during late adolescence, from ages 15 to 24, when young people are transitioning to later levels of education or to the labor market (chapter 4).

The youngest children—those born during the pandemic or a couple of years before—have had a poor start. They lost access to essential services such as vaccinations against preventable childhood diseases and pre-primary education. Their cognitive, motor, and social-emotional development has suffered compared to how children had been developing before the pandemic. Because of the initial steepness in the curve depicted for human capital accumulation and because the entire curve has shifted down and likely become flatter, in the absence of an ambitious recovery program the resulting human capital accumulation among this age group will be substantially lower than what would have been predicted for them before the pandemic.

Faced with unprecedented school closures, school-age children lost months and sometimes years of instruction—which translated one-for-one into months and years of lost learning, on average. They also now face new challenges such as anxiety and depression. Just as with children who were in the early childhood period during the pandemic, school-age children face sizable declines in human capital.

Meanwhile, many young people ages 15 to 24 lost education, work experience, or both due to increases in idle time when they were neither studying nor working during the pandemic. They risk dropping out of school or finding lower-quality and lower-paying jobs, which in turn can depress earnings for 10 to 15 years.[29] Again, because human capital is still building among this age group, the pandemic lowered youths' future trajectories compared to what would have been the case in the absence of the pandemic.

COUNTRIES HAVE THREE POTENTIAL PATHS FOLLOWING THE PANDEMIC: A PERMANENTLY LOWER TRAJECTORY, PARTIAL RECOVERY, OR COMPLETE RECOVERY

Whether these shocks permanently alter future stocks of human capital, however, depends on *both* the *size* of the initial drop in the level of human capital and the *rate* at which human capital accumulates following the shock. For an individual, figure 1.3 visualizes both the initial drop depicted in figure 1.2 and potential subsequent paths. It zeroes in on disruptions in only one stage of the life cycle, and so the curve depicting human capital accumulation can be approximated by a line that is nearly straight. Three trajectories of human capital accumulation are possible as the world emerges out of the pandemic, illustrated by the green, yellow, and red lines that follow the steep drop during lockdowns (black arrow).

In the worst-case scenario (red line), no efforts to reverse setbacks in human capital are put in place. Human capital falls well below the level it would have reached if the pandemic had not occurred. That is, the recovery path will lead to increasing *divergence* compared to pre-pandemic trends, as the rate of human capital accumulation slows down after the shock compared to the pre-pandemic rate of accumulation. Initial problems with skills development slow the future process of acquiring skills, and the effect of the shock compounds over time. Children and young adults still acquire human capital over time—the recovery path still slopes upward, but it has a lower slope than what would have been predicted had the pandemic not happened, leading to a lower stock of human capital in the future.

> To close the large gaps in human capital induced by the pandemic before they magnify over time, large changes in the level and composition of investments will be needed. But these investments can pay for themselves.

Another possibility is that, after an initial decline following lockdowns and economic slowdowns, human capital accumulates at the same rate as before the pandemic (yellow line) on a trend parallel to the pre-pandemic path. Given the staggering losses in skills documented in chapters 2, 3, and 4 and evidence that shocks to human capital do not depreciate over time,[30] achieving this parallel recovery path would require substantial investments to address current shortfalls in skills. Although there would be *partial recovery* of losses in human capital in this scenario compared with the case of divergence, the stock of human capital would still be lower in the future.

Finally, figure 1.3 demonstrates that the only path without permanent losses in human capital is the one that attains *convergence* back to the pre-pandemic path (green line). This convergent path, however, requires a substantial increase in the slope of the path. That is, human capital would have to accumulate at a faster rate than what was happening before the pandemic. Without very ambitious policies, purposeful interventions, and higher investment, however, this optimistic recovery path is unlikely to materialize.

FIGURE I.3 **Making a full recovery requires increasing the rate of human capital accumulation compared to trajectories before the pandemic**

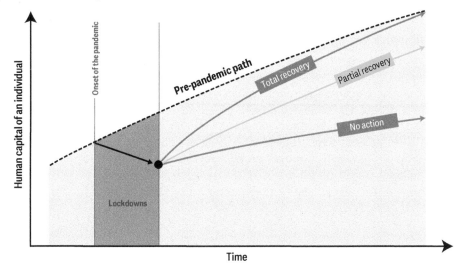

Source: Original figure for this publication.

CHOICES TODAY MATTER: GOVERNMENTS CAN CHANGE THEIR RECOVERY PATHS

Unfortunately, many governments in low- and middle-income countries find themselves in a precarious fiscal position. Budgets are limited, and there are many competing demands. Sluggish supply chains have struggled to keep up with increasing demand for food and energy, leading to capacity constraints, supply bottlenecks, and rising prices. The war in Ukraine has further restricted trade, leading to major price spikes and concerns about energy and food security.

Moreover, some interventions will have immediate payoffs, but generally the benefits of investments in human capital, even if they are very large, will only materialize in the future. Thus, governments face a trade-off between addressing poverty today and poverty in the future.[31] Because poorer families cannot protect their children from shocks as well as more affluent families can, the pandemic has eroded their human capital more, increasing inequality both today and in the future.

Although increasing the rate of human capital accumulation is ambitious, governments can do it, as subsequent chapters of this report demonstrate. Moreover, it is necessary to protect future productivity and incomes. Increasing the coverage and quality of pre-primary education can generate improvements large enough to offset the observed declines in early childhood development documented in chapter 2. In Bangladesh, for example, offering preschool for two hours per day in government schools improved the cognitive and social-emotional skills of a cohort of 4-year-old children, increasing their school readiness before they entered primary school.[32] In Tamil Nadu, India, students exhibited severe deficits in reading and math when they returned to in-person learning after pandemic-induced school closures, consistent with much of the evidence presented in chapter 3. After six months, two-thirds of the deficits were recovered, with 24 percent of the recovery attributable to a government-run after-school remediation program.[33] To support the growing ranks of youth not studying or working after the pandemic (described in chapter 4), Mexico expanded a program for 18- to 29-year-old individuals who were not in school and not working, providing 12 months of workplace training, combined with a monthly allowance and social security coverage.

After documenting the drops in human capital induced by the pandemic, chapters 2 to 4 also recommend policy options with the highest chances of reversing observed setbacks and placing countries on a recovery path that converges back to pre-pandemic trends in human capital accumulation.

When it comes to the magnitude of economic recessions, deaths, and global spread, the COVID-19 pandemic has been perhaps the largest global shock in the past century (see box 1.1). Multiple systems that normally serve to build and protect human capital failed in many countries, although some countries were able to pivot during the crisis and adjust their education systems, their delivery of health services, and their social protection programs to deal with the stresses induced by the pandemic.

The fifth chapter of this report describes features of human development systems that contributed to countries' successes in protecting human capital and reversing losses. The chapter concludes with lessons from the pandemic on creating more resilient and adaptive systems to help countries and individuals to withstand future shocks, such as conflict and climate change, that, like the COVID-19 pandemic, threaten human capital formation all along the life cycle.

Given the long list of policies needed to recover human capital for all stages of the life cycle, the sixth and final chapter of the report proposes an approach for prioritization, arguing for (1) a focus on periods in which children transition from one life-cycle stage to the next and (2) joint consideration of constraints that stem from fiscal costs, implementation complexity, and the political commitment required for some reforms.

BOX I.I How does the death toll of the COVID-19 pandemic affect human capital?

Although this report focuses on the impact of COVID-19 on human capital across the life cycle, the enormous death toll due to the pandemic is difficult to overlook. A key indicator of mortality during COVID-19 has been *excess deaths*, which captures the difference between the total number of deaths that have occurred and the number of deaths that would have been expected in the absence of the pandemic (estimated with reference to trends before the pandemic). The measure of excess deaths therefore includes officially recorded deaths due to COVID-19, deaths attributable to COVID-19 that were not officially reported, and deaths due to other causes that were indirectly associated with COVID-19 arising from broader social and health impacts of the pandemic, while it subtracts out any deaths averted due to changes in social conditions or personal behaviors associated with the pandemic (such as fewer deaths due to influenza or road traffic injuries). Because vital registries are often incomplete in low-income countries, excess deaths are likely poorly measured. Thus, in these settings, most deaths, and their causes, are not directly measured. The World Health Organization (WHO) estimates global excess deaths to be about 15 million up to December 2021.[a] This is far larger than the death toll arising from any war or natural disaster since World War II. More than 80 percent of this global excess mortality, an estimated 12 million deaths, occurred in middle-income countries.

Globally, COVID-19 mortality was much higher among the elderly, with infection fatality rates among 80-year-olds eight times higher than those among 60-year-olds and more than 100 times higher than those among 30-year-olds.[b] Mortality was also slightly higher among men than among women and significantly higher among persons with comorbidities such as chronic noncommunicable diseases.

These deaths have exacted a heavy price on individuals, families, and societies, and it would be difficult to quantify their anguish. How did this mortality affect human capital accumulation? In high-income countries, the COVID-19 pandemic led to deaths mainly in the elderly population. These deaths would have had minimal direct effects on human capital accumulation because this population had already accumulated and used their human capital in previous years and would have exited the labor market. These deaths, however, could have had substantial indirect effects given the role that the elderly, particularly grandmothers, play in childcare around the world. Many grandmothers provide care for children, which permits their mothers to participate in the labor market.[c] Therefore, when grandmothers pass away, many mothers must exit the labor market.[d]

In low- and middle-income countries, by contrast, a larger share of deaths occurred among working-age cohorts than in high-income countries.[e] Individuals under age 65 accounted for about 10 percent of deaths in high-income countries, for about 40 percent in upper-middle-income countries, and for more than 50 percent in lower-middle-income countries. Therefore, in these countries, COVID-19 deaths would have led to decreased use of human capital that had been built in previous periods.

Because of this difference in the age distribution of mortality across countries and the large populations in low- and middle-income countries, the number of orphans created by the pandemic should be higher in low- and middle-income countries. Indeed, estimates that rely on measures of excess deaths and pre-pandemic trends in fertility suggest that, as of May 2022, at least 7.5 million children had been orphaned due to the pandemic,[f] with the largest numbers in Africa and Southeast Asia. Without a parent to provide them with both the material and time investments they need to thrive, these orphans now face multiple disadvantages in physical growth, educational attainment, and protection from sexual abuse.[g]

a. WHO (2022).
b. COVID-19 Forecasting Team (2022).
c. Hank and Buber (2009); Ko and Hank (2014).
d. Talamas (2020).
e. Demombynes et al. (2021).
f. Hillis et al. (2022).
g. Beegle, De Weerdt, and Dercon (2006); Kidman and Palermo (2016).

THE TIME WINDOW FOR ADDRESSING SETBACKS IN HUMAN CAPITAL ACCUMULATION IS SHORT

Since past evidence suggests that setbacks in human capital experienced early in life tend to compound over time, the window for addressing deficits induced by the pandemic is short. Countries should embark on the path to recovery today so that the deficits do not amplify over time, with economies diverging farther and farther away from pre-pandemic progress and inalterably diminishing their future productivity. Making up for the pandemic-related losses, however, will require swift and concerted action among all of the various sectors of the economy that promote human capital. This report both quantifies the collapse in human capital induced by the pandemic and highlights evidence-based policy options for recovering from current setbacks and forestalling future ones.

NOTES

1. World Bank (2022).
2. Carneiro, Meghir, and Parey (2013); Currie and Moretti (2003); Rossin-Slater and Wust (2020).
3. Hendricks, Herrington, and Schoellman (2021).
4. Halpin et al. (2018); Laajaj and Macours (2021); Pushparatnam et al. (2021).
5. Belfield et al. (2015); Heckman and Kautz (2012); Heckman, Pinto, and Savelyev (2013); Jackson (2018).
6. Baranov et al. (2020); Ridley et al. (2020).
7. World Bank, UNESCO, and UNICEF (2021).
8. Osendarp et al. (2021).
9. COVID-19 Mental Disorders Collaborators (2021).
10. The prime-age workforce usually refers to workers who are between the ages of 25 and 55, while the workforce is composed of individuals between the ages of 15 and 65.
11. See Hendren and Sprung-Keyser (2020) for evidence from more than 130 policy changes in the United States. The high returns to investments in pre-primary education in low- and middle-income countries calculated in Holla et al. (2021) contrast with the low effectiveness of adult training programs in these settings (McKenzie 2017; McKenzie and Woodruff 2014).
12. Das et al. (2016); Forsberg and Montagu (2014); Mackintosh et al. (2016).
13. UNICEF (2019).
14. Akee et al. (2010); Akee et al. (2018); Costello et al. (2003).
15. Rossin-Slater and Wust (2020).
16. For evidence on protection from chronic diseases, see Bleker et al. (2005); Neugebauer, Hoek, and Susser (1999); Roseboom et al. (2000); and Walker et al. (2021). For studies on improvements in earnings, see Bailey, Sun, and Timpe (2021) and Heckman et al. (2010). For evidence on the relationship between education and technology adoption, see Acemoglu and Autor (2012); Caselli and Ciccone (2013); Foster and Rosenzweig (2004); and Moretti (2004). For findings on reductions in criminal activities in response to increases in education, see Carneiro and Ginja (2014) and Garcia, Heckman, and Ziff (2019).
17. Heckman et al. (2010).
18. Almond and Currie (2011).
19. Almond and Mazumder (2011); Almond, Mazumder, and Van Ewijk (2015).
20. Gertler et al. (2021).
21. Braveman and Barclay (2009).
22. Lagakos et al. (2018); von Wachter (2020).
23. Heckman and Carneiro (2003); Johnson (2001); Knudsen (2004); Shonkoff, Phillips, and National Research Council (2000); Weber et al. (2019).
24. Cunha and Heckman (2007).
25. Johnson and Jackson (2019).

26. For example, see Almond and Mazumder (2011); Almond, Mazumder, and Van Ewijk (2015); Black, Devereux, and Salvanes (2007).
27. Heckman et al. (2010); Kautz et al. (2014).
28. For evidence that gaps emerging from early adversity do not close over time, see Heckman and Carneiro (2003) and Schady et al. (2015).
29. von Wachter (2020).
30. Adhvaryu, Fenske, and Nyshadham (2019); Almond (2006).
31. World Bank (2022).
32. Spier et al. (2020).
33. Singh, Romero, and Muralidharan (2022).

REFERENCES

Acemoglu, D., and D. Autor. 2012. "What Does Human Capital Do? A Review of Goldin and Katz's *The Race between Education and Technology*." *Journal of Economic Literature* 50 (2): 426–63.

Adhvaryu, A., J. Fenske, and A. Nyshadham. 2019. "Early Life Circumstance and Adult Mental Health." *Journal of Political Economy* 127 (4): 1516–49.

Akee, R., W. Copeland, E. J. Costello, and E. Simeonova. 2018. "How Does Household Income Affect Child Personality Traits and Behaviors?" *American Economic Review* 108 (3): 775–827.

Akee, R. K., W. E. Copeland, G. Keeler, A. Angold, and E. J. Costello. 2010. "Parents' Incomes and Children's Outcomes: A Quasi-experiment Using Transfer Payments from Casino Profits." *American Economic Journal: Applied Economics* 2 (1): 86–115.

Almond, D. 2006. "Is the 1918 Influenza Pandemic Over? Long-Term Effects of *in Utero* Influenza Exposure in the Post-1940 US Population." *Journal of Political Economy* 114 (4): 672–712.

Almond, D., and J. Currie. 2011. "Killing Me Softly: The Fetal Origins Hypothesis." *Journal of Economic Perspectives* 25 (3): 153–72.

Almond, D., and B. Mazumder. 2011. "Health Capital and the Prenatal Environment: The Effect of Ramadan Observance during Pregnancy." *American Economic Journal: Applied Economics* 3 (4): 56–85.

Almond, D., B. Mazumder, and R. Van Ewijk. 2015. "*In Utero* Ramadan Exposure and Children's Academic Performance." *Economic Journal* 125 (589): 1501–33.

Bailey, M. J., S. Sun, and B. Timpe. 2021. "Prep School for Poor Kids: The Long-Run Impacts of Head Start on Human Capital and Economic Self-Sufficiency." *American Economic Review* 111 (12): 3963–4001.

Baranov, V., S. Bhalotra, P. Biroli, and J. Maselko. 2020. "Maternal Depression, Women's Empowerment, and Parental Investment: Evidence from a Randomized Controlled Trial." *American Economic Review* 110 (3): 824–59.

Beegle, K., J. De Weerdt, and S. Dercon. 2006. "Orphanhood and the Long-Run Impact on Children." *American Journal of Agricultural Economics* 88 (5): 1266–72.

Belfield, C., A. B. Bowden, A. Klapp, H. Levin, R. Shand, and S. Zander. 2015. "The Economic Value of Social and Emotional Learning." *Journal of Benefit-Cost Analysis* 6 (3): 508–44.

Black, S. E., P. J. Devereux, and K. G. Salvanes. 2007. "From the Cradle to the Labor Market? The Effect of Birth Weight on Adult Outcomes." *Quarterly Journal of Economics* 122 (1): 409–39.

Bleker, O. P., T. J. Roseboom, A. C. Ravelli, G. A. van Montfans, C. Osmond, and D. J. Barker. 2005. "Cardiovascular Disease in Survivors of the Dutch Famine." In *The Impact of Maternal Malnutrition on the Offspring: Nestlés Nutrition Workshop Series Pediatric Program*, Vol. 55, 183–95. Basel, Switzerland: Karger.

Braveman, P., and C. Barclay. 2009. "Health Disparities Beginning in Childhood: A Life-Course Perspective." *Pediatrics* 124 (Suppl 3): S163–S175.

Carneiro, P., and R. Ginja. 2014. "Long-Term Impacts of Compensatory Preschool on Health and Behavior: Evidence from Head Start." *American Economic Journal: Economic Policy* 6 (4): 135–73.

Carneiro, P., C. Meghir, and M. Parey. 2013. "Maternal Education, Home Environments, and the Development of Children and Adolescents." *Journal of the European Economic Association* 11 (Suppl 1): 123–60.

Caselli, F., and A. Ciccone. 2013. "The Contribution of Schooling in Development Accounting: Results from a Nonparametric Upper Bound." *Journal of Development Economics* 104 (1): 199–211.

Costello, E. J., S. N. Compton, G. Keeler, and A. Angold. 2003. "Relationships between Poverty and Psychopathology: A Natural Experiment." *JAMA* 290 (15): 2023–29.

COVID-19 Forecasting Team. 2022. "Variation in the COVID-19 Infection-Fatality Ratio by Age, Time, and Geography during the Pre-vaccine Era: A Systematic Analysis." *Lancet* 399 (10334): 1469–88.

COVID-19 Mental Disorders Collaborators. 2021. "Global Prevalence and Burden of Depressive and Anxiety Disorders in 204 Countries and Territories in 2020 due to the COVID-19 Pandemic." *Lancet* 398 (10312): 1700–12.

Cunha, F., and J. Heckman. 2007. "The Technology of Skill Formation." *American Economic Review* 97 (2): 31–47.

Currie, J., and E. Moretti. 2003. "Mother's Education and the Intergenerational Transmission of Human Capital: Evidence from College Openings." *Quarterly Journal of Economics* 118 (4): 1495–532.

Das, J., A. Holla, A. Mohpal, and K. Muralidharan. 2016. "Quality and Accountability in Health Care Delivery: Audit-Study Evidence from Primary Care in India." *American Economic Review* 106 (12): 3765–99.

Demombynes, G., D. de Walque, P. Gubbins, B. P. Paul, and J. Veillard. 2021. "COVID-19 Age-Mortality Curves for 2020 Are Flatter in Developing Countries Using Both Official Death Counts and Excess Deaths." World Bank, Washington, DC.

Forsberg, B. C., and D. Montagu. 2014. "Further Advances in Knowledge on the Role of the Private Sector in Health Systems." *Health Policy and Planning* 29 (Suppl 1): i1–i3.

Foster, A. D., and M. R. Rosenzweig. 2004. "Technological Change and the Distribution of Schooling: Evidence from Green-Revolution India." *Journal of Development Economics* 74 (1): 87–111.

García, J. L., J. J. Heckman, and A. L. Ziff. 2019. "Early Childhood Education and Crime." *Infant Mental Health Journal* 40 (1): 141–51.

Gertler, P., J. J. Heckman, R. Pinto, S. M. Chang, S. Grantham-McGregor, C. Vermeersch, S. Walker, and A. Wright. 2021. "Effect of the Jamaica Early Childhood Stimulation Intervention on Labor Market Outcomes at Age 31." NBER Working Paper 29292, National Bureau of Economic Research, Cambridge, MA.

Halpin, P., W. Sharon, H. Yoshikawa, N. Rojas, S. Kabay, L. Pisani, and A. Dowd. 2018. "Measuring Early Learning and Development across Cultures: Invariance of the IDELA across Five Countries." *Development Psychology* 55 (1): 23–37.

Hank, K., and I. Buber. 2009. "Grandparents Caring for Their Grandchildren: Findings from the 2004 Survey of Health, Ageing, and Retirement in Europe." *Journal of Family Issues* 30 (1): 53–73.

Heckman, J. J. 2006. "Skill Formation and the Economics of Investing in Disadvantaged Children." *Science* 312 (5782): 1900–02.

Heckman, J. J., and P. Carneiro. 2003. "Human Capital Policy." NBER Working Paper 9495, National Bureau of Economic Research, Cambridge, MA.

Heckman, J. J., and T. Kautz. 2012. "Hard Evidence on Soft Skills." *Labour Economics* 19 (4): 451–64.

Heckman, J., S. H. Moon, R. Pinto, P. Savelyev, and A. Yavitz. 2010. "Analyzing Social Experiments as Implemented: A Reexamination of the Evidence from the HighScope Perry Preschool Program." *Quantitative Economics* 1 (1): 1–46.

Heckman, J., R. Pinto, and P. Savelyev. 2013. "Understanding the Mechanisms through Which an Influential Early Childhood Program Boosted Adult Outcomes." *American Economic Review* 103 (6): 2052–86.

Hendren, N., and B. Sprung-Keyser. 2020. "A Unified Welfare Analysis of Government Policies." *Quarterly Journal of Economics* 135 (3): 1209–318.

Hendricks, L., C. Herrington, and T. Schoellman. 2021. "College Quality and Attendance Patterns: A Long-Run View." *American Economic Journal: Macroeconomics* 13 (1): 184–215.

Hillis, S., J. P. N. N'konzi, W. Msemburi, L. Cluver, A. Villaveces, S. Flaxman, and H. J. T. Unwin. 2022. "Orphanhood and Caregiver Loss among Children Based on New Global Excess COVID-19 Death Estimates." *JAMA Pediatrics* 176 (11): 1145–48.

Holla, A., M. Bendini, L. Dinarte, and I. Trako. 2021. "Is Investment in Preprimary Education Too Low? Lessons from (Quasi) Experimental Evidence across Countries." Policy Research Working Paper 9723, World Bank, Washington, DC.

Jackson, C. K. 2018. "What Do Test Scores Miss? The Importance of Teacher Effects on Non–Test Score Outcomes." *Journal of Political Economy* 126 (5): 2072–107.

Johnson, M. H. 2001. "Functional Brain Development in Humans." *Nature Reviews Neuroscience* 2 (7): 475–83.

Johnson, R. C., and C. K. Jackson. 2019. "Reducing Inequality through Dynamic Complementarity: Evidence from Head Start and Public School Spending." *American Economic Journal: Economic Policy* 11 (4): 310–49.

Kautz, T., J. J. Heckman, R. Diris, B. Ter Weel, and L. Borghans. 2014. "Fostering and Measuring Skills: Improving Cognitive and Non-Cognitive Skills to Promote Lifetime Success." NBER Working Paper 20749, National Bureau of Economic Research, Cambridge, MA.

Kidman, R., and T. Palermo. 2016. "The Relationship between Parental Presence and Child Sexual Violence: Evidence from Thirteen Countries in Sub-Saharan Africa." *Child Abuse and Neglect* 51 (January): 172–80.

Knudsen, E. I. 2004. "Sensitive Periods in the Development of the Brain and Behavior." *Journal of Cognitive Neuroscience* 16 (8): 1412–25.

Ko, P. C., and K. Hank. 2014. "Grandparents Caring for Grandchildren in China and Korea: Findings from CHARLS and KLoSA." *Journals of Gerontology Series B: Psychological Sciences and Social Sciences* 69 (4): 646–51.

Laajaj, R., and K. Macours. 2021. "Measuring Skills in Developing Countries." *Journal of Human Resources* 56 (4): 1254–95.

Lagakos, D., B. Moll, T. Porzio, N. Qian, and T. Schoellman. 2018. "Life-Cycle Human Capital Accumulation across Countries: Lessons from US Immigrants." *Journal of Human Capital* 12 (2): 305–42.

Mackintosh, M., A. Channon, A. Karan, S. Selvaraj, E. Cavagnero, and H. Zhao. 2016. "What Is the Private Sector? Understanding Private Provision in the Health Systems of Low-Income and Middle-Income Countries." *Lancet* 388 (10044): 596–605.

McKenzie, D. 2017 "How Effective Are Active Labor Market Policies in Developing Countries? A Critical Review of Recent Evidence." *World Bank Research Observer* 32 (2): 127–54.

McKenzie, D., and C. Woodruff. 2014. "What Are We Learning from Business Training and Entrepreneurship Evaluations around the Developing World?" *The World Bank Research Observer* 29 (1): 48–82.

Moretti, E. 2004. "Workers' Education, Spillovers, and Productivity: Evidence from Plant-Level Production Functions." *American Economic Review* 94 (3): 656–90.

Neugebauer, R., H. W. Hoek, and E. Susser. 1999. "Prenatal Exposure to Wartime Famine and Development of Antisocial Personality Disorder in Early Adulthood." *JAMA* 282 (5): 455–62.

Osendarp, S., J. K. Akuoku, R. E. Black, D. Headey, M. Ruel, N. Scott, M. Shekar, et al. 2021. "The COVID-19 Crisis Will Exacerbate Maternal and Child Undernutrition and Child Mortality in Low- and Middle-Income Countries." *Nature Food* 2 (7): 476–84.

Pushparatnam, A., D. A. Luna Bazaldua, A. Holla, J. P. Azevedo, M. Clarke, and A. Devercelli. 2021. "Measuring Early Childhood Development among 4–6-Year-Olds: The Identification of Psychometrically Robust Items across Diverse Contexts." *Frontiers in Public Health* February 3 (9): 569448.

Ridley, M., G. Rao, F. Schilbach, and V. Patel. 2020. "Poverty, Depression, and Anxiety: Causal Evidence and Mechanisms." *Science* 370 (6522).

Roseboom, T. J., J. H. P. van der Meulen, C. Osmond, D. J. P. Barker, A. C. J. Ravelli, and O. P. Bleker. 2000. "Plasma Lipid Profile after Prenatal Exposure to the Dutch Famine." *American Journal of Clinical Nutrition* 72 (5): 1101–06.

Rossin-Slater, M., and M. Wust. 2020. "What Is the Added Value of Preschool for Poor Children? Long-Term and Intergenerational Impacts and Interactions with an Infant Health Intervention." *American Economic Journal: Applied Economics* 12 (3): 255–86.

Schady, N., J. Behrman, M. C. Araujo, R. Azuero, R. Bernal, D. Bravo, F. Lopez-Boo, et al. 2015. "Wealth Gradients in Early Childhood Cognitive Development in Five Latin American Countries." *Journal of Human Resources* 50 (2): 446–63.

Shonkoff, J. P., D. A. Phillips, and National Research Council. 2000. "The Developing Brain." In *From Neurons to Neighborhoods: The Science of Early Childhood Development,* edited by J. P. Shonkoff and D. A. Phillips, ch. 8. Washington, DC: National Academies Press.

Singh, A., M. Romero, and K. Muralidharan. 2022. "Covid-19 Learning Loss and Recovery: Panel Data Evidence from India." NBER Working Paper 30552, National Bureau of Economic Research, Cambridge, MA. https://www.nber.org/papers/w30552.

Spier, E., K. Kamto, A. Molotsky, A. Rahman, N. Hossain, Z. Nahar, and H. Khondker. 2020. "Bangladesh Early Years Preschool Program Impact Evaluation." World Bank, Washington, DC.

Talamas, M. 2020. "Grandmothers and the Gender Gap in the Mexican Labor Market." Working paper, Northwestern University.

UNICEF (United Nations Children's Fund). 2019. *A World Ready to Learn: Prioritizing Quality Early Childhood Education.* New York: UNICEF.

von Wachter, T. 2020. "Lost Generations: Long-Term Effects of the COVID-19 Crisis on Job Losers and Labour Market Entrants, and Options for Policy." *Fiscal Studies* 41 (3): 549–90.

Walker, S. P., S. M. Chang, A. S. Wright, R. Pinto, J. J. Heckman, and S. M. Grantham-McGregor. 2021. "Cognitive, Psychosocial, and Behaviour Gains at Age 31 Years from the Jamaica Early Childhood Stimulation Trial." *Journal of Child Psychology and Psychiatry* 63 (6): 626–35.

Weber, A. M., M. Rubio-Codina, S. P. Walker, S. Van Buuren, I. Eekhout, S. M. Grantham-McGregor, M. C. Araujo, et al. 2019. "The D-Score: A Metric for Interpreting the Early Development of Infants and Toddlers across Global Settings." *BMJ Global Health* 4 (6): e001724.

WHO (World Health Organization). 2022. "14.9 Million Excess Deaths Associated with the COVID-19 Pandemic in 2020 and 2021." WHO, Geneva, May 5, 2022. https://www.who.int/news/item/05-05-2022-14.9-million-excess-deaths-were-associated-with-the-covid-19-pandemic-in-2020-and-2021.

World Bank. 2022. *Poverty and Shared Prosperity 2022: Correcting Course.* Washington, DC: World Bank.

World Bank, UNESCO (United Nations Educational, Scientific, and Cultural Organization), and UNICEF (United Nations Children's Fund). 2021. *The State of the Global Education Crisis: A Path to Recovery.* Washington, DC: World Bank; Paris: UNESCO; New York: UNICEF.

2

POOR START

The Impact of the COVID-19 Pandemic on Early Childhood Development and Subsequent Human Capital Accumulation

Alaka Holla

ABSTRACT

The earliest years of children (from gestation through age 5) set up their entire trajectory of human capital and determine much of their economic and social-emotional well-being in adulthood. However, the COVID-19 pandemic has disrupted household investments in children's nutrition, children's access to essential services, the mental health of caregivers, and the quality of care children receive at home. These deficits in inputs have also translated into declines in motor, language, cognitive, and social-emotional development in both high- and low-income settings. Available data suggest that pre-school-age children have lost from 25 to 50 percent of the early language and numeracy skills they should have acquired during their pre-primary education, making them less prepared for primary school. Where data are available, these early declines appear larger for poorer families. In the absence of policies and programs to compensate for these early developmental losses, the youngest cohorts can expect to earn as much as 17 percent less when they enter the labor market in the next 15–20 years, compared with their pre-pandemic trajectories. Past evidence also suggests that, unless remediated, these cohorts will suffer from worse physical and mental health, engage in more criminal activity, and rely more on social assistance as adults. To prevent this poor start from amplifying into greater human capital losses as these children progress along the life cycle, policies in the short to medium term should prioritize arranging transfers for households whose income has still not recovered, launching catch-up campaigns for vaccination and nutrition, organizing parenting programs to encourage more cognitive and social-emotional stimulation in the home, restoring and expanding coverage of pre-primary education, and offering parents mental health counseling programs.

It's past time that we treat childcare as what it is—an element whose contribution to economic growth is as essential as infrastructure or energy.

—Janet Yellen, US Secretary of the Treasury
Remarks, US Department of the Treasury, September 15, 2021

❝

It does not make me happy that my children are no longer going to school. Years don't wait for them. They have already lost a lot. What will become of our uneducated children?

—Mother of two preschool-age children
Interview, Human Rights Watch, North Kivu, Republic of Congo, August 2020

❝

SHOCKS OCCURRING DURING EARLY CHILDHOOD CAN PERSIST FOR DECADES—AND EVEN ACROSS GENERATIONS

In 2050, at least 20–25 percent of the prime-age workforce would have been in the womb or under age 6 during the lockdowns associated with the COVID-19 pandemic.[1] Although the full implications of the pandemic for these cohorts will not be known until far into the future, lessons from the past and current evidence that is starting to emerge point toward significant setbacks in human capital that will follow this generation of the youngest children for decades.

The total effects of the COVID-19 crisis will likely take many years to emerge for children who were very young during the pandemic as they progress through school and enter the labor market.

In 1918, Spanish influenza arrived in the United States and would eventually claim more than 675,000 lives—the highest death toll before the recent COVID-19 pandemic. Although the disease outbreak would end by 1919, for those who had been *in utero* during the pandemic the impacts of Spanish flu would be felt for decades. Compared with children born right before and after the pandemic, the children of infected mothers would go on to be 15 percent less likely to graduate from high school. They also relied more on social assistance as adults.[2] The sons of infected mothers earned 5–9 percent less 40–60 years later and exhibited much higher rates of disability as adults.

Very young children are not as resilient as one would like to believe. Shocks occurring during the early childhood period, from gestation through age 5, tend to persist, sometimes for multiple generations (for a summary of evidence, see table 2.1). For example, in Ghana fluctuations in the price of a cash crop at the time of birth (and therefore fluctuations in household income) generated fluctuations in mental health status observed 20 years later in adulthood.[3] When an earthquake in Pakistan struck close to the homes of children under age 3, they had lower test scores five years later than children who had lived farther away from the fault line.[4]

These early childhood setbacks can even undermine prospects for future generations. The Dutch Hunger Winter (1944–45) proved to be a horrific natural experiment for testing the impacts of what happens when babies in the womb are deprived of adequate nutrition. During the wartime German occupation of the Netherlands, rations in one part of the country were limited to 400–800 calories a day. Although the famine was short-lived and mortality was limited, researchers have found that children who were *in utero* during the severe food shortages went on to have, on average, significantly worse cardiovascular and mental health as adults than adjacent but unexposed cohorts.[5] They performed worse on a selective attention task in their late fifties, suggesting a low capacity for concentration.[6] Their children, the next generation, also exhibited a higher average percentage of fat tissue at birth (which is predictive of later obesity) and worse health later in life, as reported by their parents.[7]

Conversely, early positive experiences can set children up for success. In Denmark, for example, cohorts able to attend pre-primary education because of the expansion of public preschools from the 1930s to 1960s

TABLE 2.1 The impacts of early adversity and intervention can take many years to emerge and can persist across generations

		Early childhood	Childhood	Adulthood	Next generation
Early adversity		Early gestation food deprivation	Lower birthweight (US) Lower test scores at age 7 (UK)	Higher likelihood of cognitive disability (Iraq and Uganda) Higher likelihood of cardiac disease and mental illness (Netherlands) Cognitive impairment at ages 56–59 (Netherlands)	Higher percentage of fat tissue at birth and worse health outcomes (Netherlands)
		Natural disasters	Lower height (Pakistan) Lower test scores (Pakistan) Lower years of completed education (Latin America)	Increased disability (Latin America) Lower employment (Latin America) Lower wealth (Latin America)	Lower years of completed education (Latin America)
Early investments		Windfalls in household income in birth year from increase in price of cash crop	Increased schooling attainment (Ghana)	Improved mental health and higher literacy (Ghana)	
		Weekly visits for two years by counselor to increase stimulation in home for stunted children ages 9–24 months	Higher cognitive skills (Jamaica and multiple countries) Higher schooling attainment (Denmark, Jamaica)	Lower crime, higher wages and earnings, lower substance abuse, improved mental health (Jamaica)	
		Preschool attendance	Higher cognitive and social-emotional skills (multiple countries)	Higher college completion (US) Higher life expectancy (Denmark) Higher earnings (Denmark, Norway, US) Lower reliance on social assistance (Norway, US)	Higher school completion (Denmark)

Sources: Adhvaryu, Fenske, and Nyshadham 2019; Almond and Mazumder 2011; Almond, Mazumder, and Van Ewijk 2014; Andrabi, Daniels, and Das 2021; Bailey, Sun, and Timpe 2021; Bleker et al. 2005; Caruso 2017; de Rooij et al. 2010; Gertler et al. 2021; Havnes and Mogstad 2011; Holla et al. 2021; Neugebauer, Hoek, and Susser 1999; Roseboom et al. 2000; Rossin-Slater and Wust 2020; Susser, Hoek, and Brown 1998; Walker et al. 2021.

completed more schooling, earned more, and survived to age 65 more often than adjacent cohorts too old to benefit from the expansion.[8] The next generation also benefited from their parents' increased access to preschool; by age 25 they were more likely to have gone beyond the compulsory years of education than the children of the cohorts that had missed pre-primary schooling. Similarly, 30 years after the mothers of malnourished toddlers in Jamaica were shown how to increase the amount of cognitive and social-emotional stimulation they gave their children, the previously stunted children had 43 percent higher wages as adults than children who had not benefited from the early stimulation program.[9] They also exhibited lower rates of depression and substance abuse.[10]

This sensitivity of young children to both positive experiences and adversity should not be too surprising as the first five years of life are a period of rapid brain development and physical growth. Evidence from the fields of neuroscience and genetics suggests that early life experiences shape both the architecture and functions of the brain; they can even modify which genes are expressed.[11] Learning during these very early years provides the foundation for later learning as children begin to acquire knowledge about numbers, language, and social interactions and develop executive functions such as inhibition and working memory.[12]

This spectacular acquisition of skills during early childhood does not happen on its own. Children's developing brains need nurturing and protection, both by caregivers in the home and through services such as health care and education. Doctors, developmental psychologists, and researchers have agreed that for children to survive and thrive they need five elements of nurturing care: good health, adequate nutrition, responsive caregiving, opportunities for early learning, and security and safety.[13] To meet these needs, children require both material investments such as food, vaccines, and books, as well as investments of caregivers' time in play, cognitive stimulation, and social interactions.

This chapter documents the extent to which the COVID-19 pandemic has disrupted the investments in very young children that are critical for their healthy development. The chapter also presents evidence that large declines in these children's cognitive and social-emotional skills are already evident and foretell compounding losses in human capital across the life cycle that can reverberate for generations. Interventions that have demonstrated a potential for high impacts commensurate with these losses are discussed as part of a package of recovery policies for this age group.

THE PANDEMIC REDUCED CRITICAL INVESTMENTS IN YOUNG CHILDREN

Because very young children need nurturing care inside and outside the home, the recent COVID-19 pandemic could be expected to interfere with their development through three channels: loss of household income; disruptions in services such as health care and education; and strain or declines in the quality of care in the home. Lockdowns halted work outside the home and made it difficult for goods to be brought to markets, limiting the ability of households to purchase inputs such as food that contribute to children's health and physical growth. Schools, including those providing pre-primary education, closed during lockdowns, and caregivers in the home or in informal care settings rarely offer children the same level of cognitive and psychosocial stimulation that children receive in preschool.[14] School closures also interrupted the distribution of school meals. Fears of infection and an overwhelmed health care workforce kept patients away from clinics and hospitals, cutting off mothers' access to prenatal care and skilled birth attendants, as well as children's access to essential vaccinations. Increases in parents' stress levels often accompany decreases in family income.[15] Stressed and anxious parents tend to invest less time in keeping their children physically safe,[16] engage in fewer stimulating activities with them,[17] and rely on harsher modes of discipline[18]—all of which represent declines in care that could depress both the cognitive and social-emotional development of their children.

Whether these potential impacts for children under age 6 have materialized from the COVID-19 crisis is an empirical question. This question is difficult to answer, however, because the pandemic also curtailed data collection and measurement, but box 2.1 describes what past shocks reveal about what can be expected during and immediately after a crisis. Researchers are just beginning to learn the extent to which the pandemic has stifled the very start of the human capital trajectory for the under-6 age group. The total effects of the COVID-19 crisis, however, will likely take many years to emerge as this population progresses to basic education and enters the labor market and then has children of its own.

Children faced greater food insecurity during the pandemic

Evidence from 2020 and 2021 suggests that young children in low- and middle-income countries faced a higher risk of undernutrition from the pandemic. The incomes of the poorest 40 percent of the world's population fell by 7 percent, increasing the number of people living in extreme poverty by 19 percent

Shocks disrupt investments in children and lead to developmental deficits that are evident even before children start school.

Declines in maternal and child health care. The Ebola epidemic in West Africa in 2014 had effects on maternal and child services that persisted beyond the outbreak. Although rates of prenatal care and births taking place in health care facilities were improving before the Ebola outbreak, in Guinea they plummeted during the outbreak, recovered slightly afterward, and then stagnated at a lower level even one year later.[a] By 2016, essential vaccinations for children under age 1, such as those for polio, measles, and five other life-threatening diseases (the pentavalent vaccine), had also not recovered to reach the levels observed before the outbreak.

Increases in stress, injuries, and abuse. Very young children's vulnerability to shocks is not limited to low- and middle-income countries. In the United States, just the announcements of impending factory closings and mass layoffs during pregnancy decrease birthweight and the duration of pregnancies.[b] Meanwhile, exposures to stressful events such as hurricanes during pregnancy substantially increase the likelihood of complications during labor and delivery and abnormalities in the newborn period that can lead to developmental delays later in childhood.[c] Parental stress also affects children outside the womb. In the United States, nonaccidental head injuries among infants and toddlers increased during the Great Recession (2007–09),[d] as did child abuse.[e]

Increases in infant deaths. Past economic and weather-related shocks and more geographically limited outbreaks of disease foreshadow what may occur post-pandemic. For example, an analysis of more than 1.7 million births in 59 countries between 1975 and 2004 indicated that a 1 percent decrease in gross domestic product (GDP) per capita from its trend reverses year-on-year declines (progress) in infant mortality over the period by 10–15 percent.[f] Similar but more recent data suggest important variation in this relationship: infant mortality in low-income countries is much more sensitive to fluctuations in GDP than infant mortality in upper-middle-income countries.[g]

Increases in stunting. Stunted children are, by more than two standard deviations, too short for their age, compared with a healthy population of children. The first 1,000 days of a child's life, starting from conception to age 2, are a critical period for preventing stunting. For example, children under age 2 at the time of the banking and financial crisis in Ecuador in 1999 went on to become 6 percent shorter for their age.[h] Similarly, five years after the 2005 earthquake in Pakistan, despite the rollout of both housing and cash aid, children who were under age 3 when the earthquake struck and who were close to the fault line were significantly shorter than those farther away, while the height of older yet still growing children was unaffected.[i]

Declines in cognitive skills. Children under age 2 during the financial and banking crisis in Ecuador in 1999 exhibited 6 percent lower vocabulary scores than children born by the same mothers whose first 1,000 days occurred just after the crisis. Children experiencing nutritional deprivation during their first month of gestation performed worse in primary school in the United Kingdom[j] and exhibited a higher likelihood of psychological and cognitive disabilities in adulthood in Iraq and Uganda.[k]

a. Delamou et al. (2017).
b. Carlson (2015).
c. Currie and Rossin-Slater (2013).
d. Huang et al. (2011).
e. Schneider, Waldfogel, and Brooks-Gunn (2017).
f. Baird, Friedman, and Schady (2011).
g. Shapira, de Walque, and Friedman (2021).
h. Hidrobo (2014).
i. Andrabi, Daniels, and Das (2021).
j. Almond and Mazumder (2011).
k. Almond, Mazumder, and van Ewijk (2014).

FIGURE 2.1 **The share of households and children who had to skip meals or eat smaller portions increased during early lockdowns in some countries**
Percentage change in food insecurity between 2019 and 2020

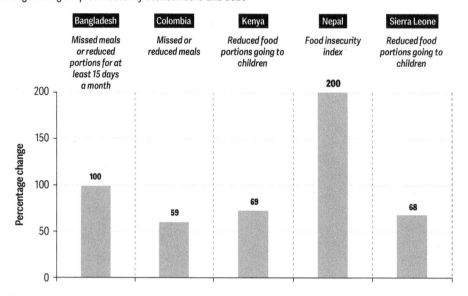

Source: Egger et al. 2021.
Note: The food insecurity index (Nepal) measures items capturing how often households had to worry about not having enough food or had to reduce portions.

between 2019 and 2020.[19] The accompanying declines in household expenditures eroded food security and dietary quality in the early pandemic period (figure 2.1). Compared with 2019, the fraction of households reporting reductions in food portions going to children increased dramatically in 2020—by 68 percent in Sierra Leone, 69 percent in Kenya, and 100 percent in Bangladesh.[20] Likewise, between 2018 and 2020 the fraction of children attaining minimum levels of dietary diversity fell by 47 percent (26 percentage points lower from a base of 81 percent) in slums in Jakarta, Indonesia.[21] The fraction of households classified as food secure fell by 62 percent (50.1 percentage points lower from a base of 81.5 percent) in rural Bangladesh between 2017 and 2020.[22]

Lockdowns prevented mothers and infants from accessing critical health care services

My wife is pregnant, and there are no consultations in clinics or hospitals.

—Eddy Roque, Peru
"Diario de la cuarentena: las historias de todos," *OjoPúblico,* April 29, 2020

❝

Before the COVID-19 pandemic, we conducted home visits for women with high-risk pregnancy or women with postpartum complications. Now, we are not able to do it. Home visits have been canceled.

—Nurul, primary health center midwife, Surabaya, Indonesia
Quoted in Hazfiarini et al. (2022)

❝

Households' investments in children's nutrition are critical for their development, but young children also rely on care outside the home—particularly health and education services. During the pandemic, lockdowns and restrictions on movement, fears of infection in the community, and shortages of frontline health care staff likely contributed to the dramatic declines in the utilization of health care services observed in some health systems across different income contexts.[23]

Declines in prenatal care and care at birth. The youngest children experienced these service disruptions while they were still *in utero* as their mothers prepared for their births. Prenatal care visits reduce the likelihood of birth complications,[24] and both maternal and infant mortality rates are lower when births take place in health care facilities with skilled staff rather than in homes.[25] Complications during labor and delivery can cause an array of developmental abnormalities in children that can imperil their ability to accumulate human capital across their life span.[26] For example, in the United States increased access to hospitals following desegregation efforts decreased postneonatal mortality among Blacks and substantially increased their cognitive scores in late adolescence.[27] Maternal deaths can be accompanied by substantial disadvantages in the surviving children's physical and mental health, education, and safety.[28]

Analysis of data from the health information systems of 18 low- and middle-income countries revealed that immediately after the onset of the pandemic, initiation of prenatal care declined by nearly 4 percent on average, and deliveries in a health care institution fell by more than 5 percent from March 2020 to July 2021 when compared with the two years before the pandemic.[29] Figure 2.2 summarizes disruptions in institutional births from this study. Declines were much higher than average in some countries. For example, institutional deliveries fell by more than 14 percent in Nigeria and 25 percent in Haiti. Box 2.2 discusses when it would be possible to distinguish declines in the use of health care services for pregnant

 FIGURE 2.2 **In low-income countries, women and infants lacked critical services during the early pandemic period**

Percentage change in births at a hospital or formal facility following the onset of the pandemic

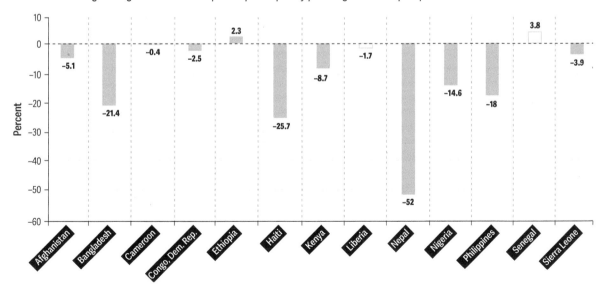

Sources: The figure is based on administrative data: the Philippines: PhilHealth claims data as reported in Uy et al. (2022); Nepal: hospital records as reported in Ashish et al. (2020). All other estimates are reported in Ahmed et al. (2021) based on data from health information management systems.
Note: Hospitals and health information systems track counts of births occurring at facilities, and studies have reported percentage changes in these counts. All statistically significant changes appear as solid bars. All changes that cannot be statistically distinguished from zero appear as empty bars.

Identifying impacts of the COVID-19 pandemic on the utilization of maternal health services

The early lockdown period and subsequent 10 months are the ideal period to examine impacts on the utilization of maternal and child health services and maternal and infant health. The pandemic—specifically, the economic dislocations, overall stress, and fears of infection—may have influenced families' decisions on whether to have, or have more, children. Indeed, there is evidence that fertility is procyclical in low- and middle-income countries.[a] Early evidence from COVID-19 also points to a (small) decline in fertility across most countries for which data are available.[b] Thus a decline in the number of prenatal visits and births in hospitals one year after lockdowns may confound a decline in fertility with a decline in mothers' and children's access to care.

a. Chatterjee and Vogl (2018).
b. UNFPA (2021).

women from declines in fertility. Similar effects on access to these essential services are evident in data from health insurance claims and hospital admissions in the Philippines and Nepal.[30, 31] These adverse birth outcomes contrast with evidence from higher-income contexts (such as Denmark, Jordan, the Netherlands, Türkiye, and the United Kingdom), where the pandemic either promoted or did not impair fetal health.[32]

Reductions in health care after the newborn period, including missed vaccinations. During the pandemic, children continued to suffer from reductions in health care after the newborn period, missing out on essential vaccinations and growth monitoring and experiencing delays in needed medical attention. A study drawing on administrative data on service delivery trends in 10 low-, middle-, and high-income countries found that, although reproductive and maternal health care (including family planning services) were generally more resilient than other services, childhood immunizations were among the most affected.[33]

Millions of young children were not fully vaccinated against diphtheria, pertussis, and tetanus (DPT) in 2020 in a reversal of global progress made over the last 10 years in combating preventable diseases (figure 2.3).[34] Because this vaccine tends to be administered during routine health visits for infants, this decline in coverage was likely accompanied by less frequent growth monitoring and other services that children should receive in their first two years. Meanwhile, polio, a debilitating disease on the brink of eradication before the pandemic, could resurge because the fraction of children receiving the full dose of this vaccine has fallen in all regions.[35]

During the early lockdowns, evidence from health clinics in rural South Africa indicates that children under age 6 attended their vaccination and growth monitoring visits 50–62 percent less often, whereas older children and adults maintained their pre-pandemic frequency of visits.[36] This shortfall in health care utilization, however, was short-lived and was no longer apparent as early as May–June 2020.

In Bangladesh, however, there is evidence that some of the delays in care for infants with diarrhea were fatal and that the delays worsened over time. Compared with the same months the year before, young children's admissions to the world's largest hospital dedicated to diarrheal disease dropped considerably from March to August 2020.[37] Because it is unlikely that lockdowns thwarted the spread of the pathogens responsible for diarrheal disease, this reduction in cases most likely reflected an increase in untreated disease. By February 2021, however, admissions exceeded pre-pandemic levels by 20 percent, and the increased severity of cases accompanying the surge in patients suggests real deterioration in health and households' capacity to prevent and treat diarrheal disease rather than a change in the composition of patients compared with the pre-pandemic period (box 2.3).

FIGURE 2.3 By 2021, coverage of essential childhood vaccines had yet to recover fully in many regions from its decline during lockdowns

DPT3 vaccine coverage, by region, 2016–21

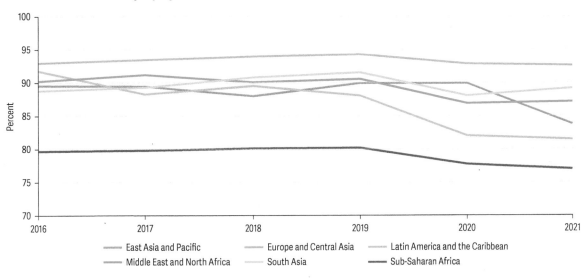

Source: Original calculations from WHO/UNICEF Estimates of National Immunization Coverage (WENIC) country summary content (WHO and UNICEF 2021).
Note: "DPT3" refers to the third dose of the three doses of the combined diphtheria, pertussis, and tetanus toxoid vaccine.

BOX 2.3 Changes in the composition of patients versus changes in underlying health

Fears of infection and triage protocols within health care facilities early in the pandemic could have created a situation in which only very severe cases would receive medical attention in a facility. Thus if the evidence suggests a change in the severity of cases along with a decline in case numbers, it would not be possible to ascertain whether a change in patients' outcomes reflects only a change in the composition of patients receiving care in facilities or whether the underlying health of the population has suffered.

When patient loads are equal to or greater than pre-pandemic levels, however, and no trends or events would have caused population numbers to swell (such as an influx of migrants), then any changes in severity can be interpreted as a real deterioration in health.

School closures compromised pre-primary education, even after lockdowns

We have always faced comments like, "It's okay if they don't go [to preschool] …" and we see that parents give more importance to primary school, so much so that the elementary school next door has had full enrollment since they reopened. But they just didn't send them to preschool.

—Rita Romo, preschool teacher, Mexico
EXPANSION Politica, Mexico, "Preescolar, el nivel educativo que dejó más salones vacíos luego de la pandemia," June 20, 2022

During the first 11 months of the pandemic, closures of preschools cut average instructional time by more than half around the world.[38] In some settings, preschools were closed longer than primary and secondary schools. These closures meant that children between the ages of 3 and 5 did not develop the early literacy, numeracy, and social-emotional skills required to succeed in elementary school.

The idea of a child missing a year or two of pre-primary education may not induce the same concern among parents and policy makers as school closures in primary and secondary education, but it should. Global evidence from randomized control trials and natural experiments suggests that, on average, pre-primary education significantly and substantially improves cognitive and social-emotional skills in all types of countries, whether high-income, middle-income, or low-income.[39] These advantages persist into basic education as increases in learning and skill acquisition and into adulthood as increases in earnings, declines in criminal activity, and lower reliance on social assistance.[40] For example, in the United States the federal Head Start preschool program for economically disadvantaged children has been shown to increase college completion by 39 percent.[41]

Advantages from pre-primary education persist into basic education as increases in learning and into adulthood as increases in earnings, declines in criminal activity, and lower reliance on social assistance.

Although it is possible that during the pandemic caregivers could have intensified their activities to stimulate children at home to compensate for what children were not learning in school, the likelihood is low that they could have fully compensated for closures in pre-primary education, particularly in low- and middle-income countries and among low-income families. Before the pandemic, investments in the time and materials needed for early stimulation, such as having children's books at home or counting objects with a child, were low.[42] On average, households in the poorest countries have only two children's books at home.[43] Moreover, evidence gathered during the pandemic suggests that even when remote-learning opportunities were available, families and children reported feeling overwhelmed, and children spent considerably less time on learning activities.[44]

Children in middle- and high-income countries and children from less poor backgrounds in low-income countries likely lost the most instructional time from preschool closures.[45] Before lockdowns, the coverage of pre-primary education was higher in higher-income countries. Specifically, in 2019 only 20 percent of age-eligible children in low-income countries attended schools providing pre-primary education, compared with 60 percent in lower-middle-income countries, 76 percent in upper-middle-income countries, and 83 percent in high-income countries.[46] Within low-income countries, only 7.6 percent of children in the poorest quintile of wealth attended some form of pre-primary education.[47]

The coverage of preschool seemed to be below expected levels even after preschools reopened (figure 2.4), as revealed by an analysis of labor force surveys conducted among a nationally representative sample of

 FIGURE 2.4 **Pre-primary attendance has not recovered from the pandemic in many countries**
Difference between predicted and observed enrollment, 2021

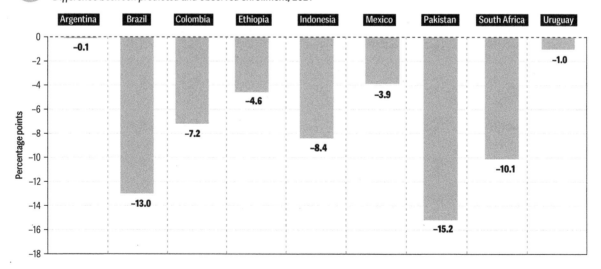

Source: Original calculations based on data from nationally representative labor force surveys.
Note: Enrollment rates in 2020 and 2021 were predicted on the basis of pre-pandemic data (2012–19 for all countries except Indonesia, where data from only 2015–19 were available to estimate time trends and seasonal effects). These estimates were then used to predict enrollment in 2020 and 2021 in the absence of the pandemic. This figure plots the difference between these predicted rates and observed rates in 2021.

Using predictions to deal with trends when estimating impacts of the pandemic

For variables such as school participation for which observations might be available from before the pandemic, it may be tempting to compare 2019 values with what was observed in 2020 and 2021 to estimate the impact of the pandemic. If rates had been increasing up to 2019, however, this strategy would underestimate the impact of the pandemic because in the absence of the pandemic the 2020 rate would have been higher than the 2019 rate. Likewise, had participation rates been declining over time before the pandemic, this strategy would overestimate the impact of the pandemic.

To account for pre-pandemic trends, one would need data from well before 2019, and information from past increases (or decreases) in rates would be used to predict the increase (or decrease) in participation between 2019 and 2020 had the pandemic not happened. It is this predicted set of participation rates for 2020 and 2021 that should be compared with what has actually been observed to estimate the impacts of the pandemic.

households (see box 2.4 on using predictions to deal with trends when estimating impacts of the pandemic). Compared with what would have been predicted from pre-pandemic trends, observed enrollment at the end of 2021 was down by more than 15 percentage points in Pakistan, 13 percentage points in Brazil, 10 percentage points in South Africa, and 8 percentage points in Indonesia. If these children completely skip pre-primary education and instead directly enroll in first grade (as their age would permit them to do), they will fail to reap the benefits of pre-primary education and will start their formal education at a lower level of school readiness than cohorts that preceded them.

Children faced more stressors in their care environments

Much of skill development during children's earliest years occurs at home and depends on investments of time by parents and other caregivers. An analysis of the historical expansions of paid maternity leave in Norway, for example, found that when mothers were able to spend the first four months after birth at home with their infants, their children went on to earn 5 percent more 30 years later.[48] Putting the powerful positive ramifications of the extra maternal caregiving in these *first four months* of life in perspective, estimates of the return to education across countries suggest that each additional *year* of education leads to later increases in earnings of 9 percent.[49]

Even before the COVID-19 pandemic, many children in low- and middle-income countries lived in home environments that did not foster safety, security, or positive interactions. Globally, about one-third of caregivers report leaving a child under age 5 in the sole care of a child younger than age 10 for more than an hour in the previous week.[50] Three-quarters of children ages 2–4 worldwide experience violent discipline by their caregivers on a regular basis, and the mothers of one-quarter of children under age 5 are themselves victims of intimate partner violence.[51]

During the pandemic, caregivers experienced more stress (figure 2.5). In the weeks following the first lockdowns in rural Colombia, for example, the probability that mothers crossed critical thresholds indicating risk of severe symptoms of anxiety, stress, and depression increased dramatically.[52] In India, the severity of local containment policies was associated with larger declines in female mental health.[53] In rural Bangladesh, in the fall of 2020 maternal depression scores were significantly higher than pre-pandemic scores.[54] More generally, a meta-analysis of nearly 60 studies from around the world comparing mental health before and after the onset of the pandemic found that, on average, the prevalence of anxiety disorders increased by 26 percent, and the prevalence of major depressive disorder increased by 28 percent.[55]

There is also evidence of an increase in violence against children and women. For example, in the United States a hospital system in a large metropolitan area reported a 97 percent increase in the share

FIGURE 2.5 Mothers' mental health declined during early lockdowns in rural Colombia and rural Bangladesh, compared with levels in 2019

Percentage change in mental health conditions compared with 2019 levels

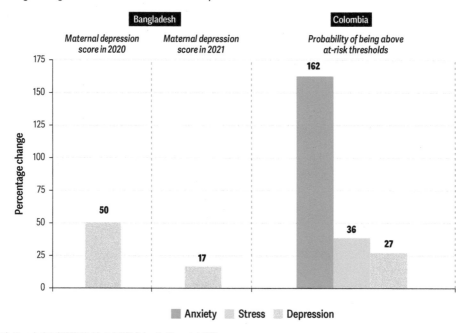

Sources: Bangladesh: Hamadani et al. 2020; Pitchik et al. 2021. Colombia: Moya et al. 2021.
Note: An increase in scores indicates increasing depression among mothers or greater probability of exhibiting severe symptoms for depression, stress, and anxiety.

of child abuse and neglect visits to the emergency department in 2020 compared with 2018 and 2019, with a 327 percent increase in the share of visits classified as neglect due to lack of supervision (which included injuries that an adult did not witness, ingestions, drownings or near drownings, falls, or gunshot wounds).[56] In a study in the Islamic Republic of Iran in which women were asked about violence perpetrated by their partners, the prevalence of reported physical intimate partner violence increased during the pandemic by 31 percent (5 percentage points higher from a base of 16.1 percent), and the prevalence of reported sexual-based violence increased by 34 percent (6 percentage points higher from a base of 17.5 percent).[57] In India, districts with the strictest mobility restrictions saw a 130 percent increase in complaints about domestic violence, compared with districts with more lenient restrictions.[58] Domestic violence complaints remained elevated compared with pre-pandemic levels, even one year after lockdowns began.

Because the COVID-19 crisis led to severe illness and the death of adults, children have also lost parents and other caregivers during the pandemic. Orphanhood has been associated with multiple disadvantages in physical growth, educational attainment, and protection from sexual abuse.[59] A study using data on COVID-19 mortality, excess deaths, and fertility rates specific to cohorts of reproductive age estimates that by May 2022, at least 7.5 million children had been orphaned because of the pandemic, with the largest numbers in the Africa and Southeast Asia regions.[60]

CHILDREN'S DEVELOPMENT SLOWED DURING LOCKDOWNS

[My daughter] has made some steps backward from a social point of view. Now, for example,
she asks me to feed her soup, and before she was doing it by herself. I think all this might have some
bigger consequences because when children spend time together, they have more stimuli... .
All this is gone, and I think my child's general development has been blocked.

—Lena Moskal, mother of a four-year-old, Bielsko-Biała, Poland
Quoted in Human Rights Watch (2021)

❝

All these stressors on very young children—the reductions in food intake, the compromised access to essential health care and pre-primary education, and the rising stress levels and violence in the home—could erode the timely formation of cognitive and social-emotional skills and depress their development. Indeed, emerging data suggest that children's skill levels are lower than the levels observed before the pandemic for children similar in age (see box 2.5 for the data requirements for detecting a pandemic-induced change in skills).

Stunting and wasting. Assessing stunting in very young children—particularly those who still cannot stand up on their own—requires in-person measurement. Because lockdowns also paused data collection, direct observations of the pandemic's effect on stunting in a general population were only just beginning to emerge in 2022. Although a study examining changes in populations admitted to a hospital finds increases in stunting and wasting, this evidence does not reveal what is happening in a more general population.[61] Two studies in Bangladesh suggest that food deprivation observed during the pandemic did not translate into increases in stunting. In rural Bangladesh, for example, 20-month-old children who had been born during a strict lockdown period were surveyed in 2022 in the same areas where 20-month-old children had been surveyed in 2019 and early 2020. The 2022 survey revealed that stunting and wasting rates among children in 2019 and 2022 were statistically indistinguishable.[62] Similarly, in urban slums in and around the capital, children under age 5 in February 2021 were just as likely to be stunted as children from the same areas measured in February 2020

BOX 2.5 Measuring changes in skills due to the pandemic

How should changes in children's development following the COVID-19 pandemic be estimated? Should the same children be tracked over time and their skill levels before the pandemic be compared with their skill levels after pandemic restrictions—that is, should researchers do a panel study? Or should the skills of children after pandemic-related restrictions were put in place be compared with those of children similar in age observed before the pandemic? That would be a repeated cross-section study.

Because a child's earliest years are a period of such rapid development, skills will improve considerably from year to year. Therefore, even if all the stressors associated with the pandemic serve to depress children's skill development, their measured skills after restrictions such as lockdowns and school closures have been lifted may still be higher than their skills before the pandemic simply because the children are older. Thus having longitudinal data on the same children does not necessarily help ascertain the effects of the pandemic because these effects might be obscured by the fact that children pick up many skills during this period of the life cycle.

On the other hand, if, for example, in a repeated cross-sectional study the skills of four-year-olds after pandemic-related restrictions have been lifted can be compared with those of a cohort of children from the same area with a similar socioeconomic background whose skills were measured before the pandemic when they were four years old, then researchers can assess whether the pandemic has slowed the acquisition of skills by age 4.

just before lockdowns, although children were significantly more likely to be wasted in 2021.[63] It is possible, however, that the full nutritional impacts of the pandemic can only be observed in the years to come.

Declines in development among toddlers. Large declines in child development for very young children have been found in rural Bangladesh. Diminished cognitive, language, and motor development, as well as social-emotional skills, were found when 20-month-old children observed in 2019 and early 2020 were compared with 20-month-old children observed in the same locations in 2022. The children measured in 2022 were born during the country's lockdowns, and their decline in cognitive scores and motor skills was quite large (an average of 0.45 standard deviation and 0.55 standard deviation, respectively).[64] Declines in cognitive and motor skills were apparent across all households and were equal in size for both male and female children, but declines were greatest for children whose mothers had completed less schooling—primary school or less (figure 2.6).

To put these magnitudes in perspective and assess their implications for human capital accumulation going forward, the decline in overall development observed in 2022 among toddlers in Bangladesh (averaged across cognitive, language, and motor skills) corresponds to more than two-thirds (68 percent) of the gap between children who received extra early stimulation in their homes for two years and those who did not in a well-known and well-documented experiment in Jamaica in the 1980s.[65] A follow-up to that study decades later revealed that the children who received additional stimulation went on to earn 25 percent more, on average, 20 years later and 37 percent more, on average, 30 years later.[66] If these causal relationships between early cognition and later earnings hold in Bangladesh, the early developmental declines currently observed there may be expected to turn into a decline in adult earnings of 17 percent when these children first enter the labor market in the next 20 years and a decline of 25 percent when they reach prime working age.

Declines in school readiness among preschool-age children. Lockdowns also thwarted child development among children who would have benefited from in-person pre-primary education in the absence of the pandemic, leaving them less prepared to start primary education. Compared with earlier cohorts, these children acquired fewer skills in language and mathematics (figure 2.7).

FIGURE 2.6 **The pandemic induced large declines in cognitive and motor development among toddlers in rural Bangladesh, with larger effects on children whose mothers had less education**

Effect of the pandemic on skills, by level of maternal education

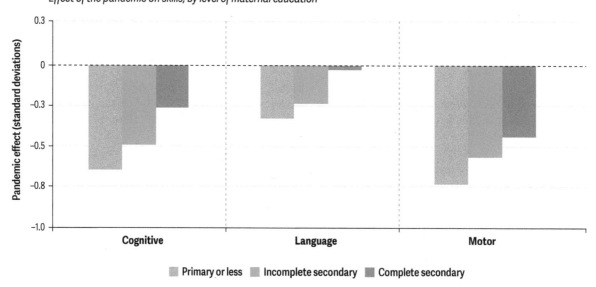

Source: Hamadani et al., forthcoming.

Note: The figure plots pandemic effects on standardized composite scores for the cognitive, language, and motor domains of the Bayley Scales of Infant Development (third edition) by level of mother's education. All plotted effects are statistically different from zero. For all skills, effects for mothers with a primary education or less were significantly different from effects for mothers who had completed a secondary education.

Collapse and Recovery: How the COVID-19 Pandemic Eroded Human Capital and What to Do about It

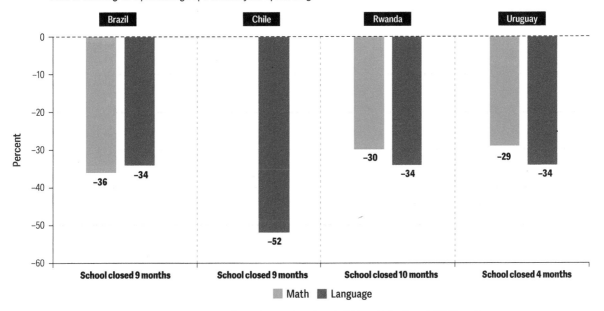

FIGURE 2.7 Children in preschool lost skills in language and math in Brazil, Chile, Rwanda, and Uruguay
Loss in learning as a percentage of a normal year of learning

	Brazil	Chile	Rwanda	Uruguay
	School closed 9 months	School closed 9 months	School closed 10 months	School closed 4 months

Math values: Brazil −36, Rwanda −30, Uruguay −29
Language values: Brazil −34, Chile −52, Rwanda −34, Uruguay −34

■ Math ■ Language

Sources: Original calculations based on Bartholo et al. 2022 (Brazil); Abufhele et al. 2022 (Chile); Holla et al. 2022 (Rwanda); González et al. 2022 (Uruguay).
Note: In Brazil, Rwanda, and Uruguay, learning losses as a percentage of learning in a normal school year were based on learning observed among students across a school year in pre-pandemic periods. In the absence of such panel data in Chile, this calculation was based on cross-sectional differences observed among children of different ages in the pre-pandemic period.

In Rio de Janeiro, Brazil, for example, researchers tracked preschool students in private and nonprofit schools during the 2019 school year. When they tracked students in the same schools during the 2020 school year in which children spent around nine months out of the classroom, they found that those students learned only 66 percent of what the 2019 cohort had learned in language before the pandemic and only 64 percent of what the 2019 cohort had learned in mathematics.[67] These losses amounted to the equivalent of four months of learning in a regular school year and appeared to have widened preexisting disparities. Economically disadvantaged children learned only 48 percent of what they would have learned in a typical year, whereas the losses among more advantaged children were smaller; they learned 75 percent of a typical year's worth of learning.

Similarly, in Rwanda where preschools were closed almost for an entire school year, children observed in public preschools in 2021 exhibited a large skill disadvantage, compared with children observed in public preschools in 2019.[68] The average decline amounted to nearly a third of a year of learning in a normal year in early numeracy skills and early literacy skills (figure 2.7).

In another city in Brazil, Sobral, learning losses were even higher for children who had started preschool in 2020, corresponding to six and seven months of lost learning in mathematics and language, respectively (figure 2.8), compared with the cohort of children unaffected by the pandemic (those in preschool in 2019). Moreover, the cohort of children starting preschool in 2021 was even worse off. This 2021 cohort would have experienced close to 16 months of remote learning and thus had only 33 percent of the in-person instructional time of the 2019 cohort. They demonstrated even lower levels of skills, compared with the 2019 cohort when measured at the same point in the school year.[69]

Skills of preschool-age children in high-income countries also declined when compared with the skills exhibited by this age group before the pandemic. In Chile, for example, where preschools were also closed for an entire school year, children exhibited in 2020 lower skills in language than children of the same age in the same municipalities surveyed with the same measurement tool in 2017.[70] These developmental deficits

CHAPTER 2 Poor Start: The Impact of the COVID-19 Pandemic on Early Childhood Development and Subsequent Human Capital Accumulation   43

FIGURE 2.8 After the pandemic, learning of preschool-age children lagged behind pre-pandemic learning in Sobral, Brazil

Learning in language during school year (2019, 2020, 2021 cohorts)

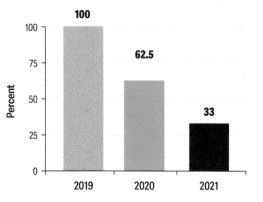

a. Average test scores, by cohort

b. Percentage of time in in-person education, by cohort

Source: Adapted from figures in Maria Cecilia Souto Vidigal Foundation (2021).

corresponded to six months of learning. Even in Uruguay, where preschools were closed for only four months, children experienced learning losses in language and math equivalent to four months of learning in pre-pandemic years.[71] In the United States, the share of kindergarten children in 41 states who scored below proficiency benchmarks increased from 28 percent in pre-pandemic years to 47 percent during the 2020–21 school year. Likewise, the share of children scoring below proficiency benchmarks in first grade (who had missed in-person instruction in the latter half of their kindergarten year and likely part of the 2020–21 school year) increased to 43 percent from 26 percent in pre-pandemic years. The declines in proficiency among Black and Latino students (who historically have been disadvantaged populations in the United States) were more than double the declines observed among White students.[72]

Taken together, these studies suggest that preschool-age children are completing early education at a marked skill disadvantage, compared with children similar in age in the same contexts born just a few years earlier. In some settings such as Uruguay, losses in skills appear commensurate with closures and lockdowns—that is, for every month of closure, children lost about a month of skill development. In other contexts, such as Brazil, the declines in skills did not track months of closure one-for-one, but losses were nevertheless very steep.

Declines in social-emotional skills and motor development. Equally worrisome are declines observed among preschool-age children in social-emotional skills and motor development. Social-emotional skills, such as emotional regulation, perseverance, and prosocial behavior, determine much of individuals' success in school and the labor market,[73] their extent (if any) of criminal activity, and their mental health in adulthood.[74] In Chile, for example, preschool-age children assessed in 2022 demonstrated more behavioral and emotional problems than children of the same age assessed in 2017.[75] In Uruguay, children demonstrated fewer externalizing behaviors such as physical or verbal aggression or defiant behavior, but they also exhibited more internalizing behaviors such as anxiety, sadness, or behavioral inhibition. In Rwanda, children in preschool in 2021 also had lower social-emotional skills than children observed in 2019.[76]

In addition, declines in motor development have been large in Bangladesh,[77] Brazil,[78] Rwanda,[79] and Uruguay,[80] perhaps because children have spent more time indoors and less time playing with other children.

THESE EARLY SETBACKS WILL HAVE LONG-LASTING RAMIFICATIONS FOR HUMAN CAPITAL ACCUMULATION, EARNINGS, AND ECONOMIC GROWTH

As discussed in chapter 1, unless remedied, the declines in maternal and child services, the closures of preschools, and the setback in skills already apparent in the youngest children following lockdowns will inhibit their ability to accumulate human capital across their entire life cycle.

Most immediately, young children will enter primary school less prepared to learn. Without interventions to compensate for missing critical health services and pre-primary education and to reverse their developmental declines, these children will complete fewer years of education and learn less when they are in school.[81] Compared with cohorts born in the years before the pandemic, they will also be more likely to suffer from substance abuse and chronic illnesses such as cardiovascular disease and depression[82] and to engage in criminal activities,[83] all of which will lead to higher burdens on public services and government budgets.

Once they enter the labor market in the next 20 years, unless interventions are put in place to remediate the observed losses from the pandemic, these children will earn lower wages due to both their lower years of schooling and lower cognitive skills.[84] Because setbacks during the earliest stages of human capital formation can transmit across generations (table 2.1), the pandemic-induced shocks that are only starting to be observed may reverberate for decades to come. How and whether this poor start permanently sets human capital accumulation off track will depend on the dynamics of recovery in the short to medium term. Implications for individual earnings and other outcomes depend on the extent to which children can bounce back from these early setbacks—that is, after a downward shift in skill acquisition very early in life, will losses persist as children find themselves on a path lower than, but parallel to, the one expected in the absence of the pandemic? Or will the losses grow over time, leading to considerable divergence with respect to pre-pandemic trends? Or will the losses be partially or completely reversed so that children converge back to their pre-pandemic trajectories? Policies and programs for children age 5 and younger today will determine which path of human capital accumulation they will take in the future.

HOW CAN POLICY GET YOUNG CHILDREN BACK ON TRACK?

During lockdowns and subsequent economic slowdowns, children lost inputs and opportunities essential for their development. The declines observed today in their cognitive, motor, and social-emotional skills have been deep and foretell future struggles in education and in the labor market. Although some losses cannot be "recovered" (such as antenatal care visits, care for an acute childhood illness, or birth complications that lead to disabilities), many of them can. It will be important to identify investments that ensure that losses observed today do not amplify over time and deepen in the future. Ideally, programs and policies implemented in the next few years would help children completely recover their losses and converge back to their pre-pandemic trajectories before they start primary education. Even when this is not possible, a partial recovery of skills would be advantageous. To identify a policy agenda to put the youngest children back on track, it is useful to examine how governments addressed the needs of this population during the pandemic and to assess how these efforts can be augmented to close the remaining deficits going forward.

Lessons from early government responses

Faced with an unprecedented crisis that could endanger children on multiple dimensions, governments around the world reacted swiftly to try to ensure that households could continue to meet basic needs and to relieve potentially stressful situations for caregivers who had to remain home with children during lockdowns. Most governments also shut down schools, including those providing pre-primary education.

Transfers. Transfer programs after the pandemic were either newly established by governments or widely expanded to achieve unparalleled coverage, reaching more than 1.3 billion individuals globally with $3 trillion invested in social protection.[85] In low- and middle-income countries, from 75 to 94 percent of these programs were new, with in-kind transfers accounting for a larger share of programs in low-income countries (40 percent), compared with those in high-income countries (29 percent). Although evidence from before the pandemic suggests that cash transfers can generate modest improvements in physical growth among very young children,[86] transfers alone do not generally improve child cognitive and other skills at a magnitude comparable to the losses observed during the pandemic.[87]

Helplines and phone-based counseling. Child protection requires the participation of multiple services because teachers and health care providers are often trained to identify signs of neglect and abuse and report them to departments with mandates to intervene. The lockdowns associated with the pandemic disrupted these important reporting channels, imperiling the physical and mental welfare of both children and women. Numerous studies have documented decreases in calls in police reports and fewer referrals to child protection services and increases in call volumes to domestic violence helplines.[88]

Restrictions on in-person interactions forced some service providers to innovate and adapt programs— for example, by providing counseling by phone or by means of voice recordings sent through text messages. In a randomized control trial in Bangladesh, women who received four 25-minute counseling sessions delivered by locally recruited and trained paracounselors during the pandemic showed large reductions in moderate or severe stress (a decline of 19 percentage points from a base of 95 percent) and depression (a decline of 19 percentage points from a base of 58 percent), compared with women who did not receive counseling.[89] Similarly, in a trial in Guatemala mothers of children between the ages of six months and three years received 20 two-minute voice messages over a period of two months on stimulating children. Compared with mothers who did not receive the messages, mothers receiving the recordings showed lower levels of anxiety, while their children showed significant improvements in vocabulary,[90] an outcome shown to predict intelligence later in childhood.[91]

Closures and slowdowns in services. As discussed in greater detail in chapter 3, most governments reacted to the pandemic by immediately shutting down schools, although there was substantial variation in the length of closures within and across regions. By 2021, mandated closures alone (rather than dropouts due to fears of infection or due to permanent closures of private schools) would have cut pre-primary instructional time in half.[92] Given the large declines in school readiness that have been observed among children in a variety of income contexts and the small risks of severe infection associated with the COVID-19 virus itself for children under age 10, these long closures likely triggered severe setbacks in skills without any meaningful protection from illness.

Likewise, many governments redirected financial resources and personnel away from programs delivering essential childhood vaccines. In early 2020, 66 countries reported postponing at least one vaccination campaign, with only 25 countries reporting that campaigns had been reinstated by the end of the year.[93] Like for school closures, however, there is substantial variation in countries' experiences. Vaccine coverage increased in 28 countries in 2020 and partially recovered to pre-pandemic levels in 2021 in 39 countries, while 24 countries managed to exceed their pre-pandemic levels in 2021.[94]

Closing gaps early so they do not widen over time

Going forward, governments should strive to close the gaps in early childhood development stemming from the pandemic. Although the transfers and phone-based counseling implemented during the pandemic may have helped children and their families cope with economic and psychological shocks, by themselves these programs would have been insufficient to counteract the developmental declines induced by the closure of essential health care and education services.

The appropriateness of recovery strategies is likely to depend on both the age of the child and a country's level of economic development. Infants and toddlers (ages 0–3) and their parents tend to fall under the purview of policies and benefits packages organized by the health and social protection sectors, whereas the preschool-age group (ages 4–5) also relies on services organized by the education sector.

Policy priorities for children under age 3

Infants and toddlers participate only infrequently in formal childcare or early education programs. Although the coverage rates for these services are unknown in low- and middle-income countries, they are likely to be extremely low because the coverage for the population of infants to two-year-olds averages 36 percent in higher-income countries in the Organisation for Economic Co-operation and Development (OECD).[95] Therefore, for this age group governments may need to reach children individually, either through special campaigns or through the existing infrastructure of health and social protection services.

Given the losses already evident in this age group, policy priorities include (1) launching catch-up campaigns for vaccination and nutritional supplementation; (2) increasing the coverage of parenting programs to improve the quality of parent-child interactions and increase cognitive and social-emotional stimulation; and (3) expanding the coverage of cash transfers to households with young children where incomes have not yet recovered.

Targeted campaigns for vaccinations and nutritional supplementation. Evidence suggests that for standard interventions such as catch-up vaccination campaigns and nutritional supplementation, complete recovery is possible from some of the declines in vaccination coverage and nutrition observed during lockdowns and the subsequent year. Catch-up vaccinations, or vaccinating individuals who have missed doses according to their national immunization schedules, have already begun in some countries.[96] In Pakistan, for example, more than 1.2 million children missed immunizations during the first year of the pandemic, but intensive outreach efforts, in part enabled by an electronic immunization registry, contributed to successful catch-up efforts that had immunized 76 percent of these children by March 2021.[97] Doses administered through outreach efforts increased by more than 120 percent, whereas vaccines administered through regular vaccination clinics were still down by 22 percent in 2021. Administering vaccines during routine health visits continues to be an option, but setting up special days and locations focused on vaccine delivery (or vaccination camps) and providing small in-kind incentives such as plates and bags of lentils can also encourage completion of vaccination schedules.[98]

As for children's nutritional status, it did not deteriorate in Indonesia following the Asian financial crisis in 1997–98. Subsequent research found that a national supplementary feeding program implemented by midwives for children between the ages of six months and five years substantially reduced rates of severe stunting by 9 percent for children under age 1, by 15 percent for children ages 1–2, and by 27 percent for children ages 2–5.[99] More generally, evidence from randomized control trials suggests that nutritional supplementation, such as iodine supplementation, can improve cognitive scores by magnitudes commensurate with the losses documented during the pandemic.[100] Similarly, meta-analyses of experimental and quasi-experimental evidence suggest that lipid-based nutrient supplementation for children between the ages of 6 and 23 months decreases child mortality and rates of stunting, wasting, and anemia.[101] Thus, at least for declines in human capital that stem from diminished access to essential vaccines and nutrition, there is a suite of policies that can get children back on track. Because many, if not most, low-income countries already formally rely on a network of community health workers to deliver maternal and child health services and nutritional programs, these existing cadres can deliver these catch-up programs.

Increasing coverage of parenting programs. There is also substantial evidence from both high- and low-income contexts that it is possible to compensate—at least partially—for early deficits in cognitive and social-emotional skills by increasing the amount of early stimulation that children receive at home. For example, in the experiment in Jamaica discussed earlier, community health workers made weekly visits to demonstrate to mothers of stunted children how they could use household materials and play activities to stimulate their children. After two years, children who were initially stunted gained 0.73 standard deviation on a developmental index that combined multiple areas of development (cognitive, language, and motor development, for example), compared with children who were not visited by the community health workers.[102] More important, this magnitude of gains would completely offset the pandemic-induced losses observed in 2022.

If early stimulation programs more broadly can generate similar effects on a large scale, then the children demonstrating declines in various cognitive, language, and social-emotional skills following lockdowns would not only converge back to their pre-pandemic trajectories but could also surpass them. Experiences in other contexts, however, suggest that at-scale programs that promote early stimulation in the home through door-to-door visits of community health workers may only lead to partial recovery of skills among the youngest children.[103] Although systematic reviews have found significant positive effects on cognitive development and other skills,[104] the average effects (0.32 standard deviation) are much lower than what was observed in the Jamaica study (0.73 standard deviation) and the magnitude of deficits observed following the pandemic. When the content of the Jamaica program was implemented in Colombia on a larger scale through the infrastructure of an existing cash transfer program and when implemented in Peru as a national program, the impacts were much lower: 0.18 standard deviation in Colombia[105] and 0.10 standard deviation in Peru.[106]

Because declines in skills may fall across the entire income spectrum, door-to-door methods of delivering early stimulation programs can be prohibitively expensive. There are, however, ways to modify parenting programs to lower costs and increase potential for scale. Evidence from India, for example, suggests that group-based early stimulation programs in which a group of mothers and their children work with trained community health workers can be just as effective as a door-to-door variant.[107] The pandemic also forced implementers of parenting programs to innovate. Evidence generated during these experiments suggests that it is possible to reach parents remotely, influence their interactions with children, and improve skills among children.[108]

Expanding the coverage of transfers for households with young children. As chapter 4 documents, employment and income have not yet fully recovered from the pandemic in some countries or among different segments of the labor force. Because income fluctuations tend to have detrimental effects on human capital investments made for the youngest children, particularly in low-income countries,[109] and on the care they receive at home, ensuring that households with young children can benefit from cash and in-kind transfers is an investment that governments need to make today to generate returns in terms of future productivity. In response to the pandemic, South Africa, for example, increased the benefits of its Child Support Grants program, which targets primary caregivers in low-income households and reaches more than 20 percent of the population. Likewise, Mongolia expanded both the eligibility and the benefits of its Child Money Program, which targets families with children and covers more than one-third of the population.

Policy priorities for children ages 3–5

For children older than age 3 and younger than age 6, pre-primary education is the main vehicle generating large immediate impacts on skills and improving children's readiness for the next stage in the life cycle, formal education. Coverage of preschool varies considerably across countries, ranging from 14 percent in low-income countries to 66 percent in high-income countries (with rates of 29 percent in lower-middle-income countries and 41 percent in upper-middle-income countries). In all countries, fully reopening preschools and ensuring that young children attend are an important priority.

Reopening schools and expanding access to pre-primary education. Expansions in community preschools in Mozambique, for example, increased an index of cognitive and language development by 0.43 standard deviation when children were observed in first grade.[110] Children in communities that received the new community preschools as part of a randomized control trial were also 8 percentage points (13 percent) more likely to be enrolled in primary school four years later and spent an additional two hours per week (14 percent more time) in school and doing homework, compared with children in communities that had not received the new preschools.

Although the impacts of pre-primary education programs demonstrate the potential for early education to help children converge back to their pre-pandemic trajectories, coverage of pre-primary education services in low-income countries is low, suggesting that scaled provision or subsidized care may not materialize quickly enough to offset the declines in skills already observed among the youngest children. Indeed, past evidence suggests that children may gain minimally if expansions proceed without sufficient attention paid to quality or to the extent to which parents might switch their children from private to public schools or from primary to pre-primary schools.[111]

Recent evidence from Bangladesh and India, however, suggests that even low-dose and low-cost programs can lead to sizable gains in skills that are commensurate with pandemic-induced losses. In Bangladesh, for example, attending a year of additional preschool through two-hour sessions taught by government teachers in government classrooms significantly improved literacy, numeracy, and social development scores (by 0.44, 0.57, and 0.68 standard deviation, respectively).[112] In a trial in India, a cadre of half-time workers with a high school education and only one week of training in pre-primary education was added to the staff in centers implementing the country's Integrated Child Development Services, which provides health, nutrition, and day care services to more than 36 million children ages 3–6. After 18 months, this additional cadre of workers increased scores in math and language by 0.29 and 0.46 standard deviation, respectively.[113]

Globally, private provision accounts for more than 40 percent of pre-primary enrollment. During lockdowns, some providers may have ceased operations altogether. Therefore, in the short term subsidies may be needed to encourage these providers to reopen and resume services. In the medium term, particularly as countries seek ways to expand coverage more generally, governments may need to subsidize nonstate provision, as is done in many flagship early education programs in high-income countries such as Canada, Norway, and the United States.

Inserting social-emotional skills into curricula and planning transitions to primary school. Because emerging evidence suggests an increase in social-emotional and behavioral problems among preschool-age children, curricula ought to reflect this weakness in the skill set of students. Compared with previous cohorts, children affected by school closures have spent less time in a classroom environment and may lack skills such as inhibition control and attention that contribute to learning. Evidence from before the pandemic suggests there can be large gains in these skills when social-emotional learning is explicitly incorporated into the curriculum or into pedagogical practices in both middle- and high-income countries.[114]

Most important, because children may exit pre-primary education with lower skills in early literacy and numeracy, social-emotional problems, and behaviors that might hamper their learning, or because many children of pre-primary school age will have missed preschool altogether, it will be important to actively coordinate between pre-primary and primary schooling so that the transition to primary school happens smoothly. In particular, the content and pacing of lessons in grade 1 must meet children where they are instead of assuming children have acquired the same level of skills that children entering grade 1 exhibited before the pandemic (chapter 3 addresses in detail adapting teaching practices to the skill level of children).

Policy priorities for mothers and other caregivers

Attention to adults' mental health is a need that cuts across age groups and income contexts. Before the pandemic, however, nearly 90 percent of individuals diagnosed with depression or anxiety in low-income countries did not receive treatment.[115] Evidence shows that when depression among mothers is addressed, they increase investments in the human capital of their children. In a randomized control trial in Pakistan, for example, depressed mothers who received psychotherapy invested more financial resources and devoted more time to the education or stimulation of their children.[116] Although many low- and middle-income countries lack the human resources to deliver care for mental health issues to all individuals in need, randomized control trials have demonstrated that scaling low-dose mental health counseling delivered by paraprofessionals can also make headway in reducing the prevalence of depression. In India, for example, such a program successfully reduced the prevalence of depression among women, with effects persisting four to five years later.[117] When scaling care delivered by specialists is not feasible, finding ways to scale mental health counseling delivered by nonspecialists should therefore be a short-term goal for health and social protection systems.

USING THE PANDEMIC TO PRIORITIZE INVESTMENTS IN CHILDREN

Historically, governments have underinvested in young children—both because the benefits from investments in early childhood were not well understood by policy makers and because the benefits of early childhood programs accrue over long periods of time and translate into increased earnings only when individuals are old enough to enter the labor market. This neglect in this sphere of policy is no longer an option after the pandemic. Addressing the damage caused by the pandemic will require governments to reprioritize children today, as the very young children affected by the pandemic need immediate attention, and the time window to help them is very short. Many will be entering primary school in the next one to two years with significant declines in their cognitive, language, motor, and social-emotional development. Without efforts to ameliorate this poor start to formal education and skill acquisition more generally, these children will accumulate human capital at a slower rate during school and will enter the labor market at a marked disadvantage.

NOTES

1. Original calculations for this publication.
2. Almond (2006).
3. Adhvaryu, Fenske, and Nyshadham (2019).
4. Andrabi, Daniels, and Das (2021).
5. Bleker et al. (2005); Neugebauer, Hoek, and Susser (1999); Roseboom et al. (2000); Susser, Hoek, and Brown (1998).
6. de Rooij et al. (2010).
7. Painter et al. (2008).
8. Rossin-Slater and Wust (2020).
9. Gertler et al. (2021).
10. Walker et al. (2021).
11. Fox, Levitt, and Nelson (2010); Johnson (2001); Mukherjee (2016).
12. Spelke and Schutts (2022).
13. WHO, UNICEF, and World Bank (2018).
14. Holla et al. (2021); McCoy et al. (2018, 2021).
15. Dearing, McCartney, and Taylor (2006); Elder and Nguyen (1985); Jackson et al. (2000).
16. Bruckner (2008).
17. Kalil and Ryan (2020); Ward and Lee (2000).
18. Elder and Nguyen (1985); McLoyd (1990).
19. World Bank (2022).
20. Egger et al. (2021); Miguel and Mobarak (2021).
21. UNICEF (2021a).
22. Hamadani et al. (2020).
23. Ahmed et al. (2021); Fetzer and Rauh (2022); Mafham et al. (2020); Moynihan et al. (2021); Siedner et al. (2020); Uy et al. (2022).
24. Darmstadt et al. (2005); Kuhnt and Vollmer (2017).
25. Lawn et al. (2009); Rohde et al. (2008).
26. Buttha et al. (2002); Johnson and Schoeni (2011); Moster, Lie, and Markestad (2008).
27. Chay, Guryan, and Mazumder (2009).
28. Becher et al. (2004); Scott et al. (2017).
29. Ahmed et al. (2021).
30. Uy et al. (2022).
31. Ashish et al. (2020).
32. Badran et al. (2021); Been et al. (2020); Hedley et al. (2022); Stowe et al. (2020); Yalçin et al. (2022).
33. Arsenault et al. (2022).
34. WHO and UNICEF (2021).
35. WHO and UNICEF (2021).
36. Siedner et al. (2020).
37. Nuzhat et al. (2022).
38. McCoy et al. (2021).
39. Holla et al. (2021).
40. Bailey, Sun, and Timpe (2021); Heckman et al. (2010); Rossin-Slater and Wust (2020).
41. Bailey, Sun, and Timpe (2021).
42. McCoy et al. (2018).

43. UNICEF (2021b).
44. Weiland et al. (2021).
45. McCoy et al. (2021).
46. UNESCO Institute for Statistics, 2020, http://data.uis.unesco.org/.
47. McCoy et al. (2018).
48. Carneiro, Løken, and Salvanes (2015).
49. Psacharopoulos and Patrinos (2018).
50. UNICEF (2021b).
51. UNICEF (2017).
52. Moya et al. (2021). The increases were 162 percent (14 percentage points from a base of 8.6 percent) for anxiety, 36 percent (10 percentage points from a base of 27.8 percent) for stress, and 27 percent (5 percentage points from a base of 18.5 percent) for depression.
53. Bau et al. (2022).
54. Pitchik et al. (2021).
55. COVID-19 Mental Disorders Collaborators (2021).
56. Bullinger et al. (2021).
57. Fereidooni et al. (2021).
58. Ravindran and Shah (2021).
59. Beegle, De Weerdt, and Dercon (2006); Kidman and Palermo (2016).
60. Hillis et al. (2022).
61. Nuzhat et al. (2022).
62. Hamadani et al. (forthcoming).
63. Win et al. (2022).
64. Hamadani et al. (forthcoming).
65. Grantham-McGregor et al. (1991).
66. Gertler et al. (2021).
67. Bartholo et al. (2022).
68. Holla et al. (2022).
69. Maria Cecilia Souto Vidigal Foundation (2021).
70. Abufhele et al. (2022).
71. González et al. (2022).
72. Amplify (2021).
73. Belfield et al. (2015); Heckman and Kautz (2012); Heckman, Pinto, and Savelyev (2013); Jackson (2018); Pisani, Seiden, and Wolf (2022).
74. Jones, Greenberg, and Crowley (2015).
75. Abufhele et al. (2022).
76. Holla et al. (2022).
77. Hamadani et al. (forthcoming).
78. Maria Cecilia Souto Vidigal Foundation (2021).
79. Holla et al. (2022).
80. González et al. (2022).
81. Gertler et al. (2021).
82. Carneiro and Ginja (2014); Walker et al. (2021).
83. Heckman et al. (2010).
84. Bailey, Sun, and Timpe (2021); Havnes and Mogstad (2011).
85. Gentilini (2022).
86. Manley et al. (2020); Manley, Alderman, and Gentilini (2022).
87. de Walque et al. (2017); Macours, Schady, and Vakis (2012); Paxson and Schady (2010).
88. Cappa and Jijon (2021).
89. Siddique et al. (2022).
90. Arteaga and Trias (2022).

91. Bornstein et al. (2008).
92. McCoy et al. (2021).
93. WHO and UNICEF (2021).
94. WHO and UNICEF (2022).
95. OECD (2021).
96. Arsenault et al. (2022); WHO and UNICEF (2021).
97. Chandir et al. (2021).
98. Banerjee et al. (2010, 2021).
99. Giles and Satriawan (2015).
100. Bougma et al. (2013).
101. Das et al. (2019); Stewart et al. (2020).
102. Grantham-McGregor et al. (1991).
103. Breeding and Holla (2021).
104. Jeong, Pitchik, and Fink (2021).
105. Andrew et al. (2018).
106. Araujo, Rubio-Codina, and Schady (2021).
107. Grantham-McGregor et al. (1991).
108. Arteaga and Trias (2022).
109. Ferreira and Schady (2009); Shapira, de Walque, and Friedman (2021).
110. Martinez, Naudeau, and Pereira (2017).
111. Berkes et al. (2019); Bernal et al. (2019); Bouguen et al. (2018).
112. Spier et al. (2020).
113. Ganimian, Muralidharan, and Walters (2021).
114. Bierman et al. (2008); Dillon et al. (2017); Hamre et al. (2012); Raver et al. (2011).
115. Patel et al. (2009); Wang et al. (2007).
116. Baranov et al. (2020).
117. Bhat et al. (2022).

REFERENCES

Abufhele, A., D. Bravo, F. López Bóo, and P. Soto-Ramirez. 2022. "Developmental Losses in Young Children from Pre-primary Program Closures during the COVID-19 Pandemic." Technical Note 2385, Inter-American Development Bank, Washington, DC.

Adhvaryu, A., J. Fenske, and A. Nyshadham. 2019. "Early Life Circumstance and Adult Mental Health." *Journal of Political Economy* 127 (4): 1516–49.

Ahmed, T., T. Roberton, J. P. Alfred, M. L. Baye, M. Diabate, H. Kiarie, P. Mbaka, et al. 2021. "Indirect Effects on Maternal and Child Mortality from the COVID-19 Pandemic: Evidence from Disruptions in Healthcare Utilization in 18 Low- and Middle-Income Countries." Johns Hopkins Center for Humanitarian Health, Baltimore, MD.

Almond, D. 2006. "Is the 1918 Influenza Pandemic Over? Long-Term Effects of *in Utero* Influenza Exposure in the Post-1940 US Population." *Journal of Political Economy* 114 (4): 672–712.

Almond, D., and B. Mazumder. 2011. "Health Capital and the Prenatal Environment: The Effect of Ramadan Observance during Pregnancy." *American Economic Journal: Applied Economics* 3 (4): 56–85.

Almond, D., B. Mazumder, and R. Van Ewijk. 2014. "In Utero Ramadan Exposure and Children's Academic Performance." *Economic Journal* 125 (589): 1501–33.

Amplify. 2021. "COVID-19 Means More Students Not Learning to Read." https://amplify.com/wp-content /uploads/2021/02/Amplify-mCLASS_MOY-COVID-Learning-Loss-Research-Brief_022421.pdf.

Andrabi, T., B. Daniels, and J. Das. 2021. "Human Capital Accumulation and Disasters: Evidence from the Pakistan Earthquake of 2005." *Journal of Human Resources*. doi: 0520-10887R1.

Andrew, A., O. Attanasio, E. Fitzsimons, S. Grantham-McGregor, C. Meghir, and M. Rubio-Codina. 2018. "Impacts 2 Years after a Scalable Early Childhood Development Intervention to Increase Psychosocial Stimulation in the Home: A Follow-Up of a Cluster Randomised Controlled Trial in Colombia." *PLoS Medicine* 15 (4).

Araujo, M. C., M. Rubio-Codina, and N. Schady. 2021. "70 to 700 to 70,000: Lessons from the Jamaica Experiment." In *The Scale-Up Effect in Early Childhood and Public Policy*, 211–32. London: Routledge.

Arsenault, C., A. Gage, M. K. Kim, N. R. Kapoor, P. Akweongo, F. Amponsah, A. Aryal, et al. 2022. "COVID-19 and Resilience of Healthcare Systems in Ten Countries." *Nature Medicine* 29: 1314–24.

Arteaga, I., and J. Trias. 2022. "Can Technology Narrow the Early Childhood Stimulation Gap in Rural Guatemala? Results from an Experimental Approach." Unpublished manuscript.

Ashish, K. C., R. Gurung, M. V. Kinney, A. K. Sunny, M. Moinuddin, O. Basnet, P. Paudel, et al. 2020. "Effect of the COVID-19 Pandemic Response on Intrapartum Care, Stillbirth, and Neonatal Mortality Outcomes in Nepal: A Prospective Observational Study." *The Lancet Global Health* 8 (10): e1273–e1281.

Badran, E. F., R. M. Darwish, Y. Khader, R. AlMasri, M. Al Jaberi, M. AlMasri, F. AlSa'di, L. Abu Yosef, and N. Al-Badaineh. 2021. "Adverse Pregnancy Outcomes during the COVID-19 Lockdown: A Descriptive Study." *BMC Pregnancy and Childbirth* 21 (1): 1–8.

Bailey, M. J., S. Sun, and B. Timpe. 2021. "Prep School for Poor Kids: The Long-Run Impacts of Head Start on Human Capital and Economic Self-Sufficiency." *American Economic Review* 111 (12): 3963–4001.

Baird, S., J. Friedman, and N. Schady. 2011. "Aggregate Income Shocks and Infant Mortality in the Developing World." *Review of Economics and Statistics* 93 (3): 847–56.

Banerjee, A., A. G. Chandrasekhar, S. Dalpath, E. Duflo, J. Floretta, M. O. Jackson, H. Kannan, et al. 2021. "Selecting the Most Effective Nudge: Evidence from a Large-Scale Experiment on Immunization." NBER Working Paper 28726, National Bureau of Economic Research, Cambridge, MA.

Banerjee, A. V., E. Duflo, R. Glennerster, and D. Kothari. 2010. "Improving Immunisation Coverage in Rural India: Clustered Randomised Controlled Evaluation of Immunisation Campaigns with and without Incentives." *BMJ* (2010): 340.

Baranov, V., S. Bhalotra, P. Biroli, and J. Maselko. 2020. "Maternal Depression, Women's Empowerment, and Parental Investment: Evidence from a Randomized Controlled Trial." *American Economic Review* 110 (3): 824–59.

Bartholo, T., M. Koslinski, P. Tymms, and D. Lopes de Castro. 2022. "Learning Loss and Learning Inequality during the Covid-19 Pandemic." https://dro.dur.ac.uk/36314/.

Bau, N., G. Khanna, C. Low, M. Shah, S. Sharmin, and A. Voena. 2022. "Women's Well-Being during a Pandemic and Its Containment." *Journal of Development Economics* 156: 102839.

Becher, H., O. Muller, A. Jahn, A. Gbangou, G. Kynast-Wolf, and B. Kouyaté. 2004. "Risk Factors of Infant and Child." *Bulletin of the World Health Organization* 82 (4): 265–73.

Beegle, K., J. De Weerdt, and S. Dercon. 2006. "Orphanhood and the Long-Run Impact on Children." *American Journal of Agricultural Economics* 88 (5): 1266–72.

Been, J. V., L. B. Ochoa, L. C. Bertens, S. Schoenmakers, E. A. Steegers, and I. K. Reiss. 2020. "Impact of COVID-19 Mitigation Measures on the Incidence of Preterm Birth: A National Quasi-Experimental Study." *The Lancet Public Health* 5 (11): e604–e611.

Belfield, C., A. B. Bowden, A. Klapp, H. Levin, R. Shand, and S. Zander. 2015. "The Economic Value of Social and Emotional Learning." *Journal of Benefit-Cost Analysis* 6 (3): 508–44.

Berkes, J. L., A. Bouguen, D. Filmer, and T. Fukao. 2019. "Improving Preschool Provision and Encouraging Demand: Heterogeneous Impacts of a Large-Scale Program." Policy Research Working Paper 9070, World Bank, Washington, DC.

Bernal, R., O. P. Attanasio, X. Peña, and M. Vera-Hernández. 2019. "The Effects of the Transition from Home-Based Childcare to Childcare Centers on Children's Health and Development in Colombia." *Early Childhood Research Quarterly* 47 (2): 418–31.

Bhat, B., J. de Quidt, J. Haushofer, V. H. Patel, G. Rao, F. Schilbach, and P. L. P. Vautrey. 2022. "The Long-Run Effects of Psychotherapy on Depression, Beliefs, and Economic Outcomes." NBER Working Paper 30011, National Bureau of Economic Research, Cambridge, MA.

Bierman, K. L., C. E. Domitrovich, R. L. Nix, S. D. Gest, J. A. Welsh, M. T. Greenberg, C. Blair, et al. 2008. "Promoting Academic and Social-Emotional School Readiness: The Head Start REDI Program." *Child Development* 79 (6): 1802–17.

Bleker, O. P., T. J. Roseboom, A. C. Ravelli, G. A. van Montfans, C. Osmond, and D. J. Barker. 2005. "Cardiovascular Disease in Survivors of the Dutch Famine." In *The Impact of Maternal Malnutrition on the Offspring: Nestle Nutrition Workshop Series Pediatric Program* 55: 183–95. Basel, Switzerland: Karger.

Bornstein, M. H., C. S. Tamis-LeMonda, C. S. Hahn, and O. M. Haynes. 2008. "Maternal Responsiveness to Young Children at Three Ages: Longitudinal Analysis of a Multidimensional, Modular, and Specific Parenting Construct." *Developmental Psychology* 44 (867): 10.1037/0012–1649.44.3.867.

Bougma, K., F. E. Aboud, K. B. Harding, and G. S. Marquis. 2013. "Iodine and Mental Development of Children 5 Years Old and Under: A Systematic Review and Meta-analysis." *Nutrients* 5 (4): 1384–1416.

Bouguen, A., D. Filmer, K. Macours, and S. Naudeau. 2018. "Preschool and Parental Response in a Second Best World: Evidence from a School Construction Experiment." *Journal of Human Resources* 53 (2): 474–512.

Breeding, M., and A. Holla. 2021. *Lessons from Parenting Programs in Early Childhood*. Washington, DC: World Bank.

Bruckner, T. A. 2008. "Metropolitan Economic Decline and Infant Mortality due to Unintentional Injury." *Accident Analysis and Prevention* 40 (6): 1797–1803.

Bullinger, L. R., A. Boy, S. Messner, and S. Self-Brown. 2021. "Pediatric Emergency Department Visits due to Child Abuse and Neglect following COVID-19 Public Health Emergency Declaration in the Southeastern United States." *BMC Pediatrics* 21 (401): 1–9.

Buttha, A., M. Cleves, P. Casey, M. Cradock, and K. Anand. 2002. "Cognitive and Behavioral Outcomes of School-Aged Children Who Were Born Preterm." *JAMA* 288 (6): 728–37.

Cappa, C., and I. Jijon. 2021. "COVID-19 and Violence against Children: A Review of Early Studies." *Child Abuse and Neglect* 116: 105053.

Carlson, K. 2015. "Fear Itself: The Effects of Distressing Economic News on Birth Outcomes." *Journal of Health Economics* 41: 117–32.

Carneiro, P., and R. Ginja. 2014. "Long-Term Impacts of Compensatory Preschool on Health and Behavior: Evidence from Head Start." *American Economic Journal: Economic Policy* 6 (4): 135–73.

Carneiro, P., K. V. Løken, and K. G. Salvanes. 2015. "A Flying Start? Maternity Leave Benefits and Long-Run Outcomes of Children." *Journal of Political Economy* 123 (2): 365–412.

Caruso, G. D. 2017. "The Legacy of Natural Disasters: The Intergenerational Impact of 100 Years of Disasters in Latin America." *Journal of Development Economics* 127: 209–233.

Chandir, S., D. A. Siddiqi, M. Mehmood, S. Iftikhar, M. Siddique, S. Jai, V. K. Dharma, et al. 2021. "1-Year Impact of COVID-19 on Childhood Immunizations in Pakistan: Analysis of 3.7 Million Children." *European Journal of Public Health* 31 (Suppl. 3): ckab164–538.

Chatterjee, S., and T. Vogl. 2018. "Escaping Malthus: Economic Growth and Fertility Change in the Developing World." *American Economic Review* 108 (6): 1440–67.

Chay, K. Y., J. Guryan, and B. Mazumder. 2009. "Birth Cohort and the Black-White Achievement Gap: The Roles of Access and Health Soon after Birth." NBER Working Paper 15078, National Bureau of Economic Research, Cambridge, MA.

COVID-19 Mental Disorders Collaborators. 2021. "Global Prevalence and Burden of Depressive and Anxiety Disorders in 204 Countries and Territories in 2020 due to the COVID-19 Pandemic." *The Lancet* 398 (2021): 1700–12.

Currie, J., and M. Rossin-Slater. 2013. "Weathering the Storm: Hurricanes and Birth Outcomes." *Journal of Health Economics* 32 (3): 487–503.

Darmstadt, G., A. B. Zulfiqar, S. Cousens, T. Adam, N. Walker, and L. Bernis. 2005. "Evidence-Based, Cost-Effective Interventions: How Many Newborn Babies Can We Save?" *The Lancet* 365 (9463): 977–88.

Das, J. K., R. A. Salam, Y. B. Hadi, S. S. Sheikh, A. Z. Bhutta, Z. W. Prinzo, and Z. A. Bhutta. 2019. "Preventive Lipid-Based Nutrient Supplements Given with Complementary Foods to Infants and Young Children 6 to 23 Months of Age for Health, Nutrition, and Developmental Outcomes." *Cochrane Database of Systematic Reviews* (5).

Dearing, E., K. McCartney, and B. A. Taylor. 2006. "Within-Child Associations between Family Income and Externalizing and Internalizing Problems." *Developmental Psychology* 42 (2): 237–52.

Delamou, A., A. M. El Ayadi, S. Sidibe, T. Delvaux, B. S. Camara, S. D. Sandouno, A. Beavogui, et al. 2017. "Effect of Ebola Virus Disease on Maternal and Child Health Services in Guinea: A Retrospective Observational Cohort Study." *The Lancet Global Health* 5 (4): e448–e457.

de Rooij, S. R., H. Wouters, J. E. Yonker, R. C. Painter, and T. J. Roseboom. 2010. "Prenatal Undernutrition and Cognitive Function in Late Adulthood." *Proceedings of the National Academy of Sciences* 107 (39): 16881–86.

de Walque, D., L. Fernald, P. Gertler, and M. Hidrobo. 2017. "Cash Transfers and Child and Adolescent Development." *Child and Adolescent Health and Development*, 3rd ed., edited by D. A. P. Bundy, N. de Silva, S. Horton, D. T. Jamison, and G. C. Patton. Washington, DC: World Bank.

Dillon, M. R., H. Kannan, J. T. Dean, E. S. Spelke, and E. Duflo. 2017. "Cognitive Science in the Field: A Preschool Intervention Durably Enhances Intuitive but Not Formal Mathematics." *Science* 357 (6346): 47–55.

Egger, D., E. Miguel, S. S. Warren, A. Shenoy, E. Collins, D. Karlan, D. Parkerson, et al. 2021. "Falling Living Standards during the COVID-19 Crisis: Quantitative Evidence from Nine Developing Countries." *Science Advances* 7 (6): eabe0997.

Elder, G. H., Jr., and T. V. Nguyen. 1985. *Linking Family Hardship to Children's Lives*. New York: John Wiley on behalf of the Society for Research in Child Development.

Fereidooni, R., J. Mootz, R. Sabaei, K. Khoshnood, S. T. Heydari, M. J. Moradian, E. Taherifard, et al. 2021. "The COVID-19 Pandemic, Socioeconomic Effects, and Intimate Partner Violence against Women: A Population-Based Cohort Study in 2020, Iran." *American Journal of Public Health.* https://ajph .aphapublications.org/doi/10.2105/AJPH.2022.306839.

Ferreira, F. H., and N. Schady. 2009. "Aggregate Economic Shocks, Child Schooling, and Child Health." *World Bank Research Observer* 24 (2): 147–81.

Fetzer, T., and C. Rauh. 2022. "Pandemic Pressures and Public Health Care: Evidence from England." CEPR Discussion Paper No. DP16955, Center for Economic and Policy Research, Washington, DC.

Fox, S. E., P. Levitt, and C. A. Nelson, III. 2010. "How the Timing and Quality of Early Experiences Influence the Development of Brain Architecture." *Child Development* 81 (1): 28–40.

Ganimian, A. J., K. Muralidharan, and C. R. Walters. 2021. "Augmenting State Capacity for Child Development: Experimental Evidence from India." NBER Working Paper 28780, National Bureau of Economic Research, Cambridge, MA.

Gentilini, U. 2022. *Cash Transfers in Pandemic Times: Evidence, Practices, and Implications from the Largest Scale Up in History*. Washington, DC: World Bank. https://openknowledge.worldbank.org /handle/10986/37700.

Gertler, P., J. J. Heckman, R. Pinto, S. M. Chang, S. Grantham-McGregor, C. Vermeersch, S. Walker, et al. 2021. "Effect of the Jamaica Early Childhood Stimulation Intervention on Labor Market Outcomes at Age 31." NBER Working Paper 29292, National Bureau of Economic Research, Cambridge, MA.

Giles, J., and E. Satriawan. 2015. "Protecting Child Nutritional Status in the Aftermath of a Financial Crisis: Evidence from Indonesia." *Journal of Development Economics* 114: 97–106.

González, M., T. Loose, M. Liz, M. Pérez, J. I. Rodríguez-Vinçon, C. Tomás-Llerena, and A. Vásquez-Echeverría. 2022. "School Readiness Losses during the COVID-19 Outbreak: A Comparison of Two Cohorts of Young Children." *Child Development* 93 (4): 910–24.

Grantham-McGregor, S. M., C. A. Powell, S. P. Walker, and J. H. Himes. 1991. "Nutritional Supplementation, Psychosocial Stimulation, and Mental Development of Stunted Children: The Jamaican Study." *The Lancet* 338 (8758): 1–5.

Hamadani, J. D., M. I. Hasan, A. J. Baldi, S. J. Hossain, S. Shiraji, M. S. A. Bhuiyan, S. F. Mehrin, et al. 2020. "Immediate Impact of Stay-at-Home Orders to Control COVID-19 Transmission on Socioeconomic Conditions, Food Insecurity, Mental Health, and Intimate Partner Violence in Bangladeshi Women." *The Lancet Global Health* 8 (11): e1380–e1389.

Hamadani, J., M. Imrul, S. Grantham-McGregor, S. Alam, M. Tipu, D. Parra Alvarez, S. Shiraji, et al. Forthcoming. "The Effect of the COVID-19 Pandemic on Children's Development and Nutritional Status at Age 20 Months in Rural Bangladesh."

Hamre, B. K., R. C. Pianta, A. J. Mashburn, and J. T. Downer. 2012. "Promoting Young Children's Social Competence through the Preschool PATHS Curriculum and MyTeachingPartner Professional Development Resources." *Early Education and Development* 23 (6): 809–32.

Havnes, T., and M. Mogstad. 2011. "No Child Left Behind: Subsidized Child Care and Children's Long-Run Outcomes." *American Economic Journal: Economic Policy* 3 (2): 97–129.

Hazfiarini, A., R. I. Zahroh, S. Akter, C. S. Homer, and M. A. Bohren. 2022. "Indonesian Midwives' Perspectives on Changes in the Provision of Maternity Care during the COVID-19 Pandemic: A Qualitative Study." *Midwifery* 108: 103291.

Heckman, J. J., and T. Kautz. 2012. "Hard Evidence on Soft Skills." *Labour Economics* 19 (4): 451–64.

Heckman, J. J., S. H. Moon, R. Pinto, P. A. Savelyev, and A. Yavitz. 2010. "The Rate of Return to the HighScope Perry Preschool Program." *Journal of Public Economics* 94 (1–2): 114–28.

Heckman, J., R. Pinto, and P. Savelyev. 2013. "Understanding the Mechanisms through Which an Influential Early Childhood Program Boosted Adult Outcomes." *American Economic Review* 103 (6): 2052–86.

Hedley, P. L., G. Hedermann, C. M. Hagen, M. Bækvad-Hansen, H. Hjalgrim, K. Rostgaard, and A. D. Laksafoss, et al. 2022. "Preterm Birth, Stillbirth and Early Neonatal Mortality during the Danish COVID-19 Lockdown." *European Journal of Pediatrics* 181 (3): 1175–84.

Hidrobo, M. 2014. "The Effect of Ecuador's 1999 Economic Crisis on Early Childhood Development." *Economic Development and Cultural Change* 62 (4): 633–71.

Hillis, S., J. P. N. N'konzi, W. Msemburi, I. Cluver, A. Villaveces, S. Flaxman, and H. J. T. Unwin. 2022. "Orphanhood and Caregiver Loss among Children Based on New Global Excess COVID-19 Death Estimates." *JAMA Pediatrics* 176 (11): 1145–48.

Holla, A., M. Bendini, L. Dinarte, and I. Trako. 2021. "Is Investment in Preprimary Education Too Low? Lessons from (Quasi) Experimental Evidence across Countries." Policy Research Working Paper 9723, World Bank, Washington, DC.

Holla, A., L. B. Luna, M. M. Isaacs Prieto, C. Dusabe, M. Abimpaye, N. Kabarungi, and N. Schady. 2022. "The Impacts of the COVID-19 Pandemic on Skill Development in Preschool: Evidence from Rwanda." Unpublished manuscript.

Huang, M. I., M. A. O'Riordan, E. Fitzenrider, L. McDavid, A. R. Cohen, and S. Robinson. 2011. "Increased Incidence of Nonaccidental Head Trauma in Infants Associated with the Economic Recession." *Journal of Neurosurgery: Pediatrics* 8 (2): 171–76.

Human Rights Watch. 2020. "Impact of Covid-19 on Children's Education in Africa." https://www.hrw.org /news/2020/08/26/impact-covid-19-childrens-education-africa#_edn2.

Human Rights Watch. 2021. "'Years Don't Wait for Them': Increased Inequalities in Children's Right to Education due to the COVID-19 Pandemic." https://www.hrw.org/report/2021/05/17/years-dont-wait-them /increased-inequalities-childrens-right-education-due-covid.

Jackson, A., J. Brooks-Gunn, C.-C. Huang, and M. Glassman. 2000. "Single Mothers in Low-Wage Jobs: Financial Strain, Parenting, and Preschoolers' Outcomes." *Child Development* 71 (5): 1409–23.

Jackson, C. K. 2018. "What Do Test Scores Miss? The Importance of Teacher Effects on Non–test Score Outcomes." *Journal of Political Economy* 126 (5): 2072–107.

Jeong, J., H. O. Pitchik, and G. Fink. 2021. "Short-Term, Medium-Term and Long-Term Effects of Early Parenting Interventions in Low- and Middle-Income Countries: A Systematic Review." *BMJ Global Health* 6 (3): e004067.

Johnson, M. H. 2001. "Functional Brain Development in Humans." *Nature Reviews Neuroscience* 2 (7): 475–83.

Johnson, R. C., and R. F. Schoeni. 2011. "The Influence of Early-Life Events on Human Capital, Health Status, and Labor Market Outcomes over the Life Course." *BE Journal of Economic Analysis and Policy* 11 (3): 2521.

Jones, D. E., M. Greenberg, and M. Crowley. 2015. "Early Social-Emotional Functioning and Public Health: The Relationship between Kindergarten Social Competence and Future Wellness." *American Journal of Public Health* 105 (11): 2283–90.

Kalil, A., and R. Ryan. 2020. "Parenting Practices and Socioeconomic Gaps in Childhood Outcomes." *Future of Children* 30 (1): 29–64.

Kidman, R., and T. Palermo. 2016. "The Relationship between Parental Presence and Child Sexual Violence: Evidence from Thirteen Countries in Sub-Saharan Africa." *Child Abuse and Neglect* 51: 172–80.

Kuhnt, J., and S. Vollmer. 2017. "Antenatal Care Services and Its Implications for Vital and Health Outcomes of Children: Evidence from 193 Surveys in 69 Low-Income and Middle-Income Countries." *BMJ Open* 7 (11): e017122.

Lawn, J., K. Kerber, C. Enweronu-Laryea, and B. O. Masse. 2009. "Newborn Survival in Low-Resource Settings—Are We Delivering?" *BJOG: An International Journal of Obstetrics and Gynaecology* 116 Suppl 1: 49–59.

Macours, K., N. Schady, and R. Vakis. 2012. "Cash Transfers, Behavioral Changes, and Cognitive Development in Early Childhood: Evidence from a Randomized Experiment." *American Economic Journal: Applied Economics* 4 (2): 247–73.

Mafham, M. M., E. Spata, R. Goldacre, D. Gair, P. Curnow, M. Bray, S. Hollings, et al. 2020. "COVID-19 Pandemic and Admission Rates for and Management of Acute Coronary Syndromes in England." *The Lancet* 396 (10248): 381–89.

Manley, J., H. Alderman, and U. Gentilini. 2022. "More Evidence on Cash Transfers and Child Nutritional Outcomes: A Systematic Review and Meta-analysis." *BMJ Global Health* 7 (4): e008233.

Manley, J., Y. Balarajan, S. Malm, L. Harman, J. Owens, S. Murthy, D. Stewart, et al. 2020. "Cash Transfers and Child Nutritional Outcomes: A Systematic Review and Meta-analysis." *BMJ Global Health* 5 (12): e003621.

Maria Cecilia Souto Vidigal Foundation. 2021. *Learning in Early Childhood Education and the Pandemic: A Study in Sobral/CE.* São Paulo, Brazil.

Martinez, S., S. Naudeau, and V. Pereira. 2017. *Preschool and Child Development under Extreme Poverty: Evidence from a Randomized Experiment in Rural Mozambique.* Washington, DC: World Bank.

McCoy, D. C., J. Cuartas, J. Behrman, C. Cappa, J. Heymann, F. López Bóo, C. Lu, et al. 2021. "Global Estimates of the Implications of COVID-19–Related Preprimary School Closures for Children's Instructional Access, Development, Learning, and Economic Wellbeing." *Child Development* 92 (5): e883–e899.

McCoy, D. C., C. Salhi, H. Yoshikawa, P. Britto, M. Black, and G. Fink. 2018. "Home- and Center-Based Opportunities for Learning in Low- and Middle-Income Countries: A Landscape Analysis." *Children and Youth Services Review* 88: 44–56.

McLoyd, V. 1990. "The Impact of Economic Hardship on Black Families and Children: Psychological Distress, Parenting, and Socioemotional Development." *Child Development* 61 (2): 311–46.

Miguel, E., and A. M. Mobarak. 2021. "The Economics of the COVID-19 Pandemic in Poor Countries." NBER Working Paper 29339, National Bureau of Economic Research, Cambridge, MA.

Moster, D., R. T. Lie, and T. Markestad. 2008. "Long-Term Medical and Social Consequences of Preterm Birth." *New England Journal of Medicine* 359 (3): 262–73.

Moya, A., P. Serneels, A. Desrosiers, V. Reyes, M. J. Torres, and A. Lieberman. 2021. "The COVID-19 Pandemic and Maternal Mental Health in a Fragile and Conflict-Affected Setting in Tumaco, Colombia: A Cohort Study." *The Lancet Global Health* 9 (8): e1068–e1076.

Moynihan, R., S. Sanders, Z. A. Michaleff, A. M. Scott, J. Clark, E. J. To, M. Jones, et al. 2021. "Impact of COVID-19 Pandemic on Utilisation of Healthcare Services: A Systematic Review." *BMJ Open* 11 (3): e045343.

Mukherjee, S. 2016. *The Gene.* New York: Scribner.

Neugebauer, R., H. W. Hoek, and E. Susser. 1999. "Prenatal Exposure to Wartime Famine and Development of Antisocial Personality Disorder in Early Adulthood." *JAMA* 282 (5): 455–62.

Nuzhat, S., S. T. Hasan, P. Palit, F. Afroze, R. Amin, M. A. Alam, B. Alam, et al. 2022. "Health and Nutritional Status of Children Hospitalized during the COVID-19 Pandemic, Bangladesh." *Bulletin of the World Health Organization* 100 (2): 98.

OECD (Organisation for Economic Co-operation and Development). 2021. "PF3.2: Enrolment in Childcare and Pre-school." OECD Family Database. https://www.oecd.org/els/soc/PF3_2_Enrolment_childcare_preschool.pdf.

Painter, R. C., C. Osmond, P. Gluckman, M. Hanson, D. I. Phillips, and T. J. Roseboom. 2008. "Transgenerational Effects of Prenatal Exposure to the Dutch Famine on Neonatal Adiposity and Health in Later Life." *BJOG: An International Journal of Obstetrics and Gynaecology* 115 (10): 1243–49.

Patel, V., G. Simon, N. Chowdhary, S. Kaaya, and R. Araya. 2009. "Packages of Care for Depression in Low- and Middle-Income Countries." *PLoS Medicine* 6 (10): e1000159.

Paxson, C., and N. Schady. 2010. "Does Money Matter? The Effects of Cash Transfers on Child Development in Rural Ecuador." *Economic Development and Cultural Change* 59 (1): 187–229.

Pisani, L., J. Seiden, and S. Wolf. 2022. "Longitudinal Evidence on the Predictive Validity of the International Development and Early Learning Assessment (IDELA)." *Educational Assessment, Evaluation and Accountability* 34 (2): 173–94.

Pitchik, H. O., F. Tofail, F. Akter, J. Sultana, A. K. M. Shoab, T. M. Huda, J. E. Forsyth, et al. 2021. "Effects of the COVID-19 Pandemic on Caregiver Mental Health and the Child Caregiving Environment in a Low-Resource, Rural Context." *Child Development* 92 (5): e764–e780.

Psacharopoulos, G., and H. A. Patrinos. 2018. "Returns to Investment in Education: A Decennial Review of the Global Literature." *Education Economics* 26 (5): 445–58.

Raver, C. C., S. M. Jones, C. Li-Grining, F. Zhai, K. Bub, and E. Pressler. 2011. "CSRP's Impact on Low-Income Preschoolers' Preacademic Skills: Self-Regulation as a Mediating Mechanism." *Child Development* 82 (1): 362–78.

Ravindran, S., and M. Shah. 2021. "Unintended Consequences of Lockdowns: COVID-19 and the Shadow Pandemic." NBER Working Paper 27562, National Bureau of Economic Research, Cambridge, MA.

Rohde, J., S. Cousens, M. Chopra, V. Tangcharoensathien, R. Black, Z. Bhutta, and J. Lawn. 2008. "30 Years after Alma-Ata: Has Primary Health Care Worked in Countries?" *The Lancet* 372 (9642): 950–61.

Roseboom, T. J., J. H. P. van der Meulen, C. Osmond, D. J. P. Barker, A. C. J. Ravelli, J. M. Schroeder-Tanka, G. A. van Montfrans, et al. 2000. "Coronary Heart Disease in Adults after Prenatal Exposure to the Dutch Famine." *Heart* 84: 595–98.

Rossin-Slater, M., and M. Wust. 2020. "What Is the Added Value of Preschool for Poor Children? Long-Term and Intergenerational Impacts and Interactions with an Infant Health Intervention." *American Economic Journal: Applied Economics* 12 (3): 255–86.

Schneider, W., J. Waldfogel, and J. Brooks-Gunn. 2017. "The Great Recession and Risk for Child Abuse and Neglect." *Children and Youth Services Review* 72: 71–81.

Scott, S., L. Kendall, P. Gomez, S. Howie, S. Zaman, S. Ceesay, U. D'Alessandro, et al. 2017. "Effect of Maternal Death on Child Survival in Rural West Africa: 25 Years of Prospective Surveillance Data in The Gambia." *PLoS One* 12 (2): e0172286.

Shapira, G., D. de Walque, and J. Friedman. 2021. "How Many Infants May Have Died in Low-Income and Middle-Income Countries in 2020 due to the Economic Contraction Accompanying the COVID-19 Pandemic? Mortality Projections Based on Forecasted Declines in Economic Growth." *BMJ Open* 11 (8): e050551.

Siddique, A., M. Vlassopoulos, T. Rahman, D. Pakrashi, A. Islam, and F. Ahmed. 2022. "Improving Women's Mental Health During a Pandemic." https://users.monash.edu/~asaduli/pub/MH_Intervention.pdf.

Siedner, M. J., J. D. Kraemer, M. J. Meyer, G. Harling, T. Mngomezulu, P. Gabela, S. Dlamini, et al. 2020. "Access to Primary Healthcare during Lockdown Measures for COVID-19 in Rural South Africa: An Interrupted Time Series Analysis." *BMJ Open* 10 (10): e043763.

Spelke, E., and K. Schutts. 2022. "Learning in the Early Years." In *Quality Early Learning: Nurturing Children's Potential,* edited by M. Bendini and A. E. Devercelli. Washington, DC: World Bank.

Spier, E., K. Kamto, A. Molotsky, A. Rahman, N. Hossain, Z. Nahar, and H. Khondker. 2020. "Bangladesh Early Years Preschool Program Impact Evaluation." World Bank, Washington, DC.

Stewart, C. P., K. R. Wessells, C. D. Arnold, L. Huybregts, P. Ashorn, and E. Becquey. 2020. "Lipid-Based Nutrient Supplements and All-Cause Mortality in Children 6–24 Months of Age: A Meta-analysis of Randomized Control Trials." *American Journal of Clinical Nutrition* 111 (1): 207–18.

Stowe, J., H. Smith, K. Thurland, M. E. Ramsay, N. Andrews, and S. N. Ladhani. 2020. "Stillbirths during the COVID-19 Pandemic in England." *JAMA* 325 (1): 86–7.

Susser, E., H. W. Hoek, and A. Brown. 1998. "Neurodevelopmental Disorders after Prenatal Famine: The Story of the Dutch Famine Study." *American Journal of Epidemiology* 147 (3): 213–16.

UNFPA (United Nations Population Fund). 2021. "How Will COVID-19 Impact Fertility?" UNFPA Technical Brief. https://www.unfpa.org/publications/how-will-covid-19-impact-fertility.

UNICEF (United Nations Children's Fund). 2017. *A Familiar Face: Violence in the Lives of Children and Adolescents.* New York: UNICEF.

UNICEF (United Nations Children's Fund). 2021a. *Fed to Fail? The Crisis of Children's Diets in Early Life. 2021 Child Nutrition Report.* New York: UNICEF.

UNICEF (United Nations Children's Fund). 2021b. *The State of the World's Children 2021: On My Mind—Promoting, Protecting and Caring for Children's Mental Health.* New York: UNICEF.

US Department of the Treasury. 2021. "Treasury Releases Report Showing U.S. Childcare System Overburdens Families and Causes Shortages Due to Inadequate Supply." Press release, September 15, 2021. https://home.treasury.gov/news/press-releases/jy0354#:~:text=%E2%80%9CIt's%20past%20time%20that%20we,are%20now%20moving%20through%20Congress.

Uy, J., V. T. S. Van, V. G. Ulep, D. B. Bayani, and D. Walker. 2022. "The Impact of COVID-19 on Hospital Admissions for Twelve High-Burden Diseases and Five Common Procedures in the Philippines: A National Health Insurance Database Study 2019–2020." *The Lancet Regional Health–Western Pacific* 18: 100310.

Walker, S. P., S. M. Chang, A. S. Wright, R. Pinto, J. J. Heckman, and S. M. Grantham-McGregor. 2021. "Cognitive, Psychosocial, and Behaviour Gains at Age 31 Years from the Jamaica Early Childhood Stimulation Trial." *Journal of Child Psychology and Psychiatry* 63 (6): 626–35.

Wang, P. S., S. Aguilar-Gaxiola, J. Alonso, M. C. Angermeyer, G. Borges, E. J. Bromet, R. Bruffaerts, et al. 2007. "Use of Mental Health Services for Anxiety, Mood, and Substance Disorders in 17 Countries in the WHO World Mental Health Surveys." *The Lancet* 370 (9590): 841–50.

Ward, K., and S. Lee. 2020. "Mothers' and Fathers' Parenting Stress, Responsiveness, and Child Wellbeing among Low-Income Families." *Children and Youth Services Review.* doi: 10.1016/j.childyouth.2020.105218.

Weiland, C., E. Greenberg, D. Bassok, A. Markowitz, P. Guerrero Rosada, G. Luetmer, R. Abenavoli, et al. 2021. "Historic Crisis, Historic Opportunity: Using Evidence to Mitigate the Effects of the COVID-19 Crisis on Young Children and Early Care and Education Programs." Education Policy Initiative and Urban Institute Policy Brief, University of Michigan, Ann Arbor.

WHO (World Health Organization) and UNICEF (United Nations Children's Fund). 2021. "Progress and Challenges with Sustaining and Advancing Immunization Coverage during the COVID-19 Pandemic: 2021 WHO/UNICEF Estimates of National Immunization Coverage (WUENIC)." WHO and UNICEF, Geneva.

WHO (World Health Organization) and UNICEF (United Nations Children's Fund). 2022. "Progress and Challenges with Achieving Universal Immunization Coverage." WHO and UNICEF, Geneva.

WHO (World Health Organization), UNICEF (United Nations Children's Fund), and World Bank. 2018. *Nurturing Care for Early Childhood Development: A Framework for Helping Children Survive and Thrive to Transform Health and Human Potential.* Geneva: WHO.

Win, H., S. Shafique, N. Probst-Hensch, and G. Fink. 2022. "Change in Nutritional Status of Urban Slum Children before and after the First COVID-19 Wave in Bangladesh: A Repeated Cross-Sectional Assessment." *PLoS Global Public Health* 2 (7): e0000456.

World Bank. 2022. *Poverty and Shared Prosperity 2022: Correcting Course.* Washington, DC: World Bank.

Yalçin, S. S., P. Boran, B. Tezel, T. E. Şahlar, P. Özdemir, B. Keskinkiliç, and F. Kara. 2022. "Effects of the COVID-19 Pandemic on Perinatal Outcomes: A Retrospective Cohort Study from Turkey." *BMC Pregnancy and Childbirth* 22 (1): 1–12.

3

LEARNING LOSSES AND DROPOUTS

The Heavy Cost COVID-19 Imposed on School-Age Children

Shwetlena Sabarwal, Andres Yi Chang, Noam Angrist, and Ritika D'Souza

ABSTRACT

This chapter describes the authors' estimates of the cost of COVID-19–related school closures on children ages 6–14 and identifies actionable strategies for learning recovery. Between March 2020 and March 2022, an average child lost about one year of in-person schooling because of school closures. In Latin America and the Caribbean and South Asia, children lost 1.7 years. New analysis shows that, on average, each month of school closures led to a full month of lost learning, with larger losses in lower-income countries. Novel data from Bangladesh demonstrate that in some contexts, the months of learning lost were much higher than the months of school closures because students also forgot skills they had already mastered. These findings reflect the limited effectiveness of remote learning. Learning losses were higher for younger and poorer students, but there were no consistent patterns of gaps between boys and girls. Emerging evidence suggests that, without urgent action, COVID-related learning losses could compound over time. Dropout rates did not increase significantly in upper-middle-income countries. However, in Ethiopia and Pakistan, two lower-income countries with data available before and after school closures, enrollment fell by 4 percentage points and 6 percentage points, respectively, and 7.6 million children dropped out of school in Pakistan alone. Without urgent policy action, today's children could lose up to 10 percent of their future average annual earnings due to the COVID-related education shocks. This loss can be prevented by (1) keeping schools open and increasing instructional time; (2) assessing learning and matching instruction to students' learning level; (3) offering remedial education for students who have fallen the furthest behind; and (4) focusing on learning foundations and streamlining the curriculum. This chapter presents novel data on teachers' willingness to implement these policies.

SCHOOLING GENERATES ENORMOUS RETURNS FOR PEOPLE AND SOCIETIES

[I]n the long run, the best way to reduce inequalities with respect to labor as well as to increase the average productivity of the labor force and the overall growth of the economy is surely to invest in education.

—Thomas Piketty, *Capital in the Twenty-First Century* (2014)

"

For millions of people around the world, schooling is the only pathway to a better, more prosperous life. Those with more schooling consistently earn more,[1] have a lower likelihood of losing their job or, if they do lose it, have a higher probability of getting a new one.[2] Schooling is linked to better health[3] and more agency.[4] For societies, education helps promote democracy,[5] generates trust,[6] boosts social capital,[7] and helps create inclusive institutions.[8] Most fundamentally, education can be a powerful force for spurring economic growth and reducing poverty.[9]

Even before the COVID-19 pandemic, schooling was not producing enough learning. Globally, students were losing between one and six years of schooling due to poor quality.[10] In Sub-Saharan Africa, a student born in 2019 could expect to receive about eight years of schooling. However, after adjusting for the quality of learning,[11] these eight years would translate into only five years of learning-adjusted schooling. In 2019, nearly 57 percent of children in low- and middle-income countries could not read and understand a simple text by age 10. In Sub-Saharan Africa, this share was 86 percent.[12]

This chapter examines how the COVID-19 pandemic affected the schooling and learning of children ages 6–14, a span that corresponds to primary and lower-secondary education levels. Chapter 4 covers students beyond age 15.

THE COVID-19 PANDEMIC LED TO SHOCKINGLY LONG SCHOOL CLOSURES

I will not allow the opening of classes where students will be near each other... .
Unless I am sure that they are really safe, it's useless to be talking about opening of classes.

—Rodrigo Duterte, President, the Philippines
"No School until Coronavirus Vaccine Is Available," Al Jazeera.com, May 26, 2020

"

In March 2020, when the pandemic first hit, schools closed in 180 countries. One year later, in March 2021, schools were still partially or fully closed in 94 countries, with more than 1 billion students affected.[13] Although the situation improved by the summer of 2021, new variants continued to thwart and reverse school reopenings. As of March 31, 2022, two years after widespread lockdowns first started, 14 countries were still experiencing full or partial school closures.[14]

Globally, between March 2020 and March 2022 an average school-age child lost about one year (37 weeks) of in-person schooling due to COVID-19–related school closures (figure 3.1).[15] Overall, 1.3 billion children in low- and middle-income countries missed at least half a year of school, 960 million missed at least a full year, and 711 million missed a year and a half or more.[16] During this time, globally schools were fully or partially closed 52 percent of the time. This share was 84 percent in Latin America and the Caribbean and 83 percent in South Asia.[17]

Aside from their extended length, another remarkable aspect of pandemic-related school closures is how widely they varied. The global average hides big regional variations—as seen in figure 3.1, panel a—in the difference in the duration of school closures in South Asia (56 weeks) and Europe and Central Asia (14 weeks).

FIGURE 3.1 **Globally, an average school-age child lost about one year of in-person schooling**

Variations (weeks) in school closures, by region and for selected countries, March 2020–March 2022

a. Region-level variations in school closures

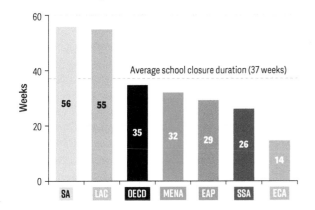

b. Country-level variations in school closures

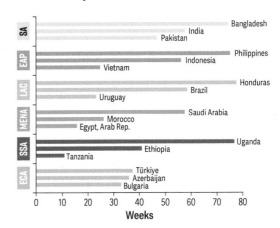

Source: Original calculations based on UIS 2022b.

Note: The figure shows school closure length by region (panel a) and by selected countries within regions (panel b), thereby indicating the range of school closure experiences. Length of school closure includes full and partial school closures. Each day of partial school closure is counted as half a day of school closure. Regional estimates are population-weighted using United Nations World Population Prospects 2022 data (https://www.un.org/development/desa/pd/content/World-Population-Prospects-2022). The dashed line in panel a indicates the mean of school closure duration (37 weeks) across all 140 countries with a school-age population of 500,000 or more. EAP = East Asia and Pacific; ECA = Europe and Central Asia; LAC = Latin America and the Caribbean; MENA = Middle East and North Africa; OECD = Organisation for Economic Co-operation and Development; SA = South Asia; SSA = Sub-Saharan Africa.

Regional variations, in turn, hide big country-level variations, even across very similar contexts. For example, between March 2020 and March 2022 schools were closed for 75 days in Tanzania but 529 days in Uganda; 178 days in Morocco but 391 days in Saudi Arabia; and 169 days in Vietnam but 510 days in the Philippines.[18]

Variation in the length of school closures was driven by different country-level policy choices. At the onset of the lockdowns (March 2020), school closures were swift and fairly uniform across countries. However, over the months that followed, noticeable variations began to emerge across countries and grew more pronounced over time. As evidence on the risks and likelihood of transmission of COVID-19 accumulated, policy makers in many countries opened public transportation, stores, restaurants, and workplaces, but kept schools closed—an active policy choice.

Even when in-person instruction began to resume, instructional hours were drastically cut. In Jordan, schools reopened in September 2021, but students attended only two to three days a week.[19] In Zimbabwe in September 2021, teaching time was slashed from the usual seven hours a day to three to four hours a day.[20] As late as February 2022, across several states of India classes were held for less than four hours a day, and in some cases only for secondary school children.[21] The problem was not just confined to low- and middle-income countries. In the United States, one year after the onset of the pandemic, nearly 60 percent of fourth-graders and 68 percent of eighth-graders were home at least part of the school week, where they were getting less instructional time than in school.[22]

With long closures, students disengaged from learning

When the schools were closed, we were worried about our daughter's education. The biggest worry was that she would lose interest in studying because … studying at home was very difficult.

—Mother of a high-achieving girl, Pakistan
Quoted in Geven et al. (2022)

Three factors played a role in student disengagement from learning during COVID-related school closures. First, remote learning was much less effective than in-person schooling. Second, students did not devote as much time to learning as they had done before the pandemic, in part because parents struggled to compensate for the instructional time with teachers that had been lost. Third, students' mental health was adversely affected. Several of these factors (with the possible exception of mental health issues) disproportionately affected poor and disadvantaged students.

Remote learning was a very poor substitute for face-to-face instruction

Once school closures went into effect, nearly all education systems pivoted to remote learning. However, remote learning was not accessible to all. Globally, more than two-thirds of children ages 3–17 (1.3 billion) lack internet access at home.[23] Even in middle-income countries such as India, approximately 29 million students did not have access to a smartphone, feature phone, television, radio, or computer.[24] In Indonesia, 57 percent of households reported the lack of access to reliable internet as a major obstacle to children learning from home successfully, with access issues largely concentrated among poorer students.[25] In Ecuador, 64 percent of students in the lowest wealth quartile accessed remote learning, compared with 81 percent in the top quartile.[26]

Even when access was not an issue, take-up of remote learning was often low, especially when delivered via television (TV) and radio. In Bangladesh, 86 percent of poor students were aware of TV lessons but only 48 percent watched them. Reminders and incentives did not improve take-up.[27] In Botswana, only 20 percent of students tuned in to educational radio programming.[28]

The quality of remote instruction could also be subpar. In many instances, remote learning did not involve direct interaction with a teacher. For example, in Poland 12 percent of students did not receive any help during online lessons despite needing it.[29] Moreover, some remote mechanisms had technical problems. In Vietnam, 38 percent of students encountered technical difficulties when joining online classes, such as no video, no audio, and internet interruptions.[30]

In some contexts, school closures also led to the shutdown of low-cost private schools.[31] The schools could not afford to continue paying rent or teachers' salaries during school closures, thereby restricting access to education for many and placing more pressure on the already overstretched public school systems.

Time spent learning declined

During school closures, the time spent studying fell, even for students engaging in remote learning. In Ghana, Liberia, and Sierra Leone, the time spent learning per day declined by 71 percent, or six hours per day, compared with time spent when schools were open.[32] In Kenya, the decrease was 61 percent, and the average student spent only two and a half to three hours per day on learning-related activities.[33]

Declines were also observed in high-income countries with remote instruction that functioned relatively well. In Germany, daily learning time fell by almost half during school closures—from an average of 7.4 hours a day to 3.6 hours a day—with significantly larger reductions for low-achievers.[34] In the United Kingdom, not only did children spend less time engaging in learning activities during the initial lockdown (about two hours less than before the pandemic), but the effect was larger for lower-income households.[35]

Evidence is mixed about whether girls or boys suffered larger declines in time spent learning. In Ghana, boys experienced a larger decline;[36] in Bangladesh, the decline was more pronounced for girls.[37] These mixed results could potentially be explained by differences in social norms and labor market opportunities.

During the pandemic, parents generally were unable to compensate for students' loss of engagement with their teachers because parents simply lacked the time or the skills (or both) to make up for it. In Indonesia, for example, 29 percent of parents reported that they had insufficient time, and 25 percent lacked the capacity to support their children in learning from home.[38] In Nepal, nearly 25 percent of parents of primary-age children spent no time helping children learn.[39] In Bangladesh, 50 percent of parents of secondary-age children could not support their children in learning a new topic.[40]

In some ways, differences in parental engagement in a child's education signal the most profound socioeconomic divide linked to learning losses. For example, in Bangladesh 39 percent of students from the bottom socioeconomic quartile received support from a family member, compared with 62 percent in the top quartile.[41] In the United States, wealthier parents reported spending more time on childcare than less affluent ones.[42] The parent participation divide has been substantial—and perhaps just as important as the digital divide—in driving increased learning inequality.

Students' mental health suffered

Declines in student mental health could also be an important driver of disengagement from learning. In both high- and low-income countries, a large share of students reported symptoms of depression, anxiety, or both. Nearly 53 percent of the surveyed households in Algeria, the Arab Republic of Egypt, Jordan, Morocco, Qatar, the Syrian Arab Republic, and Tunisia stated that their children struggled mentally and emotionally.[43] In Kenya, 50 percent of adolescents reported experiencing depression-related symptoms.[44] Most of these studies do not present a counterfactual or baseline to reveal student mental health data before the pandemic. However, evidence suggests that the likelihood of anxiety and depression among students may have increased during the pandemic. In Ecuador, a study found that 16 percent of high school students were at risk of depression.[45] This percentage is substantially higher than the 6.2 percent reported by a pre-pandemic (2017) study.[46]

In addition to depression, other types of mental health challenges were also pervasive. Studies reported that more than 50 percent of the lower-secondary students in Burkina Faso, Burundi, Côte d'Ivoire, Kenya, Senegal, and Zambia found it difficult to concentrate on their studies and schoolwork.[47] In Indonesia, 21 percent of households said children were finding it harder to concentrate, and 45 percent of households reported behavioral challenges among their children.[48] In the United States, high school students who attended school remotely reported levels of social, emotional, and academic well-being that were between 0.07 and 0.10 standard deviations below those of classmates who attended school in person.[49]

In some ways, the impacts of COVID on student health went beyond mental health. During school closures, millions of students lost access to school meals, which are an important source of nutrition, particularly for low-income children. One estimate from March 2020 suggests that early in the pandemic nearly 320 million students globally missed out on school meals due to school closures.[50] In Nigeria, a study shows that COVID-induced disruptions in educational and nutritional services exacerbated households' food insecurity.[51]

What did this disengagement from learning mean for student enrollment? This is discussed next in this chapter.

COVID-related dropouts have been lower than expected, with some notable exceptions

COVID-related school closures have been singular in multiple ways. First, their unprecedented scale and duration put the world in uncharted territory. Second, the pandemic led to both school closures and economic crisis, making household choices complex and hard to predict. Third, the pandemic also imposed steep costs on the mental and physical health of students and their families. Thus historical evidence may not be a reliable guide to the expected COVID-related school dropouts.

For estimating COVID-related dropouts, this chapter relies primarily on data from national household or labor force surveys conducted after schools reopened. These data are ideal because they are nationally representative and usually have a time series that predates the pandemic. Because of the latter, it is possible to construct a reliable counterfactual that can correct for secular trends and seasonal patterns.[52] In addition, the data allow for a disaggregation of dropouts by gender and socioeconomic status.

However, excluding high-income countries where dropouts among 6- to 14-year-olds are rare, these data are available for only nine countries: Argentina, Brazil, Colombia, Ethiopia, Indonesia, Mexico, Pakistan, South Africa, and Uruguay. Because this is a selected sample, some caution is needed in extrapolating these results to other contexts. To present a fuller picture, this analysis complements these data with high-quality one-off studies when available.

Overall, COVID-related student dropouts did not increase notably in middle-income countries. However, dropouts increased in the two lower-income countries with comparable data, Ethiopia and Pakistan. Figure 3.2 shows the difference between *predicted* school enrollment, given by historical trends, and *actual* student enrollment after schools reopened from pandemic-related disruptions[53]

Dropouts were lower than expected in middle-income contexts, but high in poorer countries.

FIGURE 3.2 COVID-19 school closures had limited impacts on dropouts in middle-income countries but negative impacts in lower-income countries

Average change in school enrollment, ages 6–14, by country

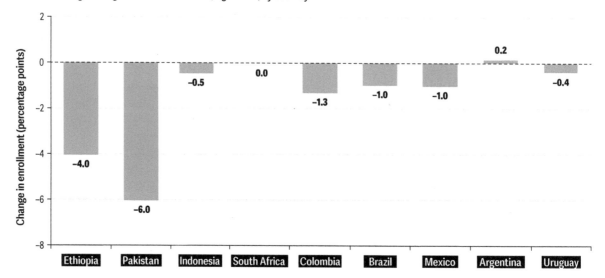

Sources: Original calculations based on the following sources: Argentina: Permanent Household Survey (EPH); Brazil: Continuous National Household Sample Survey (PNAD); Colombia: Great Integrated Household Survey (GEIH); Ethiopia: Urban Employment and Unemployment Survey and the National Labour and Migration Survey; Indonesia: National Socioeconomic Survey (SUSENAS); Mexico: National Survey of Occupation and Employment (ENOE); Pakistan: Labour Force Survey (LFS); South Africa: Quarterly Labor Force Survey (LFS); Uruguay: Continuous Household Survey (ECH).

Note: The figure shows the difference between predicted school enrollment and observed school enrollment after schools reopened. Left to right, countries are in ascending order of lowest to highest gross domestic product per capita.

for children in primary school (ages 6–11) and lower-secondary schools (ages 12–14) across the nine countries with data.

Setting aside Ethiopia and Pakistan, after schools reopened the biggest drops in enrollment for children ages 6–14 were 1.3 percentage points in Colombia and 1.0 percentage point in Brazil and Mexico. The Brazil findings are corroborated by additional ad hoc studies.[54] For the rest of the countries, the difference between predicted and observed enrollment after schools reopened is close to zero.

There were, however, relatively lower-income exceptions to this pattern. In Pakistan, school enrollment declined by 6.0 percentage points overall (6.7 percentage points at the primary level and 4.6 percentage points at the lower-secondary level). This relatively large decline is corroborated by additional one-off studies.[55] Similarly, in Ethiopia, the only low-income country in the sample, enrollment fell by 4.0 percentage points for children ages 6–14 (4.6 percentage points at the primary level and 4.0 percentage points at the lower-secondary level).[56] Another country with large dropouts among school-age children was Nigeria, where a one-off study shows that the likelihood of children ages 5–18 attending school dropped by 7 percentage points after the onset of the pandemic.[57] These findings suggest that dropouts were likely to be higher in lower-middle- and low-income countries. However, this insight is based on limited data, and results could change as more evidence emerges. Furthermore, within-country analysis in the few contexts where more disaggregated data are available suggests that dropouts were highest for children from lower socioeconomic households, proxied by household education level (see figure 3.3).

Higher levels of dropouts among poorer students are also seen in some single-country studies.[58] In rural India, the proportion of children ages 6–14 not currently enrolled in school increased from 2.5 percent to 4.6 percent between 2018 and 2021.[59] In Ghana, poorer children were more likely to drop out than richer children, and boys were slightly more likely to drop out than girls.[60]

There are no consistent patterns of gender gaps in dropouts in the available studies. In specific countries where studies show gender gaps, patterns vary. In Ethiopia and Pakistan, the two countries with a significant

FIGURE 3.3 Dropout rates are higher for households with low education levels

Average change in school enrollment, ages 6–14, by country, gender, and education level

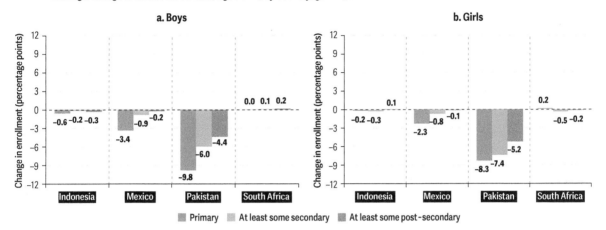

Sources: Original estimations based on the following sources: Indonesia: National Socioeconomic Survey (SUSENAS); Mexico: National Survey of Occupation and Employment (ENOE); Pakistan: Labour Force Survey (LFS); South Africa: Quarterly Labour Force Survey (QLFS).

Note: The figure shows the difference between predicted school enrollment and observed school enrollment after schools reopened for boys (panel a) and girls (panel b) ages 6–14 and by household education level (that is, maximum level of education of any household member age 25 or older). Results are shown for four selected developing countries with and without dropouts and differences by household education level.

increase in dropout rates once schools reopened, boys were slightly more affected than girls. On the other hand, a study in Kenya reports that 16 percent of adolescent girls did not return when schools reopened versus 8 percent of adolescent boys.[61]

Older children could be at a higher risk of dropping out, as documented by various studies. In Nigeria, the probability of attending school declined by 5 percentage points for children ages 5–11, but by 9 percentage points for those ages 12–18.[62] In Uganda, the dropout rate was 0.7 percent across school ages, with considerably higher rates of 3–4 percent for 15- and 16-year-olds.[63] In Pakistan, parents of children ages 13–17 were 5 percentage points more likely to report that their child would drop out, compared with the parents of younger children ages 5–12.[64] (Chapter 4 discusses this issue in more detail.)

Meanwhile, pandemic-related dropouts may not have yet become fully visible. Learning losses today could well transform into higher dropouts in the near future, particularly for the most vulnerable groups. Measuring how many students have come back to school after schools have reopened is an ongoing exercise.

School closures have caused steep learning losses

I forgot a lot because I did not study anything. I could study some things that were easy.
Additionally, my sisters and brother would explain the content that they understood.
If they did not understand it, then I would ask my friend for help....
However, I would abandon it if I did not understand it.

—Female student in a rural school, Pakistan
Quoted in Geven et al. (2022)

Even before the pandemic, many students were not learning. However, when schools shut down due to COVID, for millions learning stopped altogether. This section discusses the steep learning losses caused by COVID-related school closures.

One month of school closure led to one month of learning loss

Estimates from the study conducted for this report suggest that one month of school closures led, on average, to one month of learning lost. This finding implies that little was learned during school closures, despite widespread remote-learning efforts. This insight is based on the robust body of empirical work across countries that is synthesized in this chapter.

Estimates of "months of learning loss" during school closures were compiled using a database of 44 studies.[65] This database includes all the studies that focused on school-age children (primary to upper-secondary) and that met four criteria: (1) they had credible estimates of learning progress before school closures, which made it possible to construct a reliable counterfactual (what learning would have been in the absence of COVID-19); (2) they measured learning carefully using comparable reading, language, or math tests across years; (3) they reported learning losses in months or allowed for this conversion; and (4) they did not use a sample with special characteristics (such as students receiving some special interventions). When more than one study was available for a country, the study that had the larger sample, that measured longer-term impacts, or included more ages, grades, and so on was included.[66] Application of these criteria left 24 studies across 22 countries, representing a range of contexts (high-income to low-income) across regions.[67]

A clear pattern emerges when months of learning lost are plotted against months of school closures per country in the database (figure 3.4). Most countries with at least one study available fall somewhere near

> *Each month of school closures led, on average, to a full month of lost learning, with learning losses steeper for poorer countries and particularly among poorer and younger students.*

 FIGURE 3.4 For 30 days of school closures, students lost 34 days of learning
School closure versus learning loss, by country

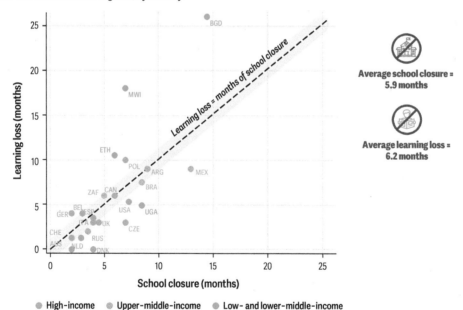

● High-income   ● Upper-middle-income   ● Low- and lower-middle-income

Sources: Original compilations based on 24 studies across 22 countries: Argentina: Argentina, Ministerio de Educación de la Nación 2022; Australia: Gore et al. 2021; Bangladesh: Djaker et al., forthcoming; Belgium: Gambi and De Witte 2021; Brazil: Brazil, Education Secretariat 2021; Lichand et al. 2022; Canada: Georgiou 2021; Czech Republic: Korbel and Prokop 2021; Denmark: Birkelund and Karlson 2021; Ethiopia: Araya et al. 2022; Germany: Ludewig et al. 2022; Italy: Contini et al. 2021; Malawi: Asim, Gera, and Singhal 2022; Mexico: Alasino, Romero, and Ramirez, forthcoming; Netherlands: Haelermans, Jacobs, et al. 2022; Poland: Gajderowicz, Jakubowski, and Wrona 2022; Russian Federation: Chaban et al. 2022; South Africa: Ardington, Wills, and Kotze 2021; Spain: Arenas and Gortazar 2022; Switzerland: Tomasik, Helbling, and Moser 2021; Uganda: Uwezo Uganda 2021; Angrist, Bergman, and Matsheng 2022; United Kingdom: Rose et al. 2021; United States: Kuhfeld and Lewis 2022.
Note: The dashed 45-degree line indicates where learning losses in months are equal to length of school closures in months. Learning losses in months are benchmarked against "typical" learning gains within each country before the pandemic. The estimates thus should not be compared across countries because, for example, three months of learning losses in the Netherlands does not compare one-to-one with three months of learning losses in South Africa, where pre-pandemic learning was lower to begin with. For country abbreviations, see International Organization for Standardization (ISO), https://www.iso.org/obp/ui/#search.

the 45-degree line, where months of learning lost are equal to the months of school closures. This finding suggests that, as a general rule, the length of school closures in months is roughly equal to learning losses in months across a wide set of countries (the few exceptions are discussed next). Overall, for every 30 days of school closures, students lost, on average, about 34 days of learning.[68] Across all these studies, the mean learning loss is 6.2 months, while the average length of school closures is 5.9 months.

Learning losses appear larger when the database of studies is restricted to include only those with larger sample sizes and the most persuasive counterfactuals. For these 14 studies across 12 countries, on average, for every 30 days of school closures students lost about 38 days of learning.[69] Across this subsample of studies, the average learning loss is 7.9 months, while the average school closure is 6.6 months.

Learning losses also seem to have been larger in countries with lower gross domestic product (GDP) per capita after controlling for the length of school closures (in the set of countries with available data). Using the sample of studies, figure 3.5 shows the negative relationship between the ratio of learning loss to school closures and the log GDP per capita (2019).[70] Although high-income, middle-income, and low-income countries all show steep learning losses, the ratio of learning losses to school closures is larger in poorer countries.[71]

A few studies show lower learning losses. National assessments from six countries in Sub-Saharan Africa—Burkina Faso, Burundi, Côte d'Ivoire, Kenya, Senegal, and Zambia—mostly show no significant learning losses.[72] These results can be explained in two ways. First, for some countries such as Burundi, school closures were extremely short.[73] Second, in this analysis learning is measured as the share of students meeting minimum proficiency levels (MPLs). If a substantial share of students was below this MPL before the pandemic and

 FIGURE 3.5 **Learning losses were higher in countries with lower GDP per capita after controlling for length of school closures**

Ratio of learning loss to school closure versus GDP per capita, by country

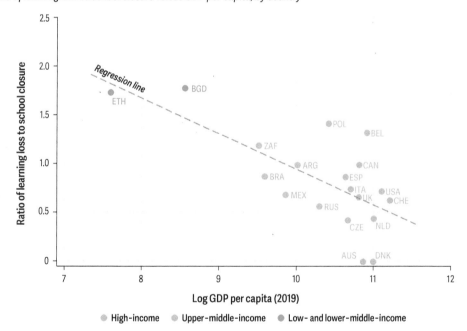

Sources: Original calculations based on 24 studies across 22 countries: Argentina: Argentina, Ministerio de Educación de la Nación 2022; Australia: Gore et al. 2021; Bangladesh: Djaker et al., forthcoming; Belgium: Gambi and De Witte 2021; Brazil: Brazil, Education Secretariat 2021; Lichand et al. 2022; Canada: Georgiou 2021; Czech Republic: Korbel and Prokop 2021; Denmark: Birkelund and Karlson 2021; Ethiopia: Araya et al. 2022; Italy: Contini et al. 2021; Mexico: Alasino, Romero, and Ramirez, forthcoming; Netherlands: Haelermans, Jacobs, et al. 2022; Poland: Gajderowicz, Jakubowski, and Wrona 2022; Russian Federation: Chaban et al. 2022; South Africa: Ardington, Wills, and Kotze 2021; Spain: Arenas and Gortazar 2022; Switzerland: Tomasik, Helbling, and Moser 2021; United Kingdom: Rose et al. 2021; United States: Kuhfeld and Lewis 2022.

Note: Learning losses in months are benchmarked against "typical" learning gains within each country before the pandemic. The dashed line is the regression line. School closure length excludes academic breaks. This list includes all studies available and used in figure 3.4 but excludes three countries (Germany, Malawi, and Uganda) that disproportionately influence the regression line and had a Cook's distance larger than 4/N, as generally suggested in the literature. For country abbreviations, see International Organization for Standardization (ISO), https://www.iso.org/obp/ui/#search.

experienced learning losses, these losses would not be visible with this measure. For example, in Zambia the proportion of grade 5 students who met the MPL during the baseline (2016) was 1.8 percent in reading and 3.5 percent in mathematics. Similarly, in Burundi only 0.3 percent of students met the MPL in reading during the baseline (2019). Under these circumstances, it is essentially impossible for studies that measure proficiency levels to capture learning losses.[74] As a result, these studies are not included in this chapter's analysis.

Comparing COVID-related education losses across countries

The full extent of COVID-related learning losses depends on the duration of school closures, the extent of dropouts, and the quality of learning before the pandemic. The latter is important because six months of school closures would cause significantly more learning loss in countries where a lot of learning was happening before the pandemic as compared with countries where not much learning was happening. Furthermore, the magnitude of learning losses and dropouts seems to be linked to a country's GDP per capita (see figures 3.2 and 3.5). Is there a way to factor these variables in and create a globally benchmarked estimate of COVID-related learning losses across countries? This analysis does that by using a single easy-to-understand metric combining information on the quantity and quality of education: the World Bank's Learning-Adjusted Years of Schooling (LAYS).[75]

> *Lost LAYS is a powerful way to convey the COVID education shock in a single, intuitive, globally benchmarked metric. Lost LAYS were largely driven by learning losses, not dropouts, but the relative proportion varies by context.*

The LAYS measure reflects the reality that children in some countries learn far less than those in other countries, despite being in school for a similar amount of time. *Quantity* of schooling is measured using *expected years of schooling* (captured by the number of years of schooling a child can expect to obtain by age 18 in a given country). *Quality* of schooling is measured using a harmonized data set of student learning based on results from comparable international and regional testing programs.[76] LAYS is simply the product of a country's expected years of schooling and its harmonized learning measure benchmarked against a standard.

School closures affected a country's LAYS in two ways: changes in dropouts and changes in learning. As explained in previous sections, both are linked to a country's income or GDP per capita. To estimate changes in dropouts, which affects expected years of schooling, this analysis uses data from national household surveys or labor force surveys to predict what enrollment would have been during the pandemic if it had not occurred. The analysis then compares these predictions with actual enrollment observed after schools reopened.[77]

With some reasonable assumptions, the preceding analysis of the nine countries where reliable enrollment data are available for the period after schools reopened can be used to predict enrollments in countries where these data are not available.[78] To do this, the analysis first obtains the coefficients from regressing changes in enrollment on log GDP per capita and the duration of school closures in the sample of nine countries. Next, these coefficients are applied to log GDP per capita and school closure data from all other countries to estimate changes in enrollment after schools reopened globally. Because data on enrollment after school reopening are available only for these nine countries, this is the best available information at the time of writing this report.

Similarly, changes in learning for every country can be estimated using data from 20 studies across 19 countries on learning losses during the pandemic.[79] The analysis begins by using these studies to calculate the ratio of learning losses to duration of school closure. It then estimates a coefficient from regressing changes in this ratio on log GDP per capita.[80] This coefficient, applied to log GDP per capita data, allows estimation of learning loss to school closure ratios for all countries. These ratios are then combined with the school closures data available across countries using the United Nations Educational, Scientific, and Cultural Organization (UNESCO) school closure database to estimate learning losses by country. As a final step, these learning losses are multiplied by pre-pandemic measures of quality of learning to standardize units across countries. For this, the analysis uses the global database on LAYS before the pandemic.[81] (Methodological details are provided in annex 3A.)

Bringing these elements together and with the caveats mentioned on data limitations, the analysis calculates the lost LAYS for the 116 low- and middle-income countries for which information on pre-pandemic LAYS

FIGURE 3.6 Regions vary in the Learning-Adjusted Years of Schooling (LAYS) they lost due to the pandemic

Lost LAYS (weighted by population) from learning losses versus dropouts, by region

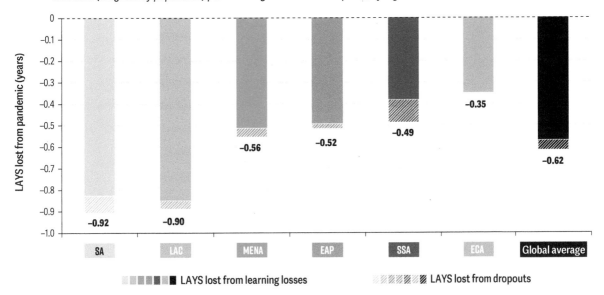

Sources: Original calculations based on D'Souza et al., forthcoming. Data on the duration of school closures are from UNESCO Global Monitoring of School Closures Caused by the COVID-19 Pandemic (https://covid19.uis.unesco.org/global-monitoring-school-closures-covid19/). Data on enrollment rates are simulated for each country using data on log GDP per capita and the duration of school closures.

Note: The figure reports the average lost LAYS by World Bank region, weighted by population. Regional averages exclude high-income countries. For each country, lost LAYS are calculated for each level of schooling and then averaged across levels, weighted by the duration of each level. Solid segments of the bars represent LAYS lost due to learning losses. Diagonal stripes represent LAYS lost due to dropouts. The total lost LAYS in years appear beneath each bar. EAP = East Asia and Pacific; ECA = Europe and Central Asia; LAC = Latin America and the Caribbean; MENA = Middle East and North Africa; SA = South Asia; SSA = Sub-Saharan Africa.

is available (see annex 3A).[82] Figure 3.6 reports average lost LAYS by region and highlights two key points.[83] First, lost LAYS are largely driven by learning losses and not by dropouts. However, the relative proportion varies by context. Dropouts account for 23 percent of lost LAYS in low-income countries, compared with 3 percent in upper-middle-income countries. Second, lost LAYS are much higher in regions with longer school closures and better quality of schooling. Sub-Saharan Africa saw relatively smaller impacts because in this region schools were closed for shorter durations and also because schools produced less learning (on average) to begin with. Therefore, the overall lost LAYS (0.5 year) is a little over half the LAYS lost in Latin America and the Caribbean.

Because of the vastly different country experiences with school closures, countries similar in LAYS before the pandemic experienced very different learning losses. This finding becomes clear in figure 3.7, which plots pre-pandemic LAYS on the horizontal axis and total LAYS lost on the vertical axis. Egypt, Honduras, and Lebanon had similar LAYS before the pandemic. However, Honduras lost significantly more learning than the other two countries, and Lebanon, in turn, lost much more than Egypt. Similarly, although China, Malaysia, and Mexico had similar LAYS before the pandemic, total LAYS lost were significantly higher in Mexico and much smaller in China, with Malaysia in the middle.

It is also possible to contrast countries that lost more in terms of *total* LAYS and those that lost more in terms of the *share* of pre-pandemic LAYS—see figure 3.8. Bulgaria and South Sudan lost a similar number of LAYS, but South Sudan lost substantially more in terms of the share of its pre-pandemic LAYS. Thus even though learning losses across the two countries are comparable, the loss to students, in terms of the share of their overall expected schooling (adjusted for quality), is much larger in South Sudan than in Bulgaria. Similarly, Serbia and Iraq lost the same number of LAYS, but this loss was a much larger proportion of Iraq's human capital (as measured by LAYS) than Serbia's.

FIGURE 3.7 Countries that had similar Learning-Adjusted Years of Schooling (LAYS) before the pandemic had vastly different experiences with learning losses

Total LAYS lost from the pandemic versus pre-pandemic LAYS, by country and region

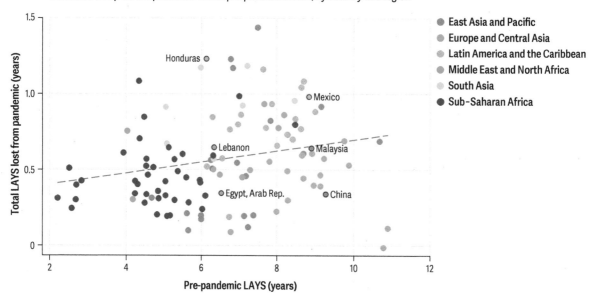

Source: Original calculations based on D'Souza et al., forthcoming.
Note: The figure shows the weak relationship between total lost LAYS from the pandemic (vertical axis) and baseline LAYS in 2020 based on data from the World Bank's Human Capital Index (HCI) (horizontal axis). The range of different experiences can be visualized by the broad distributions for different pre-pandemic LAYS levels. The dashed line represents the linear fit. Six countries are identified for illustrative purposes. This figure excludes high-income countries.

FIGURE 3.8 Countries not losing many total Learning-Adjusted Years of Schooling (LAYS) may have lost much in terms of pre-pandemic shares of LAYS (and vice versa)

Share of pre-pandemic LAYS lost versus total LAYS lost from the pandemic, by country and region

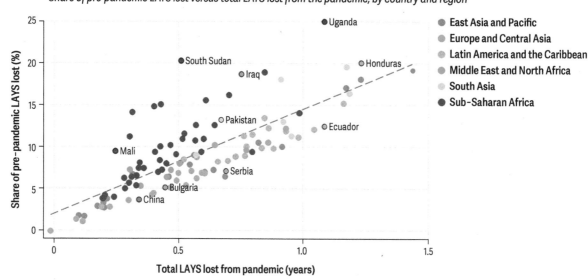

Source: Original calculations based on D'Souza et al., forthcoming.
Note: The figure shows the relationship between the percentage of pre-pandemic LAYS lost and the total LAYS lost from the COVID-19 pandemic. The dashed line represents the linear fit. Ten countries are identified for illustrative purposes. This figure excludes high-income countries. Because the positive relationship is in part mechanical, figure 3.7 is presented for comparison.

Collapse and Recovery: How the COVID-19 Pandemic Eroded Human Capital and What to Do about It

Another global metric for COVID-related education impacts is the increase in learning poverty, which measures the share of 10-year-olds who cannot read and understand a simple text. For low- and middle-income countries, learning poverty rates are estimated to have risen from 57 percent in 2019 to 70 percent in 2022.[84]

Learning forgone versus learning forgotten

Underlying an average measure of learning loss are students who learned something, students who learned nothing, and students who forgot what they used to know. Decomposing average learning losses in this way is important to fully understand them, translate them from an abstract number to real-life impacts, and design suitable policy responses.

Average learning losses have two parts: learning forgone and learning forgotten. *Forgone learning* is learning that would have happened had schools remained open. For example, if a child who could do single-digit addition was expected to master subtraction (such as 9–3) had that child remained in school for a year, learning forgone is proficiency in subtraction. However, learning loss could also include erosion of skills already mastered before schools closed.[85] This is *forgotten learning*. For example, in this hypothetical situation the student might not only not master subtraction but also forget addition.

An analysis undertaken for this report decomposed learning losses into forgone and forgotten learning using rich data from Bangladesh.[86] The two rounds of comparable assessments used for grade 6 and grade 8 students (in February 2020 and May 2022) coincided with significant school disruptions. On the whole, 14.5 months of school closures led to nearly 26 months of learning losses. Of these learning losses, 69 percent stemmed from forgone learning and 31 percent from forgotten learning (see figure 3.9 and box 3.1 for details).

The distinction between learning forgone and forgotten matters for policy. For example, students in country X were in early grade 4 when schools closed in 2020. If these students came back to grade 6 in 2022, should they learn the grade 6 curriculum? This example is playing out in most systems. However, based on global empirical evidence of steep learning losses, learning the grade 6 curriculum would be a mistake.

If students have suffered a substantial amount of forgone learning—that is, they did not learn what the curriculum expected over the two years that schools were closed—then these students should be taught

 FIGURE 3.9 **Approximately 30 percent of learning losses in Bangladesh were forgotten learning**
Share of questions answered correctly, by subject, grade, and year

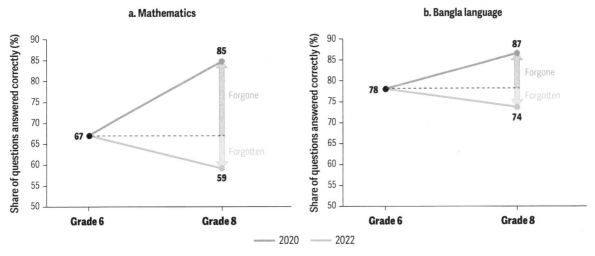

Source: Djaker et al., forthcoming.
Note: The figure shows the learning losses in Bangladesh in mathematics (panel a) and the Bangla language (panel b) between grades 6 and 8 after 14.5 months of school closures. The blue line represents the normal rate of learning from grades 6 to 8 in pre-pandemic years. The dashed horizontal line represents no learning or learning losses. The orange line represents the average decline in test scores among students between grade 6 in 2020 and grade 8 in 2022. Learning losses are the sum of forgone learning (that is, learning students would have normally acquired between grades 6 and 8—blue arrow) and forgotten learning (that is, skills they had in grade 6 but had forgotten by grade 8—orange arrow). See box 3.1 for details and a fuller explanation.

BOX 3.1 **Decomposing learning losses in forgone and forgotten learning using rich data from Bangladesh**

Learning losses can be decomposed into two parts: *forgone learning* and *forgotten learning*. As noted, forgone learning is learning that students would have received had schools remained open. Forgotten learning is learning that students acquired before the COVID-19 pandemic but forgot or lost because of school closures (for example, by not using or putting in practice the material they had previously learned).

This decomposition requires (1) cross-sectional data from two comparable cohorts (one pre-COVID and one post–school reopenings) and (2) longitudinal data for at least one of those cohorts to estimate how much learning would have taken place in the absence of school closures. The latter should ideally have an assessment that can be "equated" or put on a comparable scale. This requires incorporating a set of common overlapping items and a set of items with varying levels of difficulty in the design of the assessment, in addition to a psychometric technique called item response theory (IRT).

Djaker et al. (forthcoming) is one of the few learning loss studies that allows for decomposition of learning losses into forgone learning and forgotten learning. The study uses nationally representative pre-pandemic test score data from Bangladesh for grade 6 students (in February 2020) and then follows and tests the same students again in grade 8 (in May 2022) after 14.5 months of school disruptions. Furthermore, it has data from a different cohort in grade 8 (in February 2020), before school closures.

These rich data allow the decomposition of learning losses into learning forgone and learning forgotten in three steps as shown in, for example, panel a of figure 3.9. First, in 2020 grade 6 students answered 67 percent of math questions correctly, on average, and grade 8 students answered 85 percent of questions correctly.[a] The grade 8 average score in 2020 (versus the grade 6 student score) can be taken as a proxy for student learning during two normal (nonpandemic) academic years and considered the counterfactual (blue line). Second, the dashed horizontal line represents where no learning nor learning losses occurred: children did not forget, but neither did they learn anything new. Third, the 2022 assessment shows that the average score for students in grade 8 declined by 8 percentage points (orange line).[b] Thus the average score of students in grade 8 is 85 percent in a nonpandemic year versus 59 percent in a pandemic year for a learning loss of 26 percentage points or 26 academic months.[c] This loss can be decomposed as follows:

- Forgone learning amounts to 18 percentage points (a score of 85 percent by grade 8 in a nonpandemic year versus 67 percent in grade 6). This finding is the estimate of how much learning would have improved between grades 6 and 8 if schooling had not been disrupted.
- Forgotten learning amounts to 8 percentage points (a score of 67 percent in grade 6 before the pandemic, while grade 8 students scored 59 percent after schools reopened). This finding is the estimate of how much learning is lost because some students no longer have the skills they used to have.

The same decomposition can be conducted for Bangla language scores in panel b of figure 3.9. On the whole, 14.5 months of school closures led to nearly 26 months of learning lost, with 69 percent due to forgone learning and 31 percent due to forgotten learning. These findings have deep policy implications, as explained in this chapter.

a. Results are presented here using the percentage of correct answers for simplicity. Common items and projections across years and grades are used to estimate these numbers. Djaker et al. (forthcoming) presents a more formal analysis that equates test scores across years and grades using the IRT. This analysis confirms the results and shows even larger learning losses.

b. Due to the time difference, this estimate is likely a lower bound because it is not correcting for the additional two months of classes that grade 8 students would have had in 2022 under normal circumstances versus the 2020 cohort (because the dates of the assessments were May 2022 versus February 2020).

c. This estimation assumes that the improvement in test scores between grades 6 and 8 before the pandemic are the typical learning rate in two academic years.

the curricula of grades 4 and 5 in 2022 before they are taught the grade 6 curriculum. If, on the other hand, students have forgotten a substantial amount of learning, then they would need to learn not only the material from grades 4 and 5 but also the material from grade 3. Because learning is cumulative and skills beget skills, unless the lost foundational skills are remedied when schools reopen, new instruction would be wasted, and students would be at risk of lagging further and further behind until they cannot keep up with the material, learn nothing, or drop out of school altogether.

Learning losses were higher for younger and poorer students

I am frustrated that teachers are not taking enough measures to educate us, even though they are getting paid regularly. Poor students ... need help.

—Older brother of a secondary student, Bangladesh
Quoted in Aedo, Nahata, and Sabarwal (2020)

❝

For younger students, learning losses were higher in foundational skills. In Kenya, a study found that a higher proportion of students exhibited learning losses in math in grade 4 (69 percent) than in grade 8 (31 percent).[87] In Brazil, students in grade 5 lost three to four times as much learning as their grades 9 and 12 counterparts during pandemic-related school closures, compared with previous cohorts in these same grades who were not exposed to the pandemic.[88]

Aside from Kenya and Brazil, this body of evidence is largely from high-income contexts. In Switzerland, a study revealed that learning losses of primary students (grades 3–6) were six times larger than those of their secondary counterparts (grades 7–9).[89] Similarly, in the United States the declines for grades 3–5 were larger than those for older students in grades 7 and 8 by 1–3 percentile points in reading and 3–4 percentile points in math.[90] In the Netherlands, students in grades 2 and 3 experienced learning losses in spelling during the pandemic, whereas students in grades 4 and 5 experienced learning gains.[91] Learning losses for younger students may have been steeper because these students need greater support to learn, and so they found it harder to make up for the time lost with teachers.

Learning losses were also higher for poorer students.[92] In Bangladesh, a study conducted for this report found that students with low maternal education, a proxy for socioeconomic status, lost more than twice as much learning as students with a highly educated mother.[93] In Pakistan, when compared with pre-pandemic expected learning levels, children from the poorest households fell further behind in math during the pandemic relative to children from the richest households.[94] Similar patterns are also observed in high-income contexts such as Belgium,[95] Denmark,[96] Germany,[97] Japan,[98] the Netherlands,[99] and the United Kingdom.[100] In the United States, students in poorer schools were affected by the pandemic up to five times more than students in nonpoor schools, particularly in the elementary grades.[101] Higher learning losses for poorer students put them at a particular disadvantage when it comes to foundational skills. In Argentina, the percentage of low socioeconomic students in grade 6 with language knowledge below the basic level was more than three times larger in 2021 than in 2018, increasing from 13 percent to 43 percent.[102]

There is no evidence of consistent gender differences in learning losses across countries. Of the 56 studies analyzed for this chapter, four report larger losses for boys, nine report larger losses for girls, 16 report no significant differences, and the remaining studies do not allow for gender disaggregation.[103] For example, in the Netherlands and Bangladesh, learning losses were larger for boys than girls, whereas in Brazil and Ethiopia losses were larger for girls than boys.[104] Gender differences also varied by subject. In the state of Guanajuato, Mexico, a forthcoming study shows that students lost, on average, 0.75 and 1.05 years of schooling in Spanish and mathematics, respectively, between grades 5 and 6.[105] These losses were about 47 percent larger for girls than for boys, but only in math.

In some contexts, learning losses are also higher for other disadvantaged groups. In Ethiopia, for students in rural settings learning progressed at about 33 percent of the speed that would have been expected had they continued at the same pace as before the pandemic, while the learning of students in urban areas progressed by 50 percent.[106] Learning losses in Uganda were three times larger for students whose parents had no education or only an informal education than the losses for students whose parents had a primary education. No learning losses were observed for students whose parents had a secondary education.[107] In the United States, learning gaps between White students and their Black and Hispanic counterparts are now wider than before the pandemic.[108]

PANDEMIC-RELATED LEARNING LOSSES ARE AN ECONOMIC TIME BOMB

Learning losses can derail not only students' learning trajectory but also their lives by diminishing their economic prospects, lifetime earnings, and chances of escaping poverty. If swift and effective actions are not taken, the pandemic-related schooling shock could leave students and economies permanently scarred. The need for urgent action is underscored by two possible outcomes. First, if not remediated, learning losses could grow over time. Second, learning losses at this scale could translate into significantly lower lifetime earnings for hundreds of millions of people, which means lower productivity, greater inequality, and possibly greater social unrest for decades to come.

Learning losses, if not remediated, will compound over time

Past evidence suggests that learning losses cannot be made up through business-as-usual schooling in the medium term. In fact, because learning is cumulative by nature, current learning losses, if left unremediated, will increase and prevent future learning from happening—especially if losses occur in linked foundational skills. Various studies support this conclusion. For example, following an earthquake in Pakistan in 2005, schools near the fault line were closed for about two months. Four years later, students from these schools were from one and a half to two years behind in terms of learning, compared with their counterparts who did not experience school closures.[109] Children in the regions affected by the earthquake must have learned less every year after returning to school. Most likely this occurred because if every child had to be promoted in the new school year and if teachers taught the curriculum for the new grade, students fell further behind every subsequent year.[110]

Without action, learning losses will compound over time. Today's students could lose as much as 10 percent of their future average annual earnings due to COVID-related learning losses. But with decisive, evidence-based action, learning recovery is possible.

There is a great danger that if schools simply go back to business as usual, learning losses will compound over time. In Ethiopia, a study found that students in grades 1 and 4 not only lost learning (levels) due to the long school closures, but they are now learning at a slower rate than they did before the pandemic.[111] In Malawi, once students returned to school after seven months of school closures, learning trajectories were dramatically slower (6.9 points of learning for every 100 days of schooling once schools reopened versus 13.4 points of learning for every 100 days of schooling in the period before the pandemic).[112] If this trend continues, students affected by the pandemic could continue falling further behind their expected pre-pandemic learning trajectories.

On the other hand, emerging evidence suggests that if swift remedial action is taken, learning losses can be fully recovered. In the Indian state of Tamil Nadu, extra classes after school-focused remediation between December 2021 and May 2022 helped students recover about two-thirds of lost learning linked to 18 months of school closures.[113] In the city of Nara, Japan, immediately after three months of school closures grade 6 students experienced learning losses in mathematics, compared with the learning level of a group from before the pandemic.[114] However, the city government took swift action, shortened the summer break to extend the academic calendar, and provided every student with a laptop to help with distance learning. When measured again after six months and being exposed to these remedial policies, students not only recovered but actually also surpassed the comparison group from before the pandemic. Similarly, in the Netherlands, through concerted government efforts, learning losses grew smaller over time.[115] This finding suggests that with focused, evidence-based action, learning recovery is possible. Specific policy options are discussed in the final section of this chapter.

Learning losses will reduce lifetime earnings for hundreds of millions of people

Learning losses now will translate into lower earnings in adulthood. Unless those losses are remediated, hundreds of millions of children exposed to school closures and learning losses stemming from the COVID-19 crisis will likely have lower wages and productivity when they enter the labor market. By way of comparison, a study in Argentina found that 88 days of primary schooling lost from teacher strikes reduced the labor earnings of males by 3.2 percent and females by 1.9 percent.[116] In Cambodia, each year of disruption to primary education during civil conflicts reduces average future earnings by from 6.6 to 8.6 percent for men.[117]

Estimates that take the cumulative nature of learning losses into account suggest that the long-term cost of human capital losses will dwarf the economic shock from the COVID-19 pandemic.[118] World Bank projections suggest that, globally, pandemic-related learning losses will lead to between US$23,514 and US$31,800 in lost earnings over a typical student's lifetime. Overall, without urgent policy action, today's students could lose as much as 10 percent of their future average annual earnings due to COVID-related learning losses. In terms of present value, these earnings could amount to US$21 trillion—equivalent to 17 percent of today's global GDP.[119]

Left unchecked, learning losses will perpetuate the vicious cycle of poverty and inequality, disrupting economic development for years to come. Past major pandemics, even though much smaller in scale, have led to a significant increase in social unrest by reducing output and increasing inequality.[120] Learning losses have not only disproportionately affected low- and middle-income countries but also vulnerable groups within each country. The children who need education the most to climb out of poverty will be the ones most likely to be deprived of it by the crisis. In many low- and middle-income countries, the combination of a youth bulge and poor prospects could prove a combustible mix. Governments can act today to prevent these problems. The next two sections discuss precisely how.

HOW HAVE GOVERNMENTS RESPONDED TO THE PANDEMIC SO FAR?

Countries responded to the pandemic in a variety of ways. Some of these were impressive and some disappointing. All hold lessons for imagining better and more effective education systems going forward.

As schools closed, education systems acted quickly, and in some ways, impressively

> *We made the platform Aprendo en línea available to the educational community,*
> *which has resources for students from 1st grade through the final year of secondary level....*
> *As of end March [2020], the platform has been used by more than 2 million users.*

—Raúl Figueroa, Minister of Education, Chile
UNESCO blog, April 3, 2020

❝

Countries acted fast to maintain learning continuity during COVID school closures. Most school closures began in March 2020. By June 2020, 96 percent of countries (from a set of 118) had implemented some form of remote learning, including online platforms, TV, radio, and paper-based delivery. No middle-income country lacked a remote learning platform in June 2020, and only 7 percent of low-income and 10 percent of lower-middle-income countries were without one.[121] This effort amounts to a truly heroic response amid tremendous uncertainty, especially for countries that built these systems from scratch, almost overnight.

Most countries tried to reach every child regardless of household income by using multiple modes for remote learning. In April 2021, more than half of countries (from a set of 143) were providing more than five modes of remote learning.[122] Innovative ideas were being used to reach hard-to-reach students. For example, villages in Gujarat, India, paired students with and without digital devices together to promote access. Furthermore, these villages also used mobile learning vehicles to engage students.[123] Kenya deployed Google's Loon Balloons carrying 4G base stations over Kenyan airspace to provide students and families with internet connectivity.[124]

A variety of actors came together to offer new solutions to new-ish problems. Several governments and international organizations acted to support student mental health through hotlines, as in the Dominican Republic and Nepal.[125] SMS (text) messages were sent to parents reminding or guiding them to stay involved in their children's education[126] and were accompanied by live phone tutoring sessions.[127] Countries such as Bangladesh[128] and Indonesia[129] embraced online training to build teachers' skills. Despite steps such as these, the policy response to COVID school closures fell short in several tangible ways.

Four mistakes governments made in their COVID-schooling response

The first mistake was to keep schools closed for too long. Three months into the pandemic, 84 percent of countries had not fully reopened schools. A full year into the pandemic, 52 percent had not. Two full years on, 12 percent still had not.[130]

Keeping schools closed while the rest of the economy reopened was a mistake. Evidence shows that, in various settings, schools with appropriate mitigation measures could reopen with minimal risk of transmitting COVID-19, particularly during low-transmission periods.[131] Furthermore, in Germany, schools that had regular and mandatory rapid testing of students mitigated the growth in case numbers prior to the country's fourth pandemic wave in the fall of 2021.[132] As discussed, these closures imposed a significant cost on students and future economic growth through massive learning losses. These costs far exceed any potential benefits in terms of preventing the spread of COVID-19.

Extended school closures were not an inevitability; they were an active policy choice (see box 3.2). Uruguay first reopened schools after only three months.[133] By contrast, in Honduras, schools were fully closed for 15 months and were still not fully open as of March 2022. Similarly, Vietnam reopened schools after 47 days, whereas in the Philippines schools were physically closed for 510 days.[134]

The second mistake was not trying harder to fix the grave problems with remote learning. As described, providing remote learning did not automatically mean that students could or would access it. Many low- and middle-income countries prioritized online platforms even though only a small share of students could access them.[135] More than one-third of low- and lower-middle-income countries that provided lessons through television or radio reported that less than half of primary school students were reached.[136] Most governments could have done more to track and improve the take-up and quality of remote learning. They could also have put in place complementary measures to keep at-risk students engaged, such as phone-based tutoring or more active involvement of families and communities.

The third mistake was not ensuring student-teacher engagement during school closures. Following school closures in 2020, only 25 percent of low-income countries required teachers to teach remotely or online, whereas 49 percent of high-income countries did so.[137] Consequently, many students had little interaction of any kind with their teachers during school closures. In Nepal, only 31 percent of students claimed to have had any teacher interaction at all during closures, and the share was significantly lower for students disadvantaged in terms of wealth and caste. This finding is particularly concerning because these students were also less likely to have received parental support for learning during this time.[138] Teachers are extremely important for students, not just for learning but also for support and for maintaining attachment to schooling. Not ensuring that the student-teacher connection was maintained during school closures was a huge miss.

The fourth mistake was promoting students to advanced curricula without accounting for learning losses. The significant learning losses from COVID-related school closures were documented earlier in this chapter. And yet, many education systems are bringing students back to advanced grades as if no learning losses had occurred. A student who was in grade 2 in 2020—and then experienced two years of school closures, with much learning forgone and some learning forgotten—is now expected to handle a grade 4 curriculum in 2022. This approach could spell disaster. These students will understand little, become disengaged, and keep falling further and further behind, until they drop out.

BOX 3.2 The length of school closures is not correlated with country income or governance quality

One hypothesis is that length of school closures was linked to the governance "capacity" of governments. To explore this hypothesis, the analysis undertaken for this report plotted the length of school closures against the log gross domestic product (GDP) per capita across all regions. This analysis was complemented with a proxy of government capacity using data from the World Bank's Worldwide Governance Indicators (https://databank.worldbank.org/source/worldwide-governance-indicators). Specifically, the values from the government effectiveness indicator were averaged for 2015–19. The duration of school closures was then plotted against the measure of government effectiveness, as shown in figure B3.2.1.

In figure B3.2.1, panel a shows that, on average, higher- and lower-income countries fully closed schools for about the same amount of time. There is huge variability across countries of similar income levels in terms of school closure duration. The coefficient on a regression of school closures on log per capita income, after including region fixed effects, is -0.80 and far from significant.

Panel b makes the same point regarding government effectiveness. When translating this figure into a regression with region fixed effects, the coefficient on governance effectiveness is –2.08. However, the coefficient is relatively small, as it implies that moving a country from the median to the 95th percentile of government effectiveness reduced the duration of school closures by 5.8 weeks. The explanatory power of the regression excluding region fixed effects is very low (R-squared, 0.04). Moreover, using the same specification, the relationship between government effectiveness and school closures is not significant.

These results suggest that there is no deterministic relationship between a country's "capacity," as proxied by income or government effectiveness, and length of school closures. Some so-called low-capacity countries reopened schools quickly, while some "high-capacity" countries kept them closed for far too long.

FIGURE B3.2.1 There is no systematic relationship between the length of school closures and log GDP per capita and an indicator of governance effectiveness

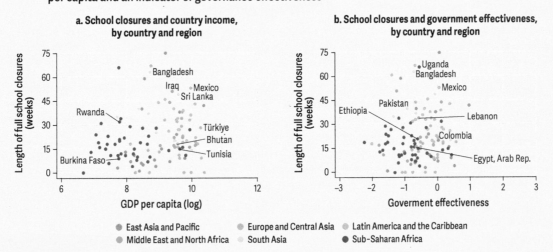

Sources: Original estimates based on data on school closures from the United Nations Educational, Scientific, and Cultural Organization (UNESCO) Institute for Statistics (UIS), https://uis.unesco.org/. Panel a, gross domestic product (GDP) per capita data: World Bank's DataBank, https://databank.worldbank.org/home. Panel b, government effectiveness: World Bank's Worldwide Governance Indicators, https://databank.worldbank.org/source/worldwide-governance-indicators.
Note: The figure shows the relationship between the length of full school closures in weeks and log GDP per capita (panel a) and the government effectiveness index from the Worldwide Governance Indicators (panel b). Both panels show the weak correlation between the variables, suggesting that government capacity as proxied by these two measures was not related to school closures.

WHAT SHOULD GOVERNMENTS DO NOW? PRIORITIZE EFFECTIVE ACTION

While many other sectors have rebounded when lockdowns eased, the damage to children's education is likely to reduce children's wellbeing and productivity for decades, making education disruption and learning loss due to school closures one of the biggest threats to medium- and long-term recovery from COVID-19 unless governments act swiftly.

—Abhijit Banerjee, Nobel Laureate
"Learning Loss Biggest Global Threat to Pandemic Recovery: Nobel Laureate Abhijit Banerjee,"
Telegraph India, February 9, 2022

66

Governments must act now. This requires setting clear priorities in two ways. First, learning recovery must be prioritized in the overall development agenda. Second, specific actions (outlined in the discussion that follows) must be prioritized within education planning and spending.

To date, global guidance on learning recovery has been broadly consistent. An analysis of key recommendations for learning recovery from eight influential global reports from 2021–22 shows a great deal of overlap.[139] The most recent report, published in June 2022 by the World Bank jointly with five other global agencies and organizations,[140] outlines five policy actions for learning recovery based on the evidence—the so-called RAPID Framework: Reach all children; Assess learning; Prioritize the fundamentals; Increase the efficiency of instruction; and Develop psychosocial health and well-being.[141] Several of these recommendations go beyond recovering pandemic losses. If implemented, they would help build better education systems that put countries on a trajectory for learning acceleration beyond restoring the status quo.[142]

As countries struggle with multiple demands and restricted fiscal space, enacting all recommended policies may be difficult for some. The discussion that follows lays out the most important nonnegotiable policy actions needed in the short term. Longer-term policy options are outlined in chapter 5.

Two types of policy responses based on country groups

Countries need to customize policies to their specific contexts. This is particularly true on one dimension: what share of lost LAYS stems from dropouts. This question has a crucial bearing on the design of optimal policy responses. Consider the following comparisons:

- Bulgaria and Mozambique both lost around 0.46 LAYS. However, in Mozambique 30 percent of lost LAYS stemmed from dropouts, whereas in Bulgaria all the lost LAYS were from learning losses. Moreover, in Bulgaria the lost LAYS were relatively smaller (equivalent to 5.5 percent of its total pre-pandemic LAYS) than in Mozambique (where losses amounted to 10.6 percent of its total pre-pandemic LAYS).
- In China and Madagascar, schools were closed for about the same amount of time. In both cases, they translated into 0.31 lost LAYS. However, in Madagascar more than one-third of these lost LAYS were from dropouts, whereas in China nearly all the lost LAYS were from learning losses.

Based on the share of lost LAYS due to dropouts, countries fall into two broad groups, with implications for the optimal blend of policies to respond to the COVID-19 crisis. In the first group, a relatively small share of lost LAYS (less than 10 percent) is from increased dropouts. Of the 116 countries covered by this analysis, 52 countries fall in this category, of which 40 are upper-middle-income countries and the remaining 12 are lower-middle-income countries. These countries—such as Bulgaria and China in the preceding examples—need to focus most of their COVID education response on learning recovery.

In the second group, a larger and decidedly nontrivial share of lost LAYS are from increased dropouts. This group is bigger and consists mostly of

> *Policy makers should calibrate policy responses based on the share of lost LAYS that are driven by dropouts vis-à-vis learning losses.*

low-income and some lower-middle-income countries, such as Madagascar and Mozambique, that need to focus on both learning recovery and bringing children back to school (reversing dropouts). This group has quite a large range. At one end of the spectrum is Bangladesh, where about 10 percent of lost LAYS are due to dropouts. At the other end are the Central African Republic and Niger, where nearly 60 percent of lost LAYS are due to increased dropouts. Clearly, the relative focus and resources needed to reverse dropouts would vary based on the precise context, but an evidence-based response on this dimension is urgently needed.

Both groups of countries can structure their policy responses using the nonnegotiable priorities for learning recovery and dropout minimization described next. However, the relative emphasis across these two dimensions needs to be calibrated based on the decomposition of lost LAYS into learning loss vis-à-vis dropouts.

Four nonnegotiable priorities to address learning losses

Keep schools open and increase instructional hours. Most countries have reopened schools,[143] and there seems to be real recognition by society of the important work schools and teachers do.[144] Teachers also seem to recognize the importance of in-person learning vis-à-vis the COVID-related risks. In Bangladesh, India (Delhi), and Nepal, most teachers (93 percent) believe schools should remain open even if COVID-19 rates are increasing at a low rate. However, only 24 percent of teachers believe schools should remain open if COVID-19 rates are increasing at a high rate.[145] Meanwhile, emerging evidence suggests that the pandemic took a heavy toll on teachers' motivation and increased burnout rates.[146] This finding suggests that more work is needed around public messaging on health and safety for school reopenings and for the well-being of teachers and students.

Face-to-face instructional hours are still limited in some contexts. As of March 2022, schools were still fully closed in Honduras and the Philippines and only partially open in 12 countries.[147] Furthermore, in many contexts, despite schools being open, students are receiving less instructional time than before. For example, in Botswana, although UNESCO data officially state that schools are fully open, the country adopted a double-shift system to enable social distancing, effectively cutting instructional hours in half.[148] Up to 69 percent of middle-income countries adopted similar "attendance in shifts" policies, many of which have yet to be reversed.[149]

To promote learning recovery, it is critical to keep schools open and restore or increase instructional hours so that students can catch up on the learning they have lost. Some countries are already pursuing this approach. In Kenya and Mexico, the government has expanded the academic calendar by shortening holidays.[150] Some 21 percent of the 122 countries interviewed in March 2021 claimed to be implementing expanded instructional hours nationwide.[151] Ensuring schooling access may require innovative strategies in fragile and conflict-affected contexts such as school-in-a-box or temporary learning centers.[152]

Assess learning and match instruction to students' level. It is very difficult to recover learning losses without first measuring them. But most countries are failing to measure and assess learning losses. By June 2021, of 143 countries, only 35 percent reported having taken steps to measure learning levels in primary or lower-secondary education.[153] Thus teachers, parents, and students themselves are flying blind as they try to address learning losses.

It is critical to equip and encourage teachers to undertake formative classroom assessments so they can determine who needs help and what type of help is needed. Where possible, assessments should focus on foundational and critical skills so that they can be remediated as a matter of priority.

In parallel, national assessments could help generate both political will and technical guidance for policy action. For this to happen, two conditions must be met. First, the technical design needs to be strong, allowing for tracking learning over time. If possible, these assessments should allow for decomposing learning losses into learning forgone and learning forgotten and allow links to be established with global and regional learning tools for reliable benchmarking against global standards, such as the Early Grade Reading Assessment (EGRA), Latin American Laboratory for Assessment of the Quality of Education (LLECE), Programme for the Analysis of Education Systems (PASEC), Pacific Islands Literacy and Numeracy Assessment (PILNA), Progress in International Reading Literacy Study (PIRLS), Programme for International Student Assessment (PISA), Southern and Eastern Africa Consortium for Monitoring Educational Quality (SACMEQ), and Trends in International Mathematics and Science Study (TIMSS). Second, national assessment data can have much greater impacts if the findings are disseminated publicly in an accessible way to generate engagement, discussion, and solutions from a range of stakeholders.

Next, learning data must lead to action in the classroom by helping teachers target instruction to the level of the child. Without this step, data can do little to address learning losses. The key is to use the findings from learning assessments to reorganize students so that the instruction they receive matches their current level. A pause in the curriculum, even if for just one hour a day, to reorganize grades and classrooms by student level rather than grade could be transformative for recovering learning losses.

Often called Teaching at the Right Level (TARL),[154] this model involves grouping students in school by learning levels and engaging in level-appropriate activities, often in small groups. Delivery models include in-school instruction as well as out-of-school catch-up camps and delivery by teachers, teachers' aides, or volunteers. This approach has been shown to be highly effective for improving student learning.[155] It is also highly cost-effective, delivering the equivalent of more than three years of high-quality schooling per US$100 spent.[156]

Implementation of TARL for recovering COVID-related learning losses shows promising results. In India, between August and October 2021, just before schools began to open, the nongovernmental organization (NGO) Pratham recruited 25,000 volunteers to run a two-month TARL catch-up campaign. The result was a 12 percent increase in the number of grades 3–5 students who could read a paragraph.[157] In the northeastern region of Botswana, students were assessed when schools reopened, and the results were used to inform and implement TARL. Foundational numeracy improved significantly.[158]

Some countries are embracing the idea of grouping students by level and targeting instruction. For example, in 2021 Chile launched Escuelas Arriba, a national program in which for each Learning Objective, a three-part methodology consists of (1) a catch-up or "leveling" phase, (2) a phase in which new content is learned, and (3) a phase of a formative assessment. The results determine whether the class continues learning or returns to the catch-up phase.[159] In Ghana, the Ministry of Education rolled out a targeted instruction intervention, rapid student assessment, and remedial education in more than 10,000 schools across the country.[160] The sustained adoption and implementation of some form of TARL could help improve learning beyond the pre-pandemic status quo and help build more effective education systems overall.

Targeted instruction in classrooms can be complemented with focused remedial support to help lagging students catch up. Computer-aided instruction can be very effective in targeting instruction much more precisely to a child's level through the use of adaptive learning software.[161]

A related set of interventions includes tutoring, which, by providing one-on-one or small-group instruction, also effectively targets teaching to a child's level.[162] Given its adaptability and flexibility, studies have shown that well-designed and well-targeted tutoring programs can be a cost-effective way to improve learning outcomes in the short run.[163] Larger effects were found in programs where tutoring was implemented by teachers or paraprofessionals, in earlier grades, and offered during regular class hours. In Colombia, a small-group remedial tutoring intervention targeting struggling third-grade students showed positive and persistent impact on literacy scores and positive spillovers on mathematics.[164] In low-income settings, phone-based tutoring has also been shown to be promising in various contexts, providing an additional option to remediate learning losses.[165]

Focus on foundations and streamline the curricula. Closely linked is the issue of streamlining curricula. Rather than pausing a curriculum to target instruction, an alternative approach is to repeat it. If most students are below grade level, it would make sense to repeat streamlined versions of past-grade curricula for all. For example, in Kenya the Ministry of Education announced a two-year accelerated "crash program" to help students catch up without repeating grades.[166] Similarly, the South African government introduced a three-year Curriculum Recovery Plan that consolidates curricula to focus on fundamental content knowledge, skills, and attitudes by grade and subject.[167] The Ministry of Education of India conducted a large-scale Foundational Learning Study that provides information on the current levels of children's foundational skill levels, forming the basis of follow-on, targeted interventions.[168] Systems should also take this opportunity to fundamentally reform or rethink overloaded curricula so that they are more realistic and focused on foundations.

Learning recovery strategies also need to be tailored to the context. For example, low-income settings may face additional barriers to learning recovery. These include initially larger learning gaps, larger class sizes, and fewer qualified and trained teachers, among others. These contexts may also have other pressing needs, such as addressing malnutrition. Thus low-income countries may benefit more from approaches such as structured pedagogy that are very helpful where there are deep gaps in teacher training.[169] Similarly, in some low-income contexts school feeding could be an effective way to address both enrollment and malnutrition.[170]

Learning recovery plans should also vary by the degree and type of learning loss. If most of the learning loss is forgone learning, immediate policy actions could range from revisiting past grade curricula to fully holding back students, depending on the magnitude of learning forgone. If, however, students are struggling with both forgone and forgotten learning, this strategy would not suffice. In addition to repeating a past curriculum or grade(s), targeted remedial support for students who have forgotten past skills would be needed. In all cases, assessing learning levels is a crucial first step and should be accompanied by some degree of streamlining curricula to focus on fundamentals and to compensate for lost time.

Create a political commitment for learning recovery. This step is based on the premise that learning recovery is not just a technical undertaking; it is also political. Recovering COVID-induced learning losses requires political alignment across multiple stakeholders with different priorities. This is not a trivial step.[171] Teachers may push back on additional tasks if they do not have the necessary support and tools. Parents, especially wealthy ones, may push back on curriculum streamlining and repetition—steps that are often stigmatized.

Crucially, education financing may be under threat. Forty percent of low- and lower-middle-income countries reduced their education spending in 2020 after the onset of the pandemic. Spending declined by 13.5 percent, on average. Although cross-country data on actual education spending in 2021 and 2022 are not yet available, the data that are available on the share of education in national budgets indicate that education lost space in the national budgets of low- and lower-middle-income countries in 2021 and 2022—this share had also fallen in 2020. Spending rebounded slightly in 2021, but fell again in 2022 below 2019 levels.[172] With many countries hit by multiple crises in 2022—including food, energy, conflict, and climate crises—education financing may remain at great risk.

Because politics is likely to be a problem, it is imperative that politics be a part of the solution. To this end, countries should harness learning measurement to build political will for action. Learning losses, no matter how steep, may currently be invisible to parents and policy makers. Clear data and messaging on the extent of learning losses and their economic costs are critical to galvanize action.

It is also important to enlist political leadership beyond ministries of education, especially at the highest level of political leadership. Political coalitions that include families, educators, civil society, the private sector, and other ministries can help this effort.

Whenever possible, governments should work closely with teachers,[173] teachers' unions, local governments, teacher-parent associations, NGOs, and civil society organizations (CSOs). Many NGOs and CSOs have done heroic work on learning recovery during the crisis. Promising local solutions can be recognized and scaled up.

Many teachers are willing and eager to implement learning recovery policies. In Nepal, Bangladesh, and India (Delhi), only about half of 926 teachers surveyed are using assessments to diagnose learning levels or conducting remedial classes. Yet more than 75 percent of them believe these actions are critical. And these are not just beliefs. An embedded experiment also elicited the teachers' willingness to engage in further remedial activities.[174] About 90 percent of teachers in Nepal, 80 percent in Bangladesh, and 60 percent in Delhi were willing and ready to spend extra time assessing students or conducting additional remedial classes.[175]

Two nonnegotiable priorities to minimize dropouts

Even though the overall extent of COVID-related student dropouts has not been very high in middle-income settings, dropouts are a big concern in lower-income settings and for specific student populations, in particular those from disadvantaged backgrounds. To address this concern, countries should prioritize the following steps.

Track students at risk of dropping out. As noted, dropouts are usually higher for older and poorer students. In some contexts, dropouts are higher for boys and in others for girls. It is crucial to monitor at-risk student groups closely so that the system can intervene early and effectively through targeted support. Brazil, Chile, Peru, and several other countries have created early warning systems that use attendance, performance, and a range of other factors to predict a student's risk of dropping out.[176] Once in place, these monitoring tools could continue ensuring that at-risk students are identified in a timely manner and supported to prevent them from dropping out. These tools could help to build better, more inclusive education systems overall.

Alleviate financial constraints and provide incentives for students to attend school. Targeted financial support, such as stipends or scholarships, can help boost enrollment, particularly among those facing financial constraints. For example, Indonesia's Jaring Pengamanan Sosial (JPS) scholarship and fee-forgiveness program, implemented during the 1990s economic crisis, reduced dropouts in lower-secondary grades by 38 percent.[177] In China, tuition waivers and subsidies had a significantly positive impact on school enrollment among rural girls in 2006.[178]

Conditional cash transfers are highly effective in improving school enrollment.[179] Large multidimensional programs such as Auxílio Brasil (formerly Bolsa Familia) in Brazil, the Programme of Advancement Through Health and Education (PATH) in Jamaica, and Pantawid Pamilyang Pilipino in the Philippines tie cash support for families to school enrollment as well as improved student attendance and schooling attainment. Similar programs worldwide have succeeded in preventing dropouts. Recently, Lebanon committed US$23 million in cash support aimed at helping youth ages 13–18 from extremely poor families and at risk of dropping out to remain in school.[180]

Nonfinancial incentives, such as school feeding programs, can serve multiple goals. Because of the COVID-19 pandemic, 370 million children from 150 countries are missing out on a daily school meal.[181] Ramped-up school feeding programs can improve school reenrollment and attendance while addressing malnutrition.[182]

Effective solutions to address early dropouts also tend to be highly specific to the context. In some contexts, early dropouts are mainly driven by social norms; in others, they are linked to labor market opportunities. In some contexts, it is vital to engage religious leaders; in others, it is more important to reach youth directly. Effective messaging can vary widely. To be successful, policy actions should be adapted to the specific circumstances.

INACTION IS ALSO A DECISION (A POOR ONE)

The pandemic was the largest shock to learning in modern history. All the evidence available suggests that if nothing is done, children will not make up their learning losses on their own. COVID-19 school closures have pushed students off their learning trajectory. As discussed in chapter 1, countries could end up on one of three possible trajectories. If countries continue with business as usual, they will likely end up with a whole generation of students who never recover the learning they lost, diminishing their future productivity and lifetime wages. On the other hand, taking effective action would not only return students (and future workers) to their learning trajectory, but could also help them surpass it. Several studies show that systemwide reforms such as targeting instruction to the student level or high-dosage tutoring for lagging students can help improve learning beyond the status quo that prevailed before the pandemic. Schools after the pandemic could be fundamentally better. They could be safer, more inclusive, and more effective. The key is to act now—and turn this crisis into opportunity.

ANNEX 3A. METHODOLOGY FOR ESTIMATING LOST LEARNING-ADJUSTED YEARS OF SCHOOLING (LAYS)

The Learning-Adjusted Years of Schooling (LAYS) measure was introduced by the World Bank by Filmer et al.[183] LAYS is calculated as the product of average years of school and a particular measure of learning relative to a numeraire, so that

$$LAYS = S_c \times R_c^n,$$

(3A.1)

where S_c is a measure of the average years of schooling acquired by a relevant cohort of the population of country c, and R_c^n is a measure of learning for a relevant cohort of students in country c relative to a numeraire (or benchmark) n.

Measuring losses to average schooling

When schools reopened after COVID-19–related closures, some children returned to school and others did not. This analysis classifies these children into three groups:

- *Group 1*—children enrolled after schools reopened who would have been enrolled even if the pandemic had not occurred.
- *Group 2*—children not enrolled after schools reopened who would have been enrolled in the absence of the pandemic.
- *Group 3*—children not enrolled after schools reopened who would not have been enrolled even if the pandemic had not occurred.

The size of each of these groups can be measured building on the analysis estimating COVID-related dropouts using national household surveys or labor force surveys as described in this chapter.[184] Time series data on enrollment before the pandemic allow predictions of what enrollment should have been during the pandemic and comparison of these predictions with actual enrollment observed after schools reopened.[185] Thus the size of group 1 is simply observed enrollment. The size of group 2 is the difference between predicted and observed enrollment. Subtracting predicted enrollment from 100 percent yields the size of group 3. It is possible to measure the size of these groups directly for the nine countries for which enrollment data are available after schools reopened[186] and use these data to produce estimates for countries missing enrollment data for this period. The analysis begins by regressing changes in enrollment on log GDP per capita and the duration of school closures for the nine countries and then applying the coefficients from this regression to country-level school closure and GDP per capita data to estimate changes in enrollment and the size of each of the groups for the rest of the sample.

The losses of learning due to the COVID-19 pandemic will differ among these groups. Group 1—children who were back in schools after they reopened—missed out on learning during the period of school closures. Data on the duration of school closures are available by country for the period March 2020 to March 2022 from the UNESCO Global Monitoring of School Closures Caused by the COVID-19 Pandemic database (https://covid19.uis.unesco.org/global-monitoring-school-closures-covid19/). The analysis in this chapter of studies documenting learning losses during the pandemic reveals that the ratio of learning losses to school closures is higher in poorer countries. To estimate this ratio for all the countries in the sample, the analysis first calculates the ratio of learning losses to the duration of school closure for 20 high-quality learning loss studies, then regresses this ratio on log GDP per capita, and finally applies the coefficient from this regression to country-level log GDP per capita data. For each country, multiplying the duration of school closures by this learning loss to school closure ratio yields the lost learning for group 1. For group 2, losses to learning include those sustained during school closures as for group 1, as well as the subsequent years of schooling missed by children having dropped out of school.[187] Finally, group 3 experiences no additional loss of schooling because children in this group would not have been enrolled even in the absence of the pandemic.

Adjusting lost schooling for quality

In standard LAYS calculations, adjusting average schooling for quality reflects the reality that quality of education varies across countries, so that a year of schooling does not translate into an equal amount of learning. Similarly, adjusting lost schooling due to the COVID-19 pandemic for quality of schooling reflects the fact children who lost a year of schooling in a country with a high-quality education system before the pandemic lost more learning than children in a country with an education system of poorer quality.

To estimate the quality of schooling prior to the pandemic, the analysis uses Harmonized Learning Outcomes (HLO) from the Global Data Set on Education Quality.[188] This data set harmonizes test scores from international and regional student assessment programs into units equivalent to those used in the Trends in International Mathematics and Science Study (TIMSS), a series of international assessments of the mathematics and science knowledge of students around the world. For each country, the HLO was divided by the benchmark score of 625—the advanced proficiency score on TIMSS—to produce a quality adjustment factor.

Estimating country-level lost LAYS

Bringing together estimates of lost schooling and the quality adjustment factor, losses to LAYS from the COVID-19 pandemic can be calculated as

$$Lost\ LAYS_{g,c} = S_{g,c} \times (L_{g,c} \times R_c) \times \frac{HLO_c}{625}, \tag{3A.2}$$

where $S_{g,c}$ measures the size of group g in the relevant cohort of the population in country c; $L_{g,c}$, is the duration of lost schooling for group g in country c; R_c is the estimated ratio of lost learning to school closures for country c; and HLO_c is the Harmonized Learning Outcome for country c. Summing lost LAYS for groups 1, 2, and 3 yields total lost LAYS for school-age children at the country level. Table 3A.1 summarizes lost LAYS for Nigeria by school level.

According to UNESCO data, schools in Nigeria closed on March 26, 2020, due to the COVID-19 pandemic and remained shut for 0.48 year (column (C)). Enrollment rates estimated using the duration of school closures and log GDP per capita (as described earlier) allow the size of each group to be calculated (columns (E) through (G)). For group 1, lost learning equals the duration of school closures multiplied by the predicted ratio of lost learning to school closures in Nigeria—that is, 0.73 year (column (H)). Children in group 2 lose subsequent years of schooling because they have dropped out of school (column (I)). And group 3 records no additional losses of schooling (column (J)).

To calculate the LAYS lost for each group (columns (K) through (M)), the analysis simply multiplies the size of the group by the duration of lost schooling and the quality adjustment factor (column (D)). Column (N) sums lost LAYS from groups 1, 2, and 3. The last row reports average LAYS lost for Nigeria as an average of the four levels of school, weighted by the duration of each level. The analysis estimates that Nigeria lost an average of 0.33 year of LAYS due to the pandemic. This same methodology is applied to other countries and results by region and income group and is presented in figure 3.6.

 TABLE 3A.1 Lost Learning-Adjusted Years of Schooling (LAYS) in Nigeria due to the COVID-19 pandemic

School level	Duration of level (years)	Duration of school closure (years)	Quality adjustment factor	Group size (proportion) Group 1	Group 2	Group 3	Lost learning (years) Group 1	Group 2	Group 3	Lost LAYS Group 1	Group 2	Group 3	Total
(A)	(B)	(C)	(D)	(E)	(F)	(G)	(H)	(I)	(J)	(K)	(L)	(M)	(N)
Pre-primary	2	0.48	0.49	0.45	0.10	0.45	0.73	1.73	0.00	0.16	0.08	0.00	**0.25**
Primary	6	0.48	0.49	0.73	0.04	0.22	0.73	5.73	0.00	0.27	0.13	0.00	**0.39**
Lower-secondary	3	0.48	0.49	0.77	0.03	0.19	0.73	3.48	0.00	0.28	0.06	0.00	**0.34**
Upper-secondary	3	0.48	0.49	0.66	0.01	0.33	0.73	2.23	0.00	0.24	0.01	0.00	**0.25**
Average LAYS lost													**0.33**

Sources: Duration of school closures: UNESCO Global Monitoring of School Closures Caused by the COVID-19 Pandemic, https://covid19.uis.unesco.org/global-monitoring-school-closures-covid19/. Enrollment rates used to calculate group sizes are estimated based on duration of school closures and log gross domestic product (GDP) per capita from the World Bank's World Development Indicators database, https://databank.worldbank.org/source/world-development-indicators.
Note: Average lost LAYS, reported in the last row, is the average of lost LAYS at the four levels of schooling, weighted by the duration of each level.

NOTES

1. Psacharopoulos and Patrinos (2018).
2. Mincer (1991).
3. Vogl (2014).
4. World Bank (2018).
5. Acemoglu et al. (2005).
6. Helliwell and Putnam (1999).
7. Huang, Van den Brink, and Groot (2009).
8. Chong and Gradstein (2015).
9. Hanushek, Ruhose, and Woessmann (2015); Manuelli and Seshadri (2014); Schoellmann (2012); Schultz (1961).
10. World Bank (2018).
11. For the rationale and methodology for using Learning-Adjusted Years of Schooling (LAYS), see Filmer et al. (2020).
12. World Bank, UIS, et al. (2022).
13. UIS (2022b).
14. These 14 countries were out of the set of 140 countries with school-age population greater than 500,000.
15. The number of weeks is estimated using school-age (5–14 years old) population weighted average data from the United Nations World Population Prospects 2022 database (https://www.un.org/development /desa/pd/content/World-Population-Prospects-2022). For simplicity, it is assumed that one school year is equal to 32 academic weeks across all countries. Each day of partial opening is counted as half a day of school closure. The original calculations are based on data from the United Nations Educational, Scientific, and Cultural Organization (UNESCO) Institute for Statistics (UIS) (https://uis.unesco.org/).
16. These estimates include school-age children from pre-primary to upper-secondary education (ages 5–17) from 140 countries with a school-age population of 500,000 or more. For simplicity, it is assumed that one school year is equal to 32 academic weeks across all countries. Each day of partial opening is counted as half a day of school closure. Original calculations based on data from UIS.
17. The global and regional percentages of time closed are estimated by weighting countries equally. Original calculations are based on data from UIS.
18. Each day of partial opening is counted as half a day of school closure. Estimations in days exclude academic breaks but include weekends. Original calculations based on data from UIS.
19. UNESCO, UNICEF, and World Bank (2021).
20. Moyo and Mazvarirwofa (2021).
21. *Hindustan Times* (2022).
22. Meckler (2021).
23. UNICEF and ITU (2020).
24. UNICEF (2021a).
25. UNICEF et al. (2021).
26. Asanov et al. (2021).
27. Sabarwal et al. (2021).
28. Angrist, Bergman, and Matsheng (2022).
29. Długosz (2022).
30. UNICEF Viet Nam (2020).
31. Blanshe and Dahir (2022); Yousafzai (2020).
32. Montoya et al. (2021).
33. PASU and Population Council (2021).
34. Grewenig et al. (2021).
35. Andrew et al. (2020).
36. Wolf et al. (2021).
37. Baird et al. (2020).

38. UNICEF et al. (2021).
39. Radhakrishnan et al. (2021).
40. Biswas et al. (2020).
41. Biswas et al. (2020).
42. Agostinelli et al. (2022).
43. UNICEF (2020a).
44. PASU and Population Council (2021).
45. Asanov et al. (2021).
46. Torres et al. (2017). This comparison is only suggestive because the two studies are based on different samples.
47. UIS (2022a).
48. UNICEF et al. (2021).
49. Duckworth et al. (2021).
50. WFP (2020).
51. Abay et al. (2021).
52. Results without correcting for time trends (that is, just comparing the latest pre-pandemic period to the periods after schools reopened) yield the same main message but slightly larger dropout rates for Pakistan, South Africa, Colombia, Brazil, Mexico, and Uruguay by about 0.6 percentage point on average (ranging from 0.4 to 1.0 percentage point). However, the same exercise for Ethiopia yields a difference that is 3.0 percentage points lower than the one correcting for time trends. No or very small differences are observed for the Argentina and Indonesia estimates.
53. These results are based on historical trends. In all cases, the analysis estimates predicted enrollment using at least five data points from before the pandemic when only yearly data were available and many more data points when quarterly data were available. Because schools reopened at different times in different countries, the analysis shows the average of student enrollment for quarters after the quarter when schools reopened (partially or fully).
54. Todos pela Educacão (2021).
55. Such as Geven et al. (2022). The results are also corroborated by results from a Gallup random-number dialing phone survey. Furthermore, World Bank estimations using data from the International Labour Organization (ILO) yield similar results.
56. For Ethiopia, the data are from two different sources: Urban Employment and Unemployment Survey for 2012, 2014, 2015, 2016, 2017, and 2019 and the National Labour and Migration Survey for 2013 and 2021. No data are available for 2017 and 2020, and the predictions are calculated only by removing the trend of the series. The sample is also restricted to make it comparable, so it is only representative for urban Ethiopia without the region of Tigray. Finally, the analysis adjusts for possible survey-specific effects by estimating the potential bias or difference between predicted and observed enrollment rates in 2013 and subtracting the potential bias from the difference between observed and predicted enrollment in 2021.
57. Dessy et al. (2021).
58. Moscoviz and Evans (2022).
59. ASER Centre (2021).
60. Abreh et al. (2021).
61. PASU and Population Council (2021).
62. Dessy et al. (2021).
63. Uwezo Uganda (2021).
64. Hasan, Geven, and Tahir (2021).
65. A total of 68 studies were reviewed.
66. To avoid overweighting a particular country in the database, multiple studies from the same country were not included. Multiple studies largely covered developed contexts such as the United States, the United Kingdom, and various European countries. When studies of comparable quality were found, the average of those studies is shown such as for Brazil and Uganda.
67. This figure includes two studies each for Brazil and Uganda. For each country, the studies were averaged.

68. This estimate is derived from a simple linear regression of learning losses on school closures with no constant. The coefficient on school closures is 1.06 with a 95 percent confidence interval of between 0.71 and 1.41 using robust standard errors.

69. This estimate is also derived from a simple linear regression of learning losses on school closures with no constant. The coefficient on school closures is 1.27 with a 95 percent confidence interval of between 0.70 and 1.83 using robust standard errors.

70. This list includes all studies available and used in figure 3.4 but excludes three countries (Germany, Malawi, and Uganda) that disproportionately influence the regression line and had a Cook's distance larger than 4/N, as generally suggested in the literature.

71. This relationship is robust to a number of specifications, such as including all countries, excluding high-income countries, limiting the sample to the high-quality study, or excluding data points that disproportionately influence the regression results. The resulting coefficients are all significant and in the range of from −0.30 to −0.45.

72. See UIS (2022a). Another study showing no learning losses is from Japan, where schools were closed for only two months. The study shows lower math scores in the short term, but lost learning was recovered after the government shortened the summer break and provided students with laptops (Asakawa and Ohtake 2021). This study is described in more detail in the next section.

73. UIS (2022a).

74. In Uganda, learning loss estimates differ across studies, with some studies showing losses and others gains. A 2021 study finds learning gains despite long school closures (Uwezo Uganda 2021). However, complementary analysis shows no learning losses when accounting for grade repetition (Sandefur 2022). These results for Uganda are contradicted by newer evidence of sharp learning losses (Angrist et al. forthcoming). How can these differences be explained? One explanation is that the historical upward trends in student learning before the pandemic may mask some of the learning losses if student performance is compared just before and after schools were closed, especially given the duration of school closures (two years). Another possible explanation for different results is the point of time at which each study measured learning and the reference it used to benchmark learning losses. And yet another explanation may be the differences in how learning is measured. The Sandefur (2022) analysis using Uwezo data found small learning losses when comparing the proportion of students who could successfully complete very basic tasks such as recognizing letters and matching numbers to the correct figure at early ages (around 6–14), which are more comparable to the grade 3 and grade 4 results from Angrist et al. (forthcoming).

75. Filmer et al. (2020).

76. Angrist et al. (2021).

77. For the purposes of this analysis, enrollment rates for the quarter after schools partially or fully reopened are used.

78. High-income countries are excluded from this analysis of dropout rates for this group because of lack of credible data on dropouts.

79. This list includes all studies available and used in figure 3.4 minus three countries (Germany, Malawi, and Uganda) that had a Cook's distance larger than 4/N as generally suggested in the literature.

80. The coefficient used was −0.39, significant at the 0.01 level. It was also robust to various specifications such as including only high-quality studies, excluding high-income countries, and using all observations available, all with significant coefficients ranging from −0.28 to −0.45.

81. World Bank (2021b).

82. See also D'Souza et al. (forthcoming).

83. Note that unlike the rest of the chapter, this analysis also includes 15- to 17-year-olds because in most countries this is the age for upper-secondary schooling and is a part of the LAYS calculation.

84. The 2020 numbers are observed and compared against the predicted Learning Poverty numbers. Note that these Learning Poverty estimates are part of a different analytical exercise that applies to a different sample than the lost LAYS analysis we conduct for 116 low- and middle-income countries and that we present in the chapter. See World Bank, UIS, et al. (2022).

85. Angrist et al. (2021).

86. Djaker et al. (forthcoming). Data requirements for decomposing learning losses into forgone and forgotten are demanding, which is why this exercise cannot be carried out in most studies.

87. See Whizz Education (2021). This study was not included in the previous subsection because it covers only selected students from rural Kenya who were actively participating in the Whizz virtual tutoring program before the pandemic (and thus already had access to the internet and a smartphone or computer), who continued to receive tutoring, and who underwent an assessment after the pandemic started. Therefore, the sample has very specific characteristics that differ from those of the average student in Kenya.

88. São Paulo Education Secretariat (2021).

89. Tomasik, Helbling, and Moser (2021).

90. Lewis et al. (2021).

91. Haelermans, Jacobs, et al. (2022).

92. Moscoviz and Evans (2022); World Bank, Bill and Melinda Gates Foundation, et al. (2022).

93. Djaker et al. (forthcoming).

94. The results are for a sample of schools and households with children attending a large private school network, The Citizens Foundation, and are not nationally representative.

95. Maldonado and De Witte (2021).

96. Birkelund and Karlson (2021).

97. Schult et al. (2022).

98. Asakawa and Ohtake (2021).

99. Engzell, Frey, and Verhagen (2021); Haelermans et al. (2021).

100. Rose et al. (2021).

101. Lewis and Kuhfeld (2021).

102. See Argentina, Ministerio de Educación de la Nación (2022). Although the percentage of students with a high socioeconomic status but with language knowledge below the basic level also increased (from 2 percent to 8 percent), in terms of the absolute number of students, the increase in the percentage of low socioeconomic status students is of much more concern.

103. This sample of studies includes more studies than the sample considered for studying the relationship between learning losses and length of school closures because the requirement of converting learning losses into months is lifted. Furthermore, because for countries with multiple studies only some studies reported gender differences, each study was considered independently as opposed to the most representative and recent one. Some studies report gender differences in various dimensions (such as subjects or grades), and so any gender difference was counted for this summary.

104. Bayley et al. (2021); Djaker et al. (forthcoming); Lichand et al. (2022); Schuurman et al. (2021). Note that other studies in the Netherlands report no differences by gender.

105. Alasino, Romero, and Ramirez (forthcoming).

106. Kim et al. (2021).

107. Angrist et al. (forthcoming).

108. Amplify (2022).

109. See Andrabi, Daniels, and Das (2021). Although comparing the effects of an earthquake and a global pandemic may seem to be a stretch, both are accompanied by many other challenges, including economic losses and psychological issues.

110. Andrabi, Daniels, and Das (2021).

111. See Araya et al. (2022). This finding was calculated using comparable assessments at the beginning and end of grades 1 and 4, both before the pandemic and after schools reopened. In grade 1, the decrease was from annual gains of 11 percentage points before the pandemic to 7 percentage points after school reopenings. In grade 4, numeracy gains over a school year are 0.24 standard deviations lower once schools reopened, compared with gains of 0.36 standard deviations before the pandemic.

112. Asim, Gera, and Singhal (2022).

113. Singh, Romero, and Muralidharan (2022). Using a value-added model, the authors conservatively attribute 21–28 percent of the learning recovery to the Illam Thedi Kalvi (Education at Doorstep) afterschool remedial classes intervention, assuming no spillover effects, with the rest of the recovery remaining unexplained.

114. Asakawa and Ohtake (2021).
115. Haelermans et al. (2021); Haelermans, Jacobs, et al. (2022); Haelermans, Korthals, et al. (2022).
116. Jaume and Willén (2019).
117. See Islam et al. (2016). However, the effect of exposure to civil conflict on earnings of women was not statistically different from zero.
118. Hanushek and Woessmann (2020).
119. World Bank, UIS, et al. (2022). Note that this number corresponds to their intermediate scenario.
120. Saadi-Sedik and Xu (2020).
121. UIS (2020).
122. UNESCO et al. (2021).
123. Bharathi et al. (2020).
124. World Bank (2020).
125. UNESCO and UNICEF (2021); UNICEF (2021b).
126. Berlinski et al. (2021).
127. Angrist, Bergman, and Matsheng (2022).
128. Biswas et al. (forthcoming).
129. Yarrow et al. (2022).
130. See UIS (2022b). Countries with academic breaks during a period are excluded from the calculation. Only countries with schools open/closed and with a school-age population of 500,000 or more were considered. The reference dates were June 30, 2020; March 31, 2021; and March 31, 2022.
131. Ertem et al. (2021); Fukumoto, McClean, and Nakagawa (2021); Lessler et al. (2021); Netherlands, National Institute for Public Health and the Environment, Ministry of Health, Welfare and Sport (2022); Walsh et al. (2021); Zimmerman et al. (2021).
132. Diederichs et al. (2022).
133. Uruguay reopened schools rapidly despite the fact that with its ongoing online program, Plan Ceibal, it had one of the strongest remote-learning platforms in the region (UNICEF 2020b). School closure data as of March 31, 2022, report that the first school closure in Uruguay included eight academic days of full school closures and 92 days of partial closures (UIS 2022b).
134. These estimations exclude academic breaks but include weekends. Vietnam's first school closure included 33 days of full school closure and 14 days of partial closure. As of March 31, 2022, Vietnam added 14 days of full school closure and was partially open 229 extra days (UIS 2022b).
135. Aedo, Nahata, and Sabarwal (2020).
136. UIS (2022b).
137. See UIS (2020). Types of engagement include requiring teachers to participate in any of the following: online learning, supporting TV/radio-based learning, mobile phone engagement, take-home/paper-based material, or any other engagement while schools were closed.
138. Radhakrishnan et al. (2021).
139. These include the following reports: ECLAC and UNESCO (2020); GEEAP (2022); McKinsey (2021); OECD (2020); Save the Children (2020); UN (2020); UNICEF (2021c); World Bank, UIS, et al. (2022); World Bank, UNESCO, and UNICEF (2021).
140. The coauthors are the Bill and Melinda Gates Foundation, FCDO (Foreign Commonwealth and Development Office, Government of the United Kingdom), UNESCO (United Nations Educational, Scientific, and Cultural Organization), UNICEF (United Nations Children's Fund), and USAID (United States Agency for International Development).
141. World Bank, Bill and Melinda Gates Foundation, et al. (2022).
142. World Bank (2020).
143. As of March 31, 2022, two years since the pandemic first started, 126 countries had fully reopened their schools out of the set of 140 countries with school-age population equal to or greater than 500,000.
144. Gupta (2020); Vegas and Winthrop (2020).
145. Angrist et al. (forthcoming).
146. See Ding et al. (2022); Ma et al. (2022); Westphal et al. (2022).

147. See UIS (2022a). These numbers exclude countries in academic breaks and with a school-age population of less than 500,000. The 12 countries partially open as of March 31, 2022, were Afghanistan, Bolivia, Cambodia, China, El Salvador, Indonesia, Iraq, the Lao People's Democratic Republic, Panama, the Russian Federation, Thailand, and Vietnam.
148. Bopa (2020).
149. GEEAP (2022).
150. World Bank, UNESCO, and UNICEF (2021).
151. UNESCO et al. (2021).
152. UNICEF (2020c, 2022).
153. UNESCO et al. (2021).
154. The model was pioneered by nongovernmental organization Pratham in India. See https://www.pratham.org/about/teaching-at-the-right-level/.
155. Banerjee et al. (2017); Duflo, Kiessel, and Lucas (2021).
156. Angrist et al. (2020).
157. Pratham (2022).
158. This work was done in collaboration with an NGO in Botswana, Youth Impact (https://www.youth-impact.org/). According to the Youth Impact data dashboard, in January 2021, 51 percent of students were innumerate (they could not add, subtract, multiply, or divide), but by April 2021 only 3 percent of students were innumerate.
159. Chile, Ministry of Education (2021).
160. World Bank, UIS, et al. (2022).
161. Muralidharan, Singh, and Ganimian (2019).
162. Carlana and La Ferrara (2021).
163. Nickow, Oreopoulos, and Quan (2020).
164. Marinelli, Berlinski, and Busso (2021).
165. See Angrist, Bergman, and Matsheng (2022); Hassan et al. 2021; Radhakrishnan et al. (2021). Crawfurd et al. (2021) find no effect of phone-based tutoring in Sierra Leone.
166. World Bank (2021a).
167. Giannini, Jenkins, and Saavedra (2022).
168. India, Ministry of Education (2022).
169. Piper et al. (2018).
170. Bedasso et al. (2022).
171. World Bank (2018).
172. World Bank and UNESCO (2022).
173. Sabarwal, Abu-Jawdeh, and Kapoor (2022).
174. The experiment does so by putting a time cost on the answers provided by teachers, so that they would not deviate from their actual willingness to engage in these activities.
175. See Angrist et al. (forthcoming). This includes 356 secondary teachers in Bangladesh, 210 teachers in Nepal, and 360 teachers in India (Delhi).
176. World Bank (2022).
177. Cameron (2009).
178. Chyi and Zhou (2014).
179. Fiszbein et al. (2009); Glewwe and Muralidharan (2016).
180. World Bank, UIS, et al. (2022).
181. Borkowski et al. (2021).
182. See Bedasso et al. (2022). Evidence is less conclusive on whether they have a similar impact on academic achievement.
183. Filmer et al. (2020).
184. Data are available by age group. Group size is calculated by age for five- to-17-year-olds.
185. For the purposes of this analysis, enrollment rates for the quarter after schools partially or fully reopened are used.

186. These countries are Argentina, Brazil, Colombia, Ethiopia, Indonesia, Mexico, Pakistan, South Africa, and Uruguay.
187. The analysis assumes that children ages 5–8 not in enrolled six months after schools have reopened have simply deferred enrollment by a year, and so they lose only one year of subsequent schooling. For children ages 9–14, the analysis assumes that half of the children not enrolled after six months will return the following year (they only miss one additional year of subsequent schooling), while the other half have permanently dropped out and will miss all subsequent years of schooling. The analysis further assumes that all children ages 15–17 not enrolled in school six months after reopening have dropped out permanently and will miss all subsequent years of schooling.
188. These data are from the 2020 update of the Global Data Set on Education Quality (https://datatopics .worldbank.org/education/wQueries/qachievement), with the most recent test scores originating from before the pandemic (2019).

REFERENCES

Abay, K.A., M. Amare, L. Tiberti, and K. S. Andam. 2021. "COVID-19–Induced Disruptions of School Feeding Services Exacerbate Food Insecurity in Nigeria." *Journal of Nutrition* 151 (8): 2245–54.

Abreh, M. K., W. K. Agbevanu, A. J. Alhassan, F. Ansah, R. S. Bosu, L. Crawfurd, C. A. Mills, et al. 2021. "What Happened to Dropout Rates after COVID-19 School Closures in Ghana?" Center for Global Development, Washington, DC.

Acemoglu, D., S. Johnson, J. A. Robinson, and P. Yared. 2005. "From Education to Democracy?" *American Economic Review* 95 (2): 44–49.

Aedo, C., V. Nahata, and S. Sabarwal. 2020. "The Remote Learning Paradox: How Governments Can Truly Minimize COVID-Related Learning Losses." World Bank, *Education for Global Development* (blog), November 10, 2020. https://blogs.worldbank.org/education/remote-learning-paradox-how-governments -can-truly-minimize-covid-related-learning-losses.

Agostinelli, F., M. Doepke, G. Sorrenti, and F. Zilibotti. 2022. "When the Great Equalizer Shuts Down: Schools, Peers, and Parents in Pandemic Times." *Journal of Public Economics* 206: 104574.

Alasino, E., M. Romero, and M. J. Ramirez. Forthcoming. "A Full Year of Learning Losses: The Effect of the Pandemic in Guanajuato, Mexico."

Al Jazeera.com. 2020. "No School until Coronavirus Vaccine Is Available." May 26, 2020. https://www.aljazeera .com/news/2020/5/26/no-school-until-coronavirus-vaccine-is-available-duterte.

Amplify. 2022. "Amid Academic Recovery in Classrooms Nationwide, Risks Remain for Youngest Students with Least Instructional Time during Critical Early Years." Research brief, Amplify, Brooklyn, NY.

Andrabi, T., B. Daniels, and J. Das. 2021. "Human Capital Accumulation and Disasters: Evidence from the Pakistan Earthquake of 2005." *Journal of Human Resources* (June 9). doi: 10.3368/jhr.59.2.0520-10887R1J.

Andrew, A., S. Cattan, M. Costa Dias, C. Farquharson, L. Kraftman, S. Krutikova, A. Phimister, et al. 2020. "Inequalities in Children's Experiences of Home Learning during the COVID-19 Lockdown in England." *Fiscal Studies* 41 (3): 653–83.

Angrist, N., M. Ainomugisha, S. Bathena, P. Bergman, C. Crossley, C. Cullen, T. Letsomo, et al. Forthcoming. "Building Resilient Education Systems: Evidence from Large-Scale Randomized Trials in Five Countries."

Angrist, N., P. Bergman, and M. Matsheng. 2022. "Experimental Evidence on Learning Using Low-Tech When School Is Out." *Nature Human Behaviour* 6: 1–10. https://doi.org/10.1038/s41562-022-01381-z.

Angrist, N., S. Djankov, P. K. Goldberg, and H. A. Patrinos. 2021. "Measuring Human Capital Using Global Learning Data." *Nature* 592: 403–08.

Angrist, N., D. K. Evans, D. Filmer, R. Glennerster, F. H. Rogers, and S. Sabarwal. 2020. "How to Improve Education Outcomes Most Efficiently?" Policy Research Working Paper 9450, World Bank, Washington, DC.

Araya, M., P. Rose, R. Sabates, D. T. Tiruneh, and T. Woldehanna. 2022. "Learning Losses during COVID-19 Pandemic in Ethiopia: Comparing Student Achievement in Early Primary Grades before School Closures, and after They Reopened." RISE Insight Series, 2022/044, RISE (Research on Improving Systems of Education) Programme, Oxford, UK.

Ardington, C., G. Wills, and J. Kotze. 2021. "COVID-19 Learning Losses: Early Grade Reading in South Africa." *International Journal of Educational Development* 86: 102480.

Arenas, A., and L. Gortazar. 2022. "Learning Loss One Year after School Closures." Esade Working Paper 277, Esade Business School, Barcelona. http://hdl.handle.net/2072/521711.

Argentina, Ministerio de Educación de la Nación. 2022. *Aprender 2021: Educación Primaria: Informe nacional de resultados: análisis sobre los logros de aprendizaje y sus condiciones.* 2d ed. Ciudad Autónoma de Buenos Aires. https://www.argentina.gob.ar/sites/default/files/informe_aprender_2021_1.pdf

Asakawa, S., and F. Ohtake. 2021. "Impact of Temporary School Closure Due to COVID-19 on the Academic Achievement of Elementary School Students." Discussion Paper in Economics and Business 21, Graduate School of Economics and Osaka School of International Public Policy (OSIPP), Osaka University, Suita, Japan.

Asanov, I., F. Flores, D. McKenzie, M. Mensmann, and M. Schulte. 2021. "Remote-Learning, Time-Use, and Mental Health of Ecuadorian High-School Students during the COVID-19 Quarantine." *World Development* 138: 105225.

ASER Centre. 2021. *Annual Status of Education Report (Rural) 2021.* New Delhi: ASER Centre. http://img .asercentre.org/docs/aser2021finalreport_16.116.54pm1.pdf.

Asim, S., R. Gera, and A. Singhal. 2022. "Learning Loss from Covid in Sub-Saharan Africa: Evidence from Malawi." *Education for Global Development* (blog), April 19, 2022. https://blogs.worldbank.org/education/ learning-loss-covid-sub-saharan-africa-evidence-malawi.

Baird, S., J. Seager, S. Sabarwal, S. Guglielmi, and M. Sultan. 2020. "Adolescence in the Time of COVID-19: Evidence from Bangladesh." South Asia Gender Innovation Lab and GAGE (Gender and Adolescence: Global Evidence) Policy Brief, World Bank, Washington, DC. http://hdl.handle.net/10986/34801.

Banerjee, A., R. Banerji, J. Berry, E. Duflo, H. Kannan, S. Mukerji, M. Shotland, et al. 2017. "From Proof of Concept to Scalable Policies: Challenges and Solutions, with an Application." *Journal of Economic Perspectives* 31 (4): 73–102.

Bayley, S., D. W. Meshesha, P. Ramchandani, P. Rose, T. Woldehanna, and L. Yorke. 2021. "Socio-emotional and Academic Learning before and after COVID-19 School Closures: Evidence from Ethiopia." RISE Working Paper 21/082, RISE (Research on Improving Systems of Education) Programme, Oxford, UK. https://riseprogramme .org/publications/socio-emotional-and-academic-learning-and-after-covid-19-school-closures-evidence.

Bedasso, B., F. Afridi, U. Gentilini, and S. Sabarwal. 2022. "Are School Meals Worth the Cost?" Center for Global Development (blog), April 25, 2022. https://www.cgdev.org/blog/are-school-meals-worth-cost -contributions-biniam-bedasso-farzana-afridi-ugo-gentilini-and.

Berlinski, S., M. Busso, T. Dinkelman, and C. Martínez. 2021. "Reducing Parent-School Information Gaps and Improving Education Outcomes: Evidence from High-Frequency Text Messages." NBER Working Paper 28581, National Bureau of Economic Research, Cambridge, MA.

Bharathi, P., C. Aedo, S. Sinha, and S. Iype. 2020. "The Gujarat Model: Managing Learning Continuity during COVID-19." World Bank, *Education for Global Development* (blog), November 20, 2020. https://blogs. worldbank.org/education/gujarat-model-managing-learning-continuity-during-covid-19.

Birkelund, J. F., and K. B. Karlson. 2021. "No Evidence of a Major Learning Slide 14 Months into the COVID-19 Pandemic in Denmark." SocArXiv. https://osf.io/preprints/socarxiv/md5zn/.

Biswas, K., T. M. Asaduzzaman, D. K. Evans, S. Fehrler, D. Ramachandran, and S. Sabarwal. 2020. "TV-Based Learning in Bangladesh." World Bank, Washington, DC.

Biswas, K., P. D. Galbert, S. Sabarwal, C. Z. Glave, and T. M. Asaduzzaman. Forthcoming. "Does Online Teacher Training Work and Can Incentives Help?" Working paper, World Bank, Washington, DC.

Blanshe, M., and A. L. Dahir. 2022. "Uganda Reopens Schools after World's Longest Covid Shutdown." *New York Times,* January 10, 2022. https://www.nytimes.com/2022/01/10/world/africa/uganda-schools-reopen .html?smid=nytcore-ios-share&referringSource=articleShare.

Bopa. 2020. "Botswana: School Shifts Returns." *Daily News,* May 27, 2020. https://allafrica.com/stories /202005270817.html.

Borkowski, A., J. S. Ortiz Correa, D. A. Bundy, C. Burbano, C. Hayashi, E. Lloyd-Evans, J. Neitzel, et al. 2021. "COVID-19: Missing More than a Classroom: The Impact of School Closures on Children's Nutrition." Innocenti Working Paper 2021-01, Office of Research-Innocenti, United Nations Children's Fund (UNICEF), New York.

Brazil, Education Secretariat. 2021. "The Impact of the Pandemic on Education: Sample Assessment of Student Learning" (translation). São Paulo.

Cameron, L. 2009. "Can a Public Scholarship Program Successfully Reduce School Drop-Outs in a Time of Economic Crisis? Evidence from Indonesia." *Economics of Education Review* 28 (3): 308–17.

Carlana, M., and E. La Ferrara. 2021. "Apart but Connected: Online Tutoring and Student Outcomes during the COVID-19 Pandemic." IZA Discussion Paper No. 14094, Institute of Labor Economics (IZA), Bonn.

Chaban, T., R. Rameeva, I. Denisov, Y. Kersha, and R. Zvyagintsev. 2022. "Russian Schools during the COVID-19 Pandemic: Impact of the First Two Waves on the Quality of Education." *Voprosy obrazovaniya/Educational Studies Moscow* 1: 160–88. https://doi.org/10.17323/1814-9545-2022-1-160-188.

Chile, Ministry of Education. 2021. *Escuelas Arriba: Orientaciones Pedagógicas Programa Escuelas Arriba 2021*. División Educación General, Ministerio de Educación de Chile, Santiago. https://escuelasarriba.mineduc.cl/wp-content/uploads/sites/125/2021/03/Orientaciones-pedagogicas-EA-0203.pdf.

Chong, A., and M. Gradstein. 2015. "On Education and Democratic Preferences." *Economics and Politics* 27 (3): 362–88.

Chyi, H., and B. Zhou. 2014. "The Effects of Tuition Reforms on School Enrollment in Rural China." *Economics of Education Review* 38: 104–23.

Contini, D., M. L. Di Tommaso, C. Muratori, D. Piazzalunga, and L. Schiavon. 2021. "The COVID-19 Pandemic and School Closure: Learning Loss in Mathematics in Primary Education." IZA Discussion Paper No. 14785, Institute of Labor Economics (IZA), Bonn.

Crawfurd, L., D. Evans, S. Hares, and J. Sandefur. 2021. "Live Tutoring Calls Did Not Improve Learning during the COVID-19 Pandemic in Sierra Leone." CGD Working Paper 591, Center for Global Development, Washington, DC. https://www.cgdev.org/publication/live-tutoring-calls-did-not-improve-learning-during-covid-19-pandemic-sierra-leone.

Dessy, S., H. Gninafon, L. Tiberti, and M. Tiberti. 2021. "COVID-19 and Children's School Resilience: Evidence from Nigeria." Policy Research Working Paper 9736, World Bank, Washington, DC.

Diederichs, M., R. van Ewijk, I. E. Isphording, and N. Pestel. "Schools under Mandatory Testing Can Mitigate the Spread of SARS-CoV-2." *PNAS* 119 (26): e2201724119.

Ding, E., O. Arias, A. T. Del Toro Mijares, and E. Molina. 2022. "Putting Teachers' Well-Being and Empowerment at the Center of Learning Recovery and Acceleration." *Education for Global Development* (blog), October 13, 2022. https://blogs.worldbank.org/education/putting-teachers-well-being-and-empowerment-center-learning-recovery-and-acceleration/.

Djaker, S., S. Sabarwal, S. Ramachandra, N. Angrist, and A. Yi Chang. Forthcoming. "Forgone and Forgotten Learning: COVID-Related Learning Losses from National Assessments in Bangladesh."

Długosz, P. 2022. "Remote Education and Its Effects on Peripheral Areas: Summary of Polish Research Findings in the Project 'Preventing Post-COVID Social Exclusion Together.'" https://doi.org/10.31219/osf.io/3m5cp.

D'Souza, R., A. Kraay, S. Sabarwal, N. Schady, and A. Yi Chang. Forthcoming. "Estimating the Impacts of COVID-19 on Learning-Adjusted Years of Schooling."

Duckworth, A. L., T. Kautz, A. Defnet, E. Satlof-Bedrick, S. Talamas, B. Lira, and L. Steinberg. 2021. "Students Attending School Remotely Suffer Socially, Emotionally, and Academically." *Educational Researcher* 50 (7): 479–82.

Duflo, A., J. Kiessel, and A. Lucas. 2021. "Experimental Evidence on Alternative Policies to Increase Learning at Scale." NBER Working Paper 27298, National Bureau of Economic Research, Cambridge, MA.

ECLAC (Economic Commission for Latin America and the Caribbean) and UNESCO (United Nations Educational, Scientific, and Cultural Organization). 2020. *Education in the Time of COVID-19.* https://repositorio.cepal.org/handle/11362/45905. ECLAC and UNESCO, Santiago, Chile, and New York.

Engzell, P., A. Frey, and M. D. Verhagen. 2021. "Learning Loss Due to School Closures during the COVID-19 Pandemic." *Proceedings of the National Academy of Sciences* 118 (17): 2022376118.

Ertem, Z., E. M. Schechter-Perkins, E. Oster, P. van den Berg, I. Epshtein, N. Chaiyakunapruk, F. A. Wilson, et al. 2021. "The Impact of School Opening Model on SARS-CoV-2 Community Incidence and Mortality." *Nature Medicine* 27 (12): 2120–126.

Filmer, D., H. Rogers, N. Angrist, and S. Sabarwal. 2020. "Learning-Adjusted Years of Schooling (LAYS): Defining a New Macro Measure of Education." *Economics of Education Review* 77: 101971.

Fiszbein, A., N. R. Schady, F. H. G. Ferreira, M. Grosh, N. Keleher, P. Olinto, and E. Skoufias. 2009. *Conditional Cash Transfers: Reducing Present and Future Poverty*. Policy Research Report 47603, World Bank, Washington, DC.

Fukumoto, K., C. T. McClean, and K. Nakagawa. 2021. "No Causal Effect of School Closures in Japan on the Spread of COVID-19 in Spring 2020." *Nature Medicine* 27: 2111–19. https://doi.org/10.1038/s41591-021-01571-8.

Gajderowicz, T., M. Jakubowski, and S. Wrona. 2022. "Achievement of Secondary School Students after Pandemic Lockdown and Structural Reforms of Education System: Results from Ticks 2021 Assessment in Warsaw." Policy Note 1/2022, Evidence Institute, Warsaw, Poland.

Gambi, L., and K. De Witte. 2021. "The Resiliency of School Outcomes after the COVID-19 Pandemic: Standardised Test Scores and Inequality One Year after Long-Term School Closures." FEB Research Report, Faculty of Economics and Business (FEB), KU Leuven, Leuven, Belgium. https://lirias.kuleuven .be/3611628?limo=0.

GEEAP (Global Education Evidence Advisory Panel). 2022. *Prioritizing Learning during COVID-19: The Most Effective Ways to Keep Children Learning during and Post-Pandemic: Recommendations of the Global Education Evidence Advisory Panel*. Washington, DC: World Bank, Foreign Commonwealth and Development Office, Government of the United Kingdom (FCDO), and Office of Research-Innocenti, United Nations Children's Fund (UNICEF).

Georgiou, G. 2021. "Covid-19's Impact on Children's Reading Scores: Data Trends and Complementary Interview." *Reading League Journal* 2 (2): 34–39.

Geven, K. M., S. Fazili, A. Tahir, and T. Fasih. 2022. "SMS Girl Data Insights: February 2022." South Asia Gender Innovation Lab Policy Brief, World Bank, Washington, DC.

Giannini, S., R. Jenkins, and J. Saavedra. 2022. "100 Weeks into the Pandemic: The Importance of Keeping Schools Open and Investing in Learning Recovery Programs." World Bank, *Education for Global Development* (blog), January 24, 2022. https://blogs.worldbank.org/education/100-weeks-pandemic-im-portance-keeping-schools-open-and-investing-learning-recovery#:~:text=The%20event%20focused%20on%20the,on%20learning%20has%20been%20devastating/.

Glewwe, P., and K. Muralidharan. 2016. "Improving Education Outcomes in Developing Countries: Evidence, Knowledge Gaps, and Policy Implications. In *Handbook of the Economics of Education* 5: 653–743. Amsterdam: Elsevier.

Gore, J., L. Fray, A. Miller, J. Harris, and W. Taggart. 2021. "The Impact of COVID-19 on Student Learning in New South Wales Primary Schools: An Empirical Study." *Australian Educational Researcher* 48 (4): 605–37.

Grewenig, E., P. Lergetporer, K. Werner, L. Woessmann, and L. Zierow. 2021. "COVID-19 and Educational Inequality: How School Closures Affect Low- and High-Achieving Students." *European Economic Review* 140: 103920.

Gupta, S. 2020. "Covid Has Transformed How People Think and Work. They Also Have New Appreciation of Schools and Teachers." *Times of India*, December 12, 2020.

Haelermans, C., M. Jacobs, R. van der Velden, L. van Vugt, and S. van Wetten. 2022. "Inequality in the Effects of Primary School Closures Due to the COVID-19 Pandemic: Evidence from the Netherlands." *AEA Papers and Proceedings* 112: 303–07.

Haelermans, C., M. Jacobs, L. van Vugt, B. Aarts, H. Abbink, C. Smeets, R. van der Velden, et al. 2021. "A Full Year COVID-19 Crisis with Interrupted Learning and Two School Closures: The Effects on Learning Growth and Inequality in Primary Education." Research Memorandum 021, Graduate School of Business and Economics (GSBE), Maastricht University, Maastricht, the Netherlands.

Haelermans, C., R. Korthals, M. Jacobs, S. de Leeuw, S. Vermeulen, L. van Vugt, B. Aarts, et al. 2022. "Sharp Increase in Inequality in Education in Times of the COVID-19 Pandemic." *Plos One* 17 (2): e0261114.

Hanushek, E., J. Ruhose, and L. Woessmann. 2015. "Human Capital Quality and Aggregate Income Differences: Development Accounting for US States." Hoover Institution Economics Working Paper No. 15112, Stanford University, Stanford, CA.

Hanushek, E. A., and L. Woessmann. 2020. "The Economic Impacts of Learning Losses." Organisation for Economic Co-operation and Development, Paris.

Hasan, A., K. Geven, and A. Tahir. 2021. "SMS Girl Data Insights: How Has COVID-19 Affected Support for Girls' Education in Punjab, Pakistan?" World Bank, Washington, DC.

Hassan, H., A. Islam, A. Siddique, and L. C. Wang. 2021. "Telementoring and Homeschooling during School Closures: A Randomized Experiment in Rural Bangladesh." Institute of Labor Economics (IZA), Bonn.

Helliwell, J. F., and R. D. Putnam. 1999. "Education and Social Capital." NBER Working Paper 7121, National Bureau of Economic Research, Cambridge, MA.

Hindustan Times. 2022. "Schools Reopening Today: Check State-Wise Schools, Colleges to Reopen on Feb 1." February 1, 2022.

Huang, J., H. M. Van den Brink, and W. Groot. 2009. "A Meta-analysis of the Effect of Education on Social Capital." *Economics of Education Review* 28 (4): 454–64.

India, Ministry of Education. 2022. "Foundational Learning Study 2022." National Initiative for Proficiency in Reading with Understanding and Numeracy (NIPUN) Bharat. https://nipunbharat.education.gov.in/fls/fls.aspx.

Islam, A., C. Ouch, R. Smyth, and L. C. Wang. 2016. "The Long-Term Effects of Civil Conflicts on Education, Earnings, and Fertility: Evidence from Cambodia." *Journal of Comparative Economics* 44 (3): 800–20.

Jaume, D., and A. Willén. 2019. "The Long-Run Effects of Teacher Strikes: Evidence from Argentina." *Journal of Labor Economics* 37 (4): 1097–1139.

Kim, J., P. Rose, D. T. Tiruneh, R. Sabates, and T. Woldehanna. 2021. "Learning Inequalities Widen following COVID-19 School Closures in Ethiopia." RISE (Research on Improving Systems of Education) Programme, Oxford, UK.

Korbel, V., and D. Prokop. 2021. "Czech Students Lost 3 Months of Learning after a Year of the COVID-19 Pandemic." PAQ Research, Prague.

Kuhfeld, M., and K. Lewis. 2022. *Student Achievement in 2021–22: Cause for Hope and Continued Urgency* (technical appendix). Northwest Evaluation Association (NWEA), Portland, OR.

Lessler, J., M. K. Grabowski, K. H. Grantz, E. Badillo-Goicoechea, C. J. E. Metcalf, C. Lupton-Smith, A. S. Azman, et al. 2021. "Household COVID-19 Risk and In-Person Schooling." *Science* 372 (6546): 1092–97.

Lewis, K., and M. Kuhfeld. 2021. "Learning during COVID-19: An Update on Student Achievement and Growth at the Start of the 2021–22 School Year." NWEA Research Brief, Northwest Evaluation Association (NWEA), Portland, OR.

Lewis, K., M. Kuhfeld, E. Ruzek, and A. McEachin. 2021. "Learning during COVID-19: Reading and Math Achievement in the 2020–21 School Year." NWEA Research Brief, Northwest Evaluation Association (NWEA), Portland, OR.

Lichand, G., C. A. Doria, O. Leal-Neto, and J. P. C. Fernandes. 2022. "The Impacts of Remote Learning in Secondary Education during the Pandemic in Brazil." *Nature Human Behaviour* 6 (8): 1079–86.

Ludewig, U., R. Kleinkorres, R. Schaufelberger, T. Schlitter, R. Lorenz, C. König, A. Frey, et al. 2022. "COVID-19 Pandemic and Student Reading Achievement: Findings from a School Panel Study." *PsyArXiv,* March 15. doi:10.3389/fpsyg.2022.876485.

Ma, K., L. Liang, M. Chutiyami, S. Nicoll, T. Khaerudin, and X. V. Ha. 2022. "COVID-19 Pandemic-Related Anxiety, Stress, and Depression among Teachers: A Systematic Review and Meta-analysis." *Work* 73 (1): 3–27. doi: 10.3233/WOR-220062.

Maldonado, J. E., and K. De Witte. 2021. "The Effect of School Closures on Standardised Student Test Outcomes." *British Educational Research Journal* 48 (1): 49–94.

Manuelli, R., and A. Seshadri. 2014. "Human Capital and the Wealth of Nations." *American Economic Review* 104 (9): 2736–62.

Marinelli, H. A., S. Berlinski, and M. Busso. 2021. "Remedial Education: Evidence from a Sequence of Experiments in Colombia." *Journal of Human Resources* 0320–10801R2.

McKinsey. 2021. "COVID-19 and Education: The Lingering Effects of Unfinished Learning." McKinsey. https://www.mckinsey.com/industries/education/our-insights/covid-19-and-education-the-lingering-effects-of-unfinished-learning.

Meckler, L. 2021. "Nearly Half of All Schools Are Open Full Time, Survey Finds." *Washington Post*, March 21, 2021.

Mincer, J. 1991. "Education and Unemployment." NBER Working Paper 3838, National Bureau of Economic Research, Cambridge, MA.

Montoya, E. C., S. M. Fall, J. McManus, and F. Njogu-Ndongwe. 2021. *Challenges and Opportunities as Students Return to School: Evidence from Caregiver and Staff Surveys across Rising Academy Network Schools.* IDinsight. https://www.idinsight.org/wp-content/uploads/2021/07/Rising-Academies-Echidna-Giving-Round-I-report.pdf.

Moscoviz, L., and D. K. Evans. 2022. "Learning Loss and Student Dropouts during the Covid-19 Pandemic: A Review of the Evidence Two Years after Schools Shut Down." Working Paper 609, Center for Global Development, Washington, DC.

Moyo, F., and K. Mazvarirwofa. 2021. "Zimbabwe: Double-Shift Schools Put Students in the Hot Seat." *Global Press Journal*, September 13, 2021.

Muralidharan, K., A. Singh, and A. J. Ganimian. 2019. "Disrupting Education? Experimental Evidence on Technology-Aided Instruction in India." *American Economic Review* 109 (4): 1426–60.

Netherlands, National Institute for Public Health and the Environment, Ministry of Health, Welfare and Sport. 2022. "Children, School and COVID-19." https://www.rivm.nl/en/coronavirus-covid-19/children-and-covid-19.

New York Times. 2020. "What Students Are Saying about Remote Learning." April 9, 2020. https://www.nytimes.com/2020/04/09/learning/what-students-are-saying-about-remote-learning.html.

Nickow, A., P. Oreopoulos, and V. Quan. 2020. "The Impressive Effects of Tutoring on Pre-K–12 Learning: A Systematic Review and Meta-analysis of the Experimental Evidence." NBER Working Paper 27476, National Bureau of Economic Research, Cambridge, MA.

OECD (Organisation for Economic Co-operation and Development). 2020. *Lessons for Education from COVID-19: A Policy Maker's Handbook for More Resilient Systems.* Paris: OECD Publishing.

PASU (Presidential Policy and Strategy Unit, Kenya) and Population Council. 2021. *Promises to Keep: Impact of COVID-19 on Adolescents in Kenya.* Nairobi: Presidential Policy and Strategy Unit (Kenya) and Population Council.

Piketty, T. 2014. *Capital in the Twenty-First Century.* Cambridge, MA: Harvard University Press.

Piper, B., S. S. Zuilkowski, M. Dubeck, E. Jepkemei, and S. J. King. 2018. "Identifying the Essential Ingredients to Literacy and Numeracy Improvement: Teacher Professional Development and Coaching, Student Textbooks, and Structured Teachers' Guides." *World Development* 106: 324–36.

Pratham. 2022. "From Teaching Children to Engaging Families: Lessons from Pratham's Experiences during the Pandemic." Pratham, Mumbai, Delhi.

Psacharopoulos, G., and H. A. Patrinos. 2018. "Returns to Investment in Education: A Decennial Review of the Global Literature." *Education Economics* 26 (5): 445–58.

Radhakrishnan, K., N. Angrist, P. Bergman, C. Cullen, M. Matsheng, A. Ramakrishnan, S. Sabarwal, et al. 2021. "Learning in the Time of COVID-19: Insights from Nepal." World Bank, Washington, DC.

Rose, S., L. Twist, P. Lord, T. Paxman, J. Coulton, P. Akhtar, S. Rutt, et al. 2021. "Impact of School Closures and Subsequent Support Strategies on Attainment at KS1: Interim Findings 2." National Foundation for Educational Research, Slough.

Saadi-Sedik, T., and R. Xu. 2020. "A Vicious Cycle: How Pandemics Lead to Economic Despair and Social Unrest." IMF Working Paper No. 20-20/216, International Monetary Fund, Washington, DC.

Sabarwal, S., M. Abu-Jawdeh, and R. Kapoor. 2022. "Teacher Beliefs: Why They Matter and What They Are." *World Bank Research Observer* 37 (1): 73–106.

Sabarwal, S., K. Biswas, D. Evans, and S. Fehrler. 2021. "Can Incentives Improve the Take-Up of TV-Based Learning? Evidence from Bangladesh during the Covid-19 Pandemic." Paper prepared for Society for Research on Educational Effectiveness (SREE) 2021 Research Conference, September 2021.

Sandefur, J. 2022. "Uganda's Record-Breaking Two-Year School Closure Led to… No Decline in the Number of Kids Who Can Read." Center for Global Development, Washington, DC.

São Paulo Education Secretariat. 2021. "The Impact of the Pandemic on Education." https://www.educacao.sp.gov.br/wp-content/uploads/2021/04/Apresenta%c3%a7%c3%a3o-Estudo-Amostral.pdf.

Save the Children. 2020. "Save Our Education: Protect Every Child's Right to Learn in the COVID-19 Response and Recovery." https://resourcecentre.savethechildren.net/pdf/save_our_education_0.pdf/.

Schoellmann, T. 2012. "Education Quality and Development Accounting." *Review of Economic Studies* 79: 388–417.

Schult, J., N. Mahler, B. Fauth, and M. A. Lindner. 2022. "Did Students Learn Less during the COVID-19 Pandemic? Reading and Mathematics Competencies before and after the First Pandemic Wave." *School Effectiveness and School Improvement* 44 (4). doi.org/10.1080/09243453.2022.2061014.

Schultz, T. W. 1961. "Education and Economic Growth." *Teachers College Record* 62 (10): 46–88.

Schuurman, T. M., L. F. Henrichs, N. K. Schuurman, S. Polderdijk, and L. Hornstra. 2021. "Learning Loss in Vulnerable Student Populations after the First Covid-19 School Closure in the Netherlands." *Scandinavian Journal of Educational Research*. doi: 10.1080/00313831.2021.2006307.

Singh, A., M. Romero, and K. Muralidharan. 2022. "COVID-19 Learning Loss and Recovery: Panel Data Evidence from India." NBER Working Paper 30552, National Bureau of Economic Research, Cambridge, MA.

Todos pela Educacão. 2021. "Nota Técnica: Taxas de Atendimento Escolar." Todos pela Educacão, São Paulo, December.

Tomasik, M. J., L. A. Helbling, and U. Moser. 2021. "Educational Gains of In-Person vs. Distance Learning in Primary and Secondary Schools: A Natural Experiment during the COVID-19 Pandemic School Closures in Switzerland." *International Journal of Psychology* 56 (4): 566–76.

Torres, C., P. Otero, B. Bustamante, V. Blanco, O. Díaz, and F. L. Vázquez. 2017. "Mental Health Problems and Related Factors in Ecuadorian College Students." *International Journal of Environmental Research and Public Health* 14 (5): 530.

UIS (United Nations Educational, Scientific, and Cultural Organization–UNESCO Institute for Statistics). 2020. "Survey on National Education: Responses to COVID-19 School Closures" (1st Iteration). UIS, Montreal, Canada. http://tcg.uis.unesco.org/survey-education-covid-school-closures.

UIS (United Nations Educational, Scientific, and Cultural Organization–UNESCO Institute for Statistics). 2022a. *COVID-19 in Sub-Saharan Africa: Monitoring Impacts on Learning Outcomes. Main Report.* Montreal, Canada: UIS.

UIS (United Nations Educational, Scientific, and Cultural Organization–UNESCO Institute for Statistics). 2022b. "Global Monitoring of School Closures Caused by the COVID-19 Pandemic." UIS, Montreal, Canada. https://covid19.uis.unesco.org/data/.

UN (United Nations). 2020. *Policy Brief: Education during COVID-19 and Beyond.* New York: United Nations. https://www.un.org/development/desa/dspd/wp-content/uploads/sites/22/2020/08/sg_policy_brief_covid-19_and_education_august_2020.pdf.

UNESCO (United Nations Educational, Scientific, and Cultural Organization). 2020. "How Is Chile Facing the COVID-19 Education Emergency? UNESCO Talks with Raul Figueroa, Minister of Education of Chile." *UNESCO* (blog), April 3, 2020.

UNESCO (United Nations Educational, Scientific, and Cultural Organization) and UNICEF (United Nations Children's Fund). 2021. *Nepal Case Study: Situation Analysis on the Effects of and Responses to COVID-19 on the Education Sector in Asia.* Paris and New York: UNESCO and UNICEF. https://www.unicef.org/rosa/media/16616/file/Nepal%20Case%20Study%20.pdf.

UNESCO (United Nations Educational, Scientific, and Cultural Organization), UNICEF (United Nations Children's Fund), and World Bank. 2021. *COVID-19 Learning Losses: Rebuilding Quality Learning for All in the Middle East and North Africa.* Paris, New York, and Washington, DC: UNESCO, UNICEF, and World Bank.

UNESCO (United Nations Educational, Scientific, and Cultural Organization), UNICEF (United Nations Children's Fund), World Bank, and OECD (Organisation for Economic Co-operation and Development). 2021. *What's Next? Lessons on Education Recovery: Findings from a Survey of Ministries of Education amid the COVID-19 Pandemic.* Paris, New York, and Washington, DC: UNESCO, UNICEF, World Bank, and OECD.

UNICEF (United Nations Children's Fund). 2020a. *Impact of COVID-19 on Children in the Middle East and North Africa Report.* Amman, Jordan: UNICEF Middle East and North Africa.

UNICEF (United Nations Children's Fund). 2020b. "Reopening Schools in Uruguay during a Health Emergency." *UNICEF* (blog). https://blogs.unicef.org/blog/reopening-schools-uruguay-during-health-emergency/.

UNICEF (United Nations Children's Fund). 2020c. "School-in-a-Box Guidelines for Use." UNICEF, New York. https://www.unicef.org/supply/reports/school-box-guidelines-use.

UNICEF (United Nations Children's Fund). 2021a. *Rapid Assessment of Learning during School Closures in the Context of COVID-19.* New Delhi: UNICEF India.

UNICEF (United Nations Children's Fund). 2021b. "The Harmful Effects of COVID-19 on Mental Health in Children and Young People Could Last for Many Years." UNICEF, New York. https://www.unicef.org/dominicanrepublic/comunicados-prensa/unicef-los-efectos-nocivos-de-la-covid-19-sobre-la-salud-mental-en-los-ninos.

UNICEF (United Nations Children's Fund). 2021c. *The State of the World's Children 2021: On My Mind—Promoting, Protecting and Caring for Children's Mental Health.* New York: UNICEF.

UNICEF (United Nations Children's Fund). 2022. *Helping Children Overcome Post-Flood Distress in Pakistan.* New York: UNICEF. https://www.unicef.org/blog/helping-children-overcome-post-flood-distress-pakistan.

UNICEF (United Nations Children's Fund) and International Telecommunication Union (ITU). 2020. "How Many Children and Young People Have Internet Access at Home? Estimating Digital Connectivity during the COVID-19 Pandemic." UNICEF and ITU, New York and Geneva.

UNICEF (United Nations Children's Fund), UNDP (United Nations Development Programme), Prospera, and SMERU (SMERU Research Institute). 2021. "Analysis of the Social and Economic Impacts of COVID-19 on Households and Strategic Policy Recommendations for Indonesia." UNICEF, UNDP, Prospera, and SMERU, Jakarta.

UNICEF Viet Nam. 2020. "Rapid Assessment of the Social and Economic Impacts of COVID-19 on Children and Families in Viet Nam." UNICEF Viet Nam, Ho Chi Minh City.

Uwezo Uganda. 2021. *Are Our Children Learning? Illuminating the Covid-19 Learning Losses and Gains in Uganda. Uwezo National Learning Assessment Report, 2021.* Kampala: Uwezo Uganda.

Vegas, E., and R. Winthrop. 2020. "Global Education: How to Transform School Systems? Reimagining the Global Economy: Building Back Better in a Post–COVID-19 World." Center for Universal Education, Brookings Institution, Washington, DC.

Vogl, T. S. 2014. "Education and Health in Developing Economies." In *Encyclopedia of Health Economics,* 246–49. Amsterdam: Elsevier. https://doi.org/10.1016/B978-0-12-375678-7.00109-7.

Walsh, S., A. Chowdhury, V. Braithwaite, S. Russell, J. M. Birch, J. L. Ward, C. Waddington, et al. 2021. "Do School Closures and School Reopenings Affect Community Transmission of COVID-19? A Systematic Review of Observational Studies." *BMJ Open* 11 (8): p.e053371.

Westphal, A., E. Kalinowski, C. J. Hoferichter, and M. Vock. 2022. "K-12 Teachers' Stress and Burnout during the COVID-19 Pandemic: A Systematic Review." *Frontiers in Psychology* 2022 13: 920326. doi: 10.3389/fpsyg.2022.920326.

WFP (World Food Programme). 2020. "World Food Programme Gears Up to Support Children Left without Meals Due to COVID-19 School Closures." News release, March 20, 2020.

Whizz Education. 2021. "Measuring the Impact of COVID-19 on Learning in Rural Kenya." Whizz Education, London. https://www.whizzeducation.com/wp-content/uploads/Kenya-Covid-Impact-SCREEN.pdf.

Wolf, S., E. Aurino, N. Suntheimer, E. Avornyo, E. Tsinigo, J. Jordan, S. Samanhyia, et al. 2021. "Learning in the Time of a Pandemic and Implications for Returning to School: Effects of COVID-19 in Ghana." Working paper, Penn Graduate School of Education, Philadelphia. https://repository.upenn.edu/cpre_workingpapers/28.

World Bank. 2018. *World Development Report 2018: Learning to Realize Education's Promise.* Washington, DC: World Bank.

World Bank. 2020. *The COVID-19 Pandemic: Shocks to Education and Policy Responses.* Washington, DC: World Bank.

World Bank. 2021a. "Accelerating Learning Recovery." World Bank, Washington, DC. https://thedocs.worldbank.org/en/doc/75bdb5f2c03f19f0642db1c941193f8d-0140042021/related/Recovery-updated-09-27-2021.pdf.

World Bank. 2021b. *The Human Capital Index 2020 Update: Human Capital in the Time of COVID-19.* Washington, DC: World Bank. doi:10.1596/978-1-4648-1552-2.

World Bank. 2022. *Two Years After: Saving a Generation.* Washington, DC: World Bank. https://openknowledge .worldbank.org/handle/10986/37586.

World Bank, Bill and Melinda Gates Foundation, FCDO (Foreign Commonwealth and Development Office, Government of the United Kingdom), UNESCO (United Nations Educational, Scientific, and Cultural Organization), UNICEF (United Nations Children's Fund), and USAID (United States Agency for International Development). 2022. *Guide for Learning Recovery and Acceleration: Using the RAPID Framework to Address COVID-19 Learning Losses and Build Forward Better.* Washington, DC: World Bank.

World Bank, UIS (United Nations Educational, Scientific, and Cultural Organization–UNESCO Institute for Statistics), UNICEF (United Nations Children's Fund), FCDO (Foreign Commonwealth and Development Office, Government of the United Kingdom), USAID (United States Agency for International Development), Bill and Melinda Gates Foundation, and UNESCO. 2022. *The State of Global Learning Poverty: 2022 Update.* Conference Edition, June 23, 2022. Washington, DC: World Bank.

World Bank and UNESCO (United Nations Educational, Scientific, and Cultural Organization). 2022. *Education Finance Watch 2022.* Washington, DC, and Paris: World Bank and UNESCO.

World Bank, UNESCO (United Nations Educational, Scientific, and Cultural Organization), and UNICEF (United Nations Children's Fund). 2021. *The State of the Global Education Crisis: A Path to Recovery.* Washington, DC, Paris, and New York: World Bank, UNESCO, and UNICEF.

Yarrow, N., N. Khairina, J. Cilliers, and I. Dini. 2022. "The Digital Future of Teacher Training in Indonesia: What's Next?" World Bank, Jakarta.

Yousafzai, A. 2020. "Low-Cost Private Schools May Not Be Able to Survive COVID-19 Crisis." *The News,* April 1, 2020. https://www.thenews.com.pk/print/637486-low-cost-private-schools-may-not-be-able-to-survive -covid-19-crisis.

Zimmerman, K. O., I. C. Akinboyo, M. A. Brookhart, A. E., Boutzoukas, K. A. McGann, M. J. Smith, G. Maradiaga Panayotti, et al. 2021. "Incidence and Secondary Transmission of SARS-CoV-2 Infections in Schools." *Pediatrics* 147 (4): e2020048090.

4

LOST OPPORTUNITIES

The Protracted Effects of the Pandemic on Youth and Young Adults

Norbert Schady and Joana Silva

ABSTRACT

This chapter provides a comprehensive diagnostic of the effects of the COVID-19 pandemic on the human capital of young people ages 15–24 and identifies promising policy responses for governments. The chapter begins by describing the ways in which the crisis affected youth human capital and providing estimates of the magnitude of the losses, primarily using microdata from labor force surveys for 12 countries. It presents three key findings. First, the pandemic led to a sharp reduction in employment and an uneven recovery globally. In some countries, there is little sign of an improvement in youth employment. The reductions were compounded by declines in job quality. Second, during the pandemic the enrollment of youth in educational institutions rose in some countries but not in others. Where increases in school enrollment did occur, they were smaller than the corresponding declines in employment, implying that more young people were neither studying nor working than would have in the absence of the pandemic. Third, there is some evidence that beyond the labor market, the pandemic led to a deterioration of other outcomes for young people, including increases in teenage pregnancy, elevated risks of depression and other mental health problems, and a decline in the development of key social-emotional skills and executive functions. These effects will have severe long-term consequences if not addressed.

The appropriate policies needed to address the sharp declines in youth employment will vary by country, depending on the extent to which both adult and youth employment have recovered. For countries where neither adult nor youth employment has recovered, demand-side policies should be geared primarily toward spurring firms to start hiring again. For countries where adult employment has recovered but youth employment has not, promoting training, job intermediation, entrepreneurship programs, and new workforce-oriented initiatives adapted for youth is particularly important. For countries where both adult and youth employment have recovered, there is no emergency. These countries should monitor developments in the labor market to ensure that the rising tide is truly lifting all boats. In all countries, policies should recognize that youth are a diverse group and that skills are the best insurance against a crisis. For younger youth (ages 15–18) who may have dropped out of school, conditional cash transfers and information campaigns can be effective in encouraging them, especially disadvantaged youth, to return to school and regain lost skills. For older youth (ages 19–24), making post-secondary education relevant and engaging, partnering with service providers and the private sector to offer short-term practical credentials, and providing information about job market returns, transparency, and accountability among service providers are key.

YOUTH IS A CRITICAL MOMENT IN THE LIFE CYCLE

It's going to take longer for younger people to find productive employment,
which is obviously a financial loss to them and their families. But on top of that,
the economy is going to suffer. It holds back economic growth.

—Stephanie Aaronson, Vice President and Director, Economic Studies, Brookings Institution
Quoted in Aaronson (1998)

❝

Youth (the period spanning ages 15–24) is a critical time in the life cycle—people make the transition from mainly accumulating human capital to utilizing it.[1] Young people can be in school, employed (whether formally or informally and in high- or low-wage jobs), or Not in Education, Employment, or Training (NEETs). They can also engage (or not) in behaviors such as unprotected sex, drug use, criminal activity, and gang membership.

The decisions made by young people have long-term consequences, and the pandemic is likely to have affected them in critical ways. Some youth may complete fewer years of schooling than they would have otherwise. If these young people entered the labor market during the pandemic, they will have brought in additional income in the immediate term, but their earnings trajectory over their lifetimes will be lower because they acquired less human capital. Others will have had difficulties finding a job or may have taken lower-quality jobs. This can lead to labor market *scarring*. Various studies have documented such scarring.[2] In the United States, for example, a spell of unemployment before age 23 has been found to have negative effects on self-reported well-being, health status, and job satisfaction more than 20 years later.[3] Individuals entering the labor market in a typical recession (characterized by a 4–5 percentage point rise in unemployment rates) have initial earnings that are 10–15 percent lower than similar cohorts entering labor markets in "normal" times. These effects tend to fade away with time, but slowly—losses are still observed 10 years later in the labor market.[4] Evidence from Brazil and Ecuador shows that the global financial crisis of 2008–09 had lasting effects on formal employment and wages for the average worker (youth and adults)—effects that could be detected (at least) nine years after the onset of the crisis.[5]

This chapter discusses how the pandemic affected the opportunities that young people had and the choices they made. It reveals that there was a sharp deterioration in the labor market, resulting in deep job losses and lower wages for young people at the onset of the pandemic. The recovery has been uneven, and, in some countries, there was little sign of an improvement 18 months after the pandemic began.

Alongside employment effects, this chapter also studies the effects of the pandemic on enrollment in school or post-secondary education because young people make decisions about work and schooling jointly. In a typical recession, both *income* effects and *substitution* effects operate on the schooling decision, and these effects work in opposite directions. The income effect arises because households are generally poorer, and families may not be able to afford the direct cost of schooling or may need the income that young people can earn. These circumstances will tend to push young people out of school. The substitution effect arises because during aggregate economic shocks wages will be lower, on average, so the opportunity cost of going to school—as reflected in forgone earnings—will also be lower. These circumstances will tend to push youth into school.

A poor start in the labor market, like the one young people experienced due to the pandemic, can have long-lasting effects. For example, a spell of unemployment in the United States before age 23 has negative effects on self-reported well-being, health status, and job satisfaction up to 20 years later. Similarly, the global financial crisis of 2008–09 had lasting effects on formal employment and wages for the average worker (both youth and adults) in Brazil and Ecuador.

However, the pandemic was not a typical recession. In addition to the economic downturn, there was a health emergency, along with school closures and mobility restrictions. Results indicate that attendance in educational institutions rose in some countries and fell in others. Even where school attendance rose, the increases were smaller than the corresponding declines in employment. As a result, more young people were neither studying nor working than would have been the case in the absence of the pandemic. These youth suffered an unambiguous loss of human capital from the crisis.

There is also some evidence that the pandemic led to increases in teenage pregnancy, elevated risks of depression and other mental health problems, and declines in the development of key social-emotional skills and executive functions—the mental processes that enable people to plan, focus attention, remember, and juggle multiple tasks. However, evidence on these outcomes is generally available only for smaller samples rather than for nationally representative household or labor force surveys.

THE PANDEMIC LED TO A SHARP REDUCTION AND AN UNEVEN RECOVERY IN EMPLOYMENT GLOBALLY

Globally, the pandemic represented a huge employment shock.[6] Between the fourth quarter of 2019 and the second quarter of 2020, 191 million full-time jobs were lost in middle-income countries and 25 million in high-income countries.[7] As a result, the employment rate—the proportion of people between the ages of 15 and 65 who are working—fell by 5.1 percentage points in middle-income countries relative to the baseline (the last quarter of 2019). Since then, recovery has been uneven. Although some countries have surpassed 2019 employment rates, others have made only limited progress, and in still others, there is little evidence of a recovery in employment. Overall, in the third quarter of 2021 about 40 million fewer people were employed in middle-income countries than before the pandemic.

Employment declined more steeply and the recovery has been slower in lower-middle-income countries than in upper-middle- and high-income countries. In the second quarter of 2020, employment losses were 8 percentage points in lower-middle-income countries, compared with 2.6 percentage points in upper-middle-income countries and 4.3 percentage points in high-income countries. Even though the recovery in employment was almost complete by the third quarter of 2021 in high- and upper-middle-income countries, it was still 3.5 percentage points below pre-pandemic levels in lower-middle-income countries (figure 4.1).

FIGURE 4.1 Worldwide, employment fell sharply during the pandemic

Change in employment rate, by country income group, 2019:Q4–2021:Q3

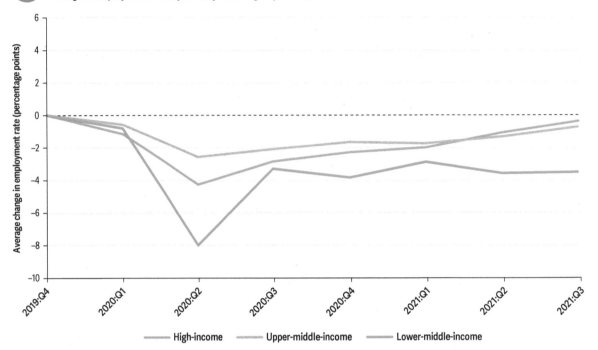

Source: Original calculations using employment data from national accounts.
Note: The figure presents the percentage point changes in employment with respect to the fourth quarter (Q4) of 2019 (as a population-weighted average) by country income group.
Data cover a total of 78 countries and represent 73 percent of the global population. Comparable data for low-income countries are not available.

YOUTH EMPLOYMENT AND WAGES FELL SHARPLY AND HAVE RECOVERED IN SOME COUNTRIES BUT NOT IN OTHERS

Global data on changes in total employment are useful for an overall view of a wide range of countries. However, these data do not allow analysis of the separate effects of the pandemic on young men and young women, or study of the evolution of other outcomes, such as wages. For this reason, this chapter now turns to a detailed analysis of quarterly data from labor force surveys for 12 low- and middle-income countries—Brazil, Bulgaria, Ethiopia, India, Jordan, Mexico, Morocco, Pakistan, the Philippines, South Africa, Türkiye, and Vietnam.[8] In each country, as discussed in annex 4A, the analysis is based on calculations of predicted and observed employment (and other outcomes), relying on a methodology that is comparable to that used in earlier chapters.

In most countries, youth employment (ages 15–24) fell sharply at the beginning of the pandemic, as evident in figure 4.2. The figure shows employment losses at three points in time: in the second quarter of 2020 (shortly after the onset of the pandemic), in the first quarter of 2021, and in the fourth quarter of 2021 (the last point in time in which data are available for most countries). These declines were particularly pronounced in the Philippines (with a decline of 11 percentage points), in Türkiye (with a decline of 7 percentage points), and in the two Latin American countries in the sample (with a 6 percentage point decline in Brazil and an 8 percentage point decline in Mexico). On the other hand, youth employment *increased* in the two lower-income countries in the sample—by 1 percentage point in Ethiopia and by 3 percentage points in Pakistan.

Collapse and Recovery: How the COVID-19 Pandemic Eroded Human Capital and What to Do about It

FIGURE 4.2 **Youth employment declined sharply during the pandemic**

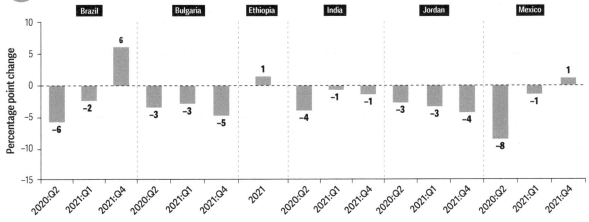

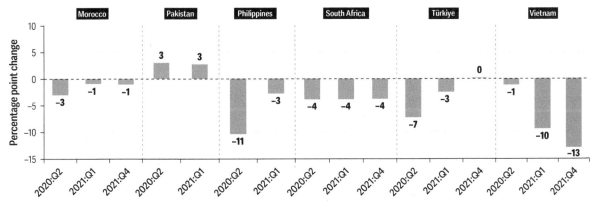

Source: Original calculations using labor force survey data.
Note: The bars represent estimates of the impact of the pandemic on youth employment at three points in time: the second quarter (Q2) of 2020 (shortly after the onset of the pandemic), the first quarter (Q1) of 2021, and the fourth quarter (Q4) of 2021 (the last point in time for which data are available for most countries). Each bar corresponds to the difference between the observed and predicted employment rate for youth in that period. Thus, when bars extend above zero, they correspond to the values of employment above their expected levels, and when they extend below zero, the reverse is true. Seasonal effects were removed. All values in the figure refer to percentage point changes.

Figure 4.2 also shows the substantial differences in the pattern of recovery. By the end of 2021, youth employment had recovered fully and exceeded pre-pandemic levels in Brazil, Mexico, and Türkiye. On the other hand, there is no evidence of a recovery in South Africa, while in Bulgaria, Jordan, and—especially—Vietnam, youth employment continued to decline throughout 2021.

Finding and keeping a job are one measure of labor market success. The *quality* of that job is also important. Measures of job quality include wages, whether the job is full-time or part-time, and whether employment is formal or informal. Unfortunately, for the pandemic period these data are available in the labor force surveys of only six of the 12 countries under analysis: Brazil, India, Mexico, the Philippines, South Africa, and Vietnam.

Figure 4.3 compares the magnitude of the changes in youth employment and wages for these six countries for the three periods shown in figure 4.2. The figure shows that in most countries declines in wages were smaller than the corresponding declines in employment. However, India is an important exception: the

FIGURE 4.3 In many countries, the employment losses of youth during the pandemic were compounded by declines in wages

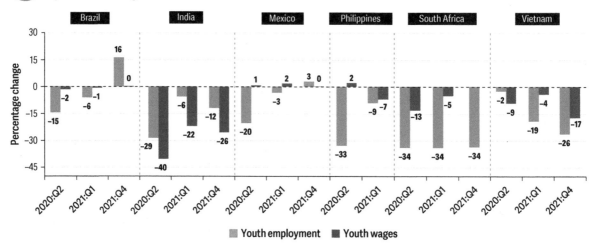

■ Youth employment ■ Youth wages

Source: Original calculations using labor force survey data.

Note: The bars represent estimates of the impact of the pandemic on youth employment and wages at three points in time: the second quarter (Q2) of 2020 (shortly after the onset of the pandemic), the first quarter (Q1) of 2021, and the fourth quarter (Q4) of 2021 (the last point in time for which data are available for most countries). Each bar corresponds to the difference between the observed and predicted employment or wage rate for youth in that period. Thus, when bars extend above zero, they correspond to the values of employment or wages above their expected levels, and when they extend below zero, the reverse is true. Seasonal effects were removed. All values in the figure refer to percentage changes. No data are available for wages in South Africa in 2021:Q4.

reduction in wages (–40 percent in the second quarter of 2020 and –22 percent in the first quarter of 2021) was even larger than the reduction in youth employment in this period (–29 percent in the second quarter of 2020 and –6 percent in the first quarter of 2021).

Other measures of job quality, such as hours worked and the proportion of young people holding a formal job, also declined in some countries. Specifically, the number of hours worked by employed young people fell—by six hours a week in Brazil, nine hours a week in South Africa, and 20 hours a week in the Philippines (from 39 to 19). Hours worked is what economists refer to as the intensive margin of employment as opposed to the extensive margin, which simply measures whether someone has a job. This evidence therefore indicates that there were large adjustments on both margins in some countries.

Another measure of job quality is whether young people are employed formally or informally. A priori, it is not clear whether the pandemic would lead to increases or decreases in the informality rate among those employed. Young people who lost a salaried job in the formal sector could have migrated to the informal sector or become self-employed. In this scenario, informality could increase among youth, even if jobs among informal workers were lost. However, the reverse is also possible. Informal sector workers, who enjoy fewer protections, could have been more likely to be laid off, and so informality could decline. In practice, both patterns occurred in different countries. In Türkiye, the proportion of employed youth with a formal job increased sharply after the onset of the pandemic and remained above expected trends at the end of 2021. By contrast, in Mexico and Vietnam formality decreased. In the other countries for which data are available (Brazil, India, and South Africa), changes in formality were small and brief.

In summary, the pandemic resulted in large declines in youth employment and job quality. These declines are a concern because they imply reductions in current income and in on-the-job learning, which, like schooling, is an investment in the human capital of young people. In addition, difficulties finding and keeping a job early in a worker's career can have long-term consequences for productivity and wages because of scarring in the labor market (box 4.1).

How labor market scarring works

To understand labor market scarring, it is useful to consider three scenarios that could occur when a young person has difficulty finding a job (figure B4.1.1). Consider a hypothetical 18-year-old who could not find a job at the beginning of the pandemic. One possibility is that she pursues more schooling, which implies a shift of her experience-wage profile to the right (because she does not earn income for the period she is in school) and upward (because schooling is an investment that yields returns).[a] This is scenario 1 (postponed labor market entry with additional schooling). However, this young person may not choose to extend her education or be able to do so. At a minimum, this implies a period of forgone earnings, thereby shifting her experience-wage profile to the right and reducing her discounted lifetime income. This is scenario 2 (postponed labor market entry without additional schooling). Alternatively, she could take a job during the pandemic—scenario 3. This job may pay lower wages. In this case, the experience-wage profile shifts downward (red line), or in the worst-case scenario, she takes a lower-quality job and her experience-wage profile shifts downward and flattens, implying lower wage growth in the future (red dashed line).

Scenario 3 is what economists have in mind when they refer to "scarring" in the labor market. Why might this happen? Much of the increase in wages that occurs with additional experience materializes as workers shop around for higher-paying jobs. But workers who start with lower wages may have less bargaining power, or they may be more risk-averse. They are "stuck" in worse jobs, and their wage losses compound.

FIGURE B4.1.1 Three scenarios show how short-term employment losses can affect a young person's future wages

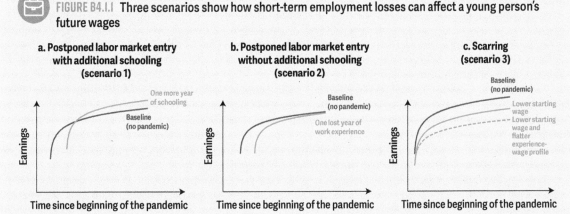

a. Postponed labor market entry with additional schooling (scenario 1)

One more year of schooling

Baseline (no pandemic)

Earnings

Time since beginning of the pandemic

b. Postponed labor market entry without additional schooling (scenario 2)

Baseline (no pandemic)

One lost year of work experience

Earnings

Time since beginning of the pandemic

c. Scarring (scenario 3)

Baseline (no pandemic)

Lower starting wage

Lower starting wage and flatter experience-wage profile

Earnings

Time since beginning of the pandemic

Source: Original calculations.
Note: The brown line represents the trajectory of wage earnings from the moment a young person enters the labor market. The red line represents three scenarios of possible shifts in the experience-wage profiles due to changes in the decisions of young adults in response to the COVID-19 shock.

a. These returns depend on the quality and relevance of this schooling.

DECLINES IN YOUTH EMPLOYMENT WERE NOT FULLY MADE UP BY INCREASES IN SCHOOL ATTENDANCE

As with effects of the pandemic on school-aged children, because of the nature of the pandemic one could expect either rising or falling school enrollment among youth, and evidence from earlier crises indicates that both can occur.[9] Yet as box 4.1 clarifies, the implications of a decline in youth employment are very different if the decline is made up by an increase in school enrollment than if it is not—the subject of this section.

Data on enrollment at any educational institution (called here "school enrollment," even when it refers to young people who are likely attending university or technical or vocational training rather than secondary school) are available for only seven—Brazil, Ethiopia, Mexico, Pakistan, the Philippines, South Africa, and Vietnam—of the 12 countries in the sample used here. Moreover, in the Philippines schools were closed during all of 2020 and 2021. It is not clear that "school enrollment" is a meaningful concept when schools are closed, and so the results that follow exclude the Philippines.

Figure 4.4 presents evidence on changes in youth employment and school enrollment, overall and by gender, for the three time periods also shown in figures 4.2. and 4.3 (as available for each country). The disaggregation by gender is important because the effects of a crisis on female and male youth could differ for several reasons. First, cultural reasons could determine how young men and young women respond to an economic shock. Second, because women generally bear a disproportionate share of childcare responsibilities and because school closures increased childcare burdens, larger declines in female employment might be expected. Finally, there are differences in the sectors in which young women and men work—for example, services versus construction—and the pandemic affected some sectors more than others.

Figure 4.4 contains some important results about the six countries of interest here. First, in one (Pakistan) there was a large decline in school enrollment (-7 percentage points in the first quarter of 2021), whereas in another (Vietnam), there was a large increase (+7 percentage points in the fourth quarter of 2021). Second, differences by gender are generally modest—with the exception of Pakistan, where the decline in school enrollment was substantially larger among young men (-9 percentage points) than among young women (-5 percentage points). Third, in countries where school enrollment increased, such as in South Africa and Vietnam, these increases were smaller in magnitude than the corresponding declines in employment.

The fact that the reductions in youth employment have generally been larger than the corresponding increases in school enrollment suggests there may be increases in some countries in the proportion of young people who are neither studying nor working—that is, Not in Education, Employment, or Training (a NEET). Figure 4.5 tackles this question directly. The figure shows that in South Africa, the share of NEETs in the fourth quarter of 2021 was 9 percentage points higher than it would have been in the absence of the pandemic, while in Vietnam it was 8 percentage points higher. In other countries, changes were smaller or faded out quickly. On average, in the six countries for which data are available, NEETs now represent 24 percent of all young people.

Figure 4.5 also shows that in Mexico and Pakistan, the increase in male NEETs was somewhat larger than the corresponding increase in female NEETs. This pattern may not hold, however, in other lower-middle- or low-income countries—settings where the labor force surveys that are the basis for the figure are collected irregularly, including during the pandemic. Indeed, two recent studies for Kenya and Uganda report worrying increases in school dropouts among female youth. In Uganda, among grade 12 students, 18 percent of girls did not come back, compared with 2 percent of boys.[10] Likewise, in a small-scale but well-designed study in Kenya, dropouts among girls ages 13–16 tripled relative to the pre-pandemic cohort, from 3.2 percent to 9.4 percent.[11] These studies suggest that countries should closely monitor the school enrollment of adolescents, including any possible differences by gender.

Although the results of the analysis suggest that the pandemic may not have differentially affected employment for young women versus young men, the structural impediments to women's participation in the labor market are far higher in many countries than they are for men's participation.

 FIGURE 4.4 **School enrollment increased in some countries and declined in others during the pandemic**

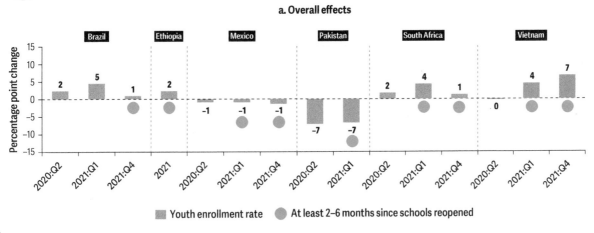

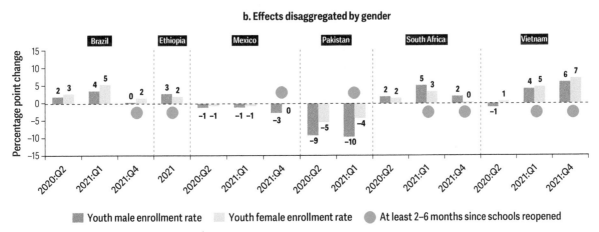

Source: Original calculations using labor force survey data.
Note: The bars represent estimates of the impact of the pandemic on youth enrollment at any educational institution at three points in time: the second quarter (Q2) of 2020 (shortly after the onset of the pandemic), the first quarter (Q1) of 2021, and the fourth quarter (Q4) of 2021 (the last point in time for which data are available for most countries). Each bar corresponds to the difference between the observed and predicted enrollment rate for youth in that period. Thus, when bars extend above zero, they correspond to the values of enrollment above their expected levels, and when they extend below zero, the reverse is true. Seasonal effects were removed. All values in the figure refer to percentage point changes.

FIGURE 4.5 The share of youth who were Not in Education, Employment, or Training (NEETs) increased sharply in some countries during the pandemic

a. Overall effects

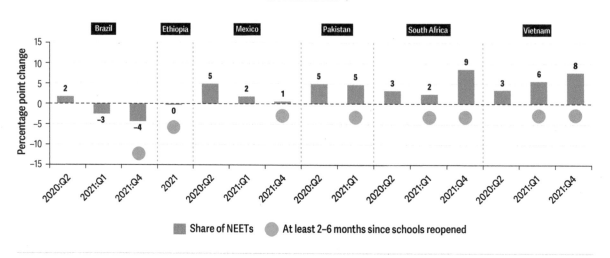

b. Effects disaggregated by gender

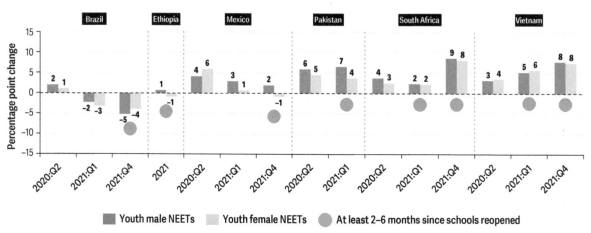

Source: Original calculations using labor force survey data.

Note: The bars show changes in the share of youth who were Not in Education, Employment, or Training (NEETs) induced by the pandemic at different points in time. In all countries for which data are available, effects are estimated in the second quarter (Q2) of 2020 (shortly after the onset of the pandemic), the first quarter (Q1) of 2021, and the fourth quarter (Q4) of 2021 (the last point in time in which data are available for most countries). Panel a reports overall effects, and panel b reports results disaggregated by gender. Each bar corresponds to the difference between the observed rate and the predicted rate of the respective indicator after the onset of the pandemic. Thus when bars extend above zero, they correspond to values above their expected levels, and when they extend below zero the reverse is true. All values in the figure refer to changes in percentage points.

BEYOND EMPLOYMENT AND SCHOOLING: OTHER ADVERSE EFFECTS OF THE PANDEMIC ON YOUTH

Many students returned back to school, but many also got married.....
All the girls who got married are in my age range....
Instead of sitting idle without school they decided to get married.

—An 18-year-old girl, Ethiopia
Quoted in Jones et al. (2021)

❝

Up to this point, this chapter has focused on the effects of the pandemic on youth employment and school enrollment. However, youth is a time in which several risks may emerge, including physical and mental health problems, teenage pregnancy, early marriage, and gender-based violence.[12] This is also the life stage at which lasting social networks of friends and coworkers are formed. These networks influence attitudes, criminal activity and gang membership, and habits related to health and substance abuse.[13] These individual choices are likely to affect lifetime outcomes and may have longer-term intergenerational effects.[14] Youth is also the stage at which individuals develop key social-emotional skills, self-regulation skills, and executive functions—skills critical for future labor market success and well-being. Emerging evidence suggests that the pandemic may have had negative effects on the development of executive functions and social-emotional skills, teenage pregnancy and marriage, and stress and violence within households.

Educational neuroscientists have shown that adolescence is an important period for the development of executive functions and noncognitive skills. Lockdowns, social distancing, and distance learning, among other changes arising from the pandemic, may have curtailed the formation of these skills. Evidence on the nature and magnitude of these impacts is not extensive and is mostly from high-income contexts. Yet the few existing studies yield important insights. For example, a 2021 study of a sample of US university students finds that executive functions declined during the pandemic.[15] Adolescents with poorer working memory before the pandemic experienced higher anxiety during the pandemic.[16] Confinement during the pandemic lowered executive functions (in addition to increasing anxiety and decreasing the quality of sleep), as reported in a study of a large sample of six- to 18-year-olds in Spain.[17] Young adults with preexisting deficits in executive functions were more vulnerable to negative changes in health behaviors during the pandemic, as reported in a longitudinal, multisite study in the United States.[18] Although some of these impacts tend to persist, the literature shows that some interventions can mitigate them, including mindfulness training and cognitive behavioral therapy.

> *In some countries, the pandemic led to increases in teenage pregnancy, worse mental health, and declines in the development of key social-emotional skills and executive functions, although data are spottier.*

More generally, various studies have found that policies restricting mobility, such as "stay-at-home" or "shelter-in-place" orders, were strongly associated with adverse impacts on mental well-being.[19] Young healthy people living alone and with an active working life before the pandemic experienced significantly higher levels of distress because of the pandemic.[20] Evidence shows that declines in student mental health led to depression. In Ecuador, 16 percent of high school students interviewed during lockdowns were depressed.[21] This level is substantially higher than the level (6.2 percent) reported before the pandemic in Ecuador in a 2017 study,[22] suggesting that depression rates increased. However, this evidence is only suggestive because the samples were different. In Kenya, 50 percent of adolescents reported experiencing depression-related symptoms during lockdowns.[23]

Attending school protects girls from early marriage, pregnancy, and sexually transmitted infections.[24] In a prior epidemic, the Ebola outbreak in Africa, evidence for the three countries most affected

(Guinea, Liberia, and Sierra Leone) suggests that school closures were associated with an increase in teenage pregnancies.[25] Once schools reopened, many "visibly pregnant girls" were banned from going back to school.[26]

Strong quantitative evidence during the current pandemic is more limited. And for some outcomes such as teenage pregnancy, even 2021 may be too early to detect the effects of school closures. More data are needed to determine whether excess teenage pregnancies occurred or will occur (in 2022, 2023, and beyond) among the cohorts affected by the pandemic. A recent study using longitudinal data on 910 girls in their last two years of secondary school in rural western Kenya between 2018 and 2021 finds that those in the COVID-19 cohort had twice the risk of becoming pregnant before completing secondary school relative to similar girls in the pre–COVID-19 cohort.[27]

A study applying a mixed-methods approach finds evidence that the pandemic changed perceptions about the risk of child marriage in Bangladesh, Ethiopia, Jordan, and the West Bank and Gaza.[28] Adolescent girls in rural Ethiopia perceived an increased risk because of intensifying economic poverty, discriminatory gender norms, and a general lack of surveillance and reporting due to an absence of teachers and health extension workers. Research participants in Jordan noted that child marriage became more likely because the cost of getting married dropped as the pandemic evolved, and it became socially acceptable to organize modest and smaller weddings. Drawing on cross-national panel data from Bangladesh and Jordan, a 2022 study finds that the pandemic worsened inequalities experienced by married girls in contexts of displacement.[29] Refugee girls were found to be at greater risk of child marriage than their counterparts in host communities. Married girls consistently were more likely to experience anxiety and were less positive and more concerned about the future.

Finally, in terms of engagement in violence, various studies find that added stress and violence within families during the pandemic increased the gap in prosociality (behaviors intended to benefit others) between adolescents of high and low socioeconomic status, which is particularly concerning because prosociality was already lower for the low-socioeconomic status adolescents prior to the pandemic.[30] A 2022 study of low- and middle-income countries finds that adolescents in urban Ethiopia and Jordan report having observed more stress within households during the pandemic. This extra stress often translated into elevated levels of verbal and sometimes physical violence.[31]

HOW HAVE GOVERNMENTS RESPONDED SO FAR TO THE PANDEMIC-RELATED LOSSES IN YOUNG PEOPLE'S HUMAN CAPITAL?

Consider, for a moment, a tale of two countries. Both have suffered a severe recession and lost jobs as a result, but not on the same scale. In Country A, employment has fallen more than 5 percent, and the unemployment rate has more than doubled. In Country B, employment has fallen only half a percent, and unemployment is only slightly higher than it was before the crisis. Don't you think Country A might have something to learn from Country B?

—Paul Krugman, US economist
"Free to Lose," *New York Times*, November 12, 2009

❝

Many of the losses of youths' human capital induced by the pandemic can be mitigated or even recovered. To identify a policy agenda to get youth back on track, it is useful to examine how governments addressed the employment and schooling challenges of youth during the pandemic and to assess how these efforts can be augmented to close the remaining gaps going forward.

Policies that promoted employment, possibly affecting the human capital of young people

Economywide countercyclical policies. In response to the pandemic, and in addition to addressing the health emergency, most countries implemented large packages of economywide countercyclical policies to mitigate employment and income losses. These policies were not specifically geared toward youth but could affect the job prospects of youth (and adults). They mostly took the form of macroeconomic policies to stimulate the economy and countercyclical income support programs that acted as automatic stabilizers (through unemployment benefits and other forms of income support).

The macroeconomic policies implemented consisted of active fiscal (tax and spending) policies and accommodative monetary policy lending. Some upper-middle-income countries were able to put in place large stimulus packages in 2020. For example, macroeconomic support as a percentage of gross domestic product (GDP) reached 9.3 percent in Brazil, 12.2 percent in Serbia, and 14.6 percent in Thailand.[32] However, countercyclical policies were generally much smaller in lower-income countries and in those with high levels of public debt or limited access to international capital markets.

These policies were supplemented by stabilizers in place before the pandemic, which differed across countries in their breadth and scope. Countercyclical income support programs, such as unemployment insurance and other transfers to households in bad times, limit the damage from contractions and help economic recovery. During the pandemic, such assistance consisted of the expansion of unemployment benefits and cash transfers to workers in high-income countries.[33] Unemployment insurance systems are not common in lower-income countries—indeed, less than a third of low- and middle-income countries have mandatory, risk-pooling unemployment insurance.[34] Focusing mainly on insuring workers by aggressively increasing the generosity of unemployment insurance was not a viable option in most low-income countries.

Policies to sustain firms and maintain employment within firms. Several governments engaged in policies to protect firms and, indirectly, maintain employment within these firms. Actions to protect firms mostly consisted of improving access to credit as governments (through their central banks) issued lines of credit or credit guarantees. In a typical program, the government established a sovereign guarantee to provide loans for working capital to private companies that were tax-compliant and solvent before the pandemic. The government guaranteed a share of the loans, with the interest rate capped. Other forms of support included payment facilities and utility and rent support.

Firm- or sector-specific support aimed at keeping businesses open and retaining jobs was the main form of government employment assistance, according to the World Bank's COVID-19 Social Protection and Jobs (SPJ) Policy Inventory under the Jobs Watch COVID-19 initiative. The inventory analyzed 3,181 social protection and jobs programs implemented by low- and middle-income countries during the pandemic.[35] This type of support, introduced by 90 percent of countries, represented, on average, an allocation of 2.6 percent of GDP (US$32.1 billion) to policies to protect firms' liquidity.

The risk associated with protecting firms is that the support provided may not be enough to ensure firm survival, and, even if it is, surviving firms can still retrench workers. Instead of protecting *firms* directly, some countries prioritized actions to preserve *employment* within firms by conditioning support on retention of workers—that is, by maintaining job matches between employees and firms. The objective of these policies was to limit employment losses and preserve firm-specific human capital by helping workers and firms maintain a link that would be easier to reestablish once the economy began to recover.

Job retention schemes often took the form of transfers to employers or workers that partially or fully covered wages and other payroll-associated costs—for example, by capping or temporarily suspending social security contributions or income taxes. These programs were widely used in member countries of the Organisation for Economic Co-operation and Development (OECD). They supported about 50 million jobs across OECD members, which are about 10 times as many as during the global financial crisis of 2008–09.[36]

Emerging evidence from impact evaluations, albeit largely limited to high-income countries, yields some important insights into the role of job retention schemes in mitigating the effects of the pandemic on labor markets and consumption. For example, according to an evaluation of the expansion of the Kurzarbeit program in Germany exploiting differences across states in exposure to the pandemic shock and program take-up, the unemployment rate would have increased by an additional 3 percentage points, on average, at the trough of the recession, and the contraction of consumption would have been two to three times larger had the program not been expanded.[37] Evidence from a similar scheme in Australia reveals that its job retention program saved the job of one in five employees who received a transfer payment.[38] Overall, without the widespread coverage of these job retention schemes, unemployment in the euro area would have peaked at about 10.5 percent in 2020, or more than 2.5 percentage points higher than the level observed.[39]

To preserve job matches and lessen the social costs created by "excess" layoffs in recessions, wage subsidies should cover a substantial share of a worker's salary (otherwise, a firm may prefer not to retain the worker because the associated costs would be too high, or the worker may choose to leave the job rather than experience large income losses). Wage subsidies should also avoid creating distortions, and the program should ensure that firms do not just use the subsidies while it is active and fire workers immediately after it stops. In low- and middle-income countries, many countries had little fiscal space to implement these programs at scale. Wage subsidies often targeted specific sectors (and often firms within sectors), covered 40–50 percent of workers' salaries (compared with 60–80 percent in high-income countries), and often did not include the requirement that firms maintain the employment relationship after the program ended (box 4.2). The jury is still out on the effect of these policies on employment changes. Early evidence from Latin America found that firm support policies had a modest (but some) impact on employment growth.[40]

Even if these policies are perfectly designed, the formal/informal divide in the labor markets in low- and middle-income countries can reduce the ability of these policies to limit layoffs. Targeting informal firms is often difficult. By targeting formal firms, many of these programs excluded a large share of the workforce and most young and low-income workers. Reaching informal workers and firms is particularly important in low- and middle-income countries, where most workers are employed informally. In the sample of 12 countries analyzed in depth in this chapter, 63 percent of employment was informal in 2019. Among youth, informality was even higher, at 77 percent.

BOX 4.2 **How wage subsidies in response to the pandemic differed by country income**

During the pandemic, wage subsidies in low- and middle-income countries were often different in nature from those in high-income countries. They were less generous and frequently did not require firms to maintain the employment relationship after the subsidies ended. In Colombia, the wage subsidy program covered 50 percent of the minimum wage per worker for businesses experiencing a decline of more than 20 percent in revenue in the previous three months. In Serbia, all employees of small and medium enterprises (SMEs) received minimum wages for three months, while employees in large private sector companies and those who were not working were paid 50 percent of the minimum wage for three months. In Thailand, SMEs could deduct from taxes three times the amount paid in salaries to workers registered with the social security office between April and July 2020, or up to US$457 per worker per month. Beneficiary firms were required to maintain employment levels equal to the number of insured workers according to social security records at the end of December 2019. In Timor-Leste, 60 percent of wage costs were covered for formal sector employees. In Brazil, formal sector workers received a temporary wage subsidy (up to a maximum of R$600 per month for a duration of three months) if they were furloughed or had their hours temporarily reduced, with the requirement that their firms maintain the employment relationship after the program ended. These measures targeting workers were complemented by subsidies to firms and other measures. Altogether, they amounted to 4.1 percent of Brazil's gross domestic product in 2020.[a]

a. World Bank (2022a).

During the pandemic, some countries were able to provide informal firms and workers with direct support. For example, Bangladesh offered suspension of loan repayments to informal firms using micro-credit institutions and informal sector organizations already serving these groups. Other countries opted to reduce, eliminate, or defer utility and rent payments for informal firms. However, evidence from Latin America indicates that despite the unprecedented amount of firm- or sector-specific support, such policies had limited impacts on small and informal firms. These firms were less aware of programs, applied less, and received less assistance.[41] This was true as well in past crises. Program evaluations suggest that earmarked loans went mostly to larger, less credit-constrained firms, many of which did not need this assistance.[42]

In general, low- and middle-income countries engaged more in policies that protected firms (employers) directly than those that protected workers (people) directly. Although the former is better at increasing the probability of firm survival, the latter is better at preserving employment. If well designed, wage subsidies may be an efficient way to respond to temporary shocks, but they may be less appropriate for responding to more persistent shocks because they impede the reallocation of resources to expanding firms, sectors, or regions. Importantly, previous crises have demonstrated that, to be successful, programs to support firms or workers within firms need to be time-bound and should quickly evolve into more targeted support to avoid becoming an obstacle to needed structural change.[43] The experience during the pandemic suggests that policies insuring workers and jobs in combination with other instruments that boost labor demand (such as hiring subsidies) may be the most efficient way to respond to recessions in the labor market.

Overall, how likely was it that the policies subsidizing jobs affected youth? It probably depends on the proportion of youth working and those close to entering the labor market. Working youth have less firm-specific human capital than adults and are less likely to be covered by permanent work contracts because they entered employment more recently. For these reasons, they are often the first to be laid off. Moreover, these policies are unlikely to directly reach youth who will soon enter the labor market and therefore do not have an ongoing contract with a specific firm.

Policies that reach informal workers through household-level social protection measures. Governments in low- and middle-income countries massively increased the coverage and generosity of cash transfers. The coverage of these programs increased by more than 230 percent, with about 15 percent of the world's population receiving at least one pandemic-related cash payment (but only 2 percent in Sub-Saharan Africa). More than 271 programs were introduced, expanded, or adapted to respond to the pandemic.[44] During the crisis, cash transfers to economically active individuals were the second-most-used labor policy response and the most common form of income support. Countries for which data are available spent, on average, 0.45 percent of GDP (US$3.5 billion) on cash transfers. About one-third of COVID-19 responses across countries included some form of cash transfers.[45] The scope and benefit amounts of these programs could be quickly expanded in countries with social or civil registries. Their simplicity, speed, and broad-based coverage made them a very popular crisis response policy.[46]

The main ways in which cash transfer programs were expanded included advance payments (as in Colombia and Indonesia); ensuring additional payments from existing schemes, often on a one-off basis (as in Argentina, Armenia, and Türkiye); temporarily providing more generous benefit levels (as in China); increasing the coverage of existing cash schemes (as in Brazil); providing a universal, one-off cash payment to all citizens (as in Singapore and Hong Kong SAR, China); and creating a new targeted transfer (as in Brazil—see box 4.3). These programs helped maintain income and consumption levels, but not employment (including youth employment) and not the income of many households in countries where there were no social registries.

To address temporary unemployment, several countries implemented public works programs. For example, in Nepal informal sector workers who lost their jobs due to the pandemic could participate in public works projects. They could choose between receiving a subsistence wage or 25 percent of the local daily wage. Low-income countries were more likely than middle-income countries to implement public works programs.[47] In general, youth participation in these types of programs is limited.

> **BOX 4.3 Brazil's measures for both informal workers at risk of poverty and low-wage formal workers**
>
> Brazil sought to protect two major vulnerable groups from the COVID-19 crisis: low-income families working in the informal economy and low-wage formal workers.
>
> It began by expanding the existing conditional cash transfer programs, Bolsa Familia, both horizontally (by adding new beneficiaries) and vertically (by providing existing beneficiaries with greater benefits). In addition, the country launched a temporary cash transfer program, Auxílio Emergencial, that targeted informal workers. It consisted of an emergency cash transfer program for poor families (defined as participants in the Bolsa Familia program) as well as those individuals without formal wage employment but normally ineligible for social assistance, such as nonpoor informal workers and formal self-employed workers.
>
> For low-wage formal workers at risk of dismissal, Brazil expanded unemployment insurance and provided wage subsidies. In addition, the country relaxed budget constraints so that already eligible and newly eligible families could gain coverage through the automatic absorption of new claims submitted to the unemployment insurance program. It also allowed for advance payments of regular entitlements, including special withdrawals from the employer-sponsored savings accounts, FGTS (Fundo de Garantia do Tempo de Serviço).

Policies that reduced the human capital accumulation of young people

Most secondary schools and training centers closed during lockdowns and tried to move to remote learning. But this move was challenging in lower-income countries. For example, across 92 low- and middle-income countries, less than 20 percent of providers of technical and vocational education and training (TVET) reported being able to switch to fully remote modalities (compared with 70 percent in high- and upper-middle-income countries). Within countries, the lack of reliable internet connectivity, the scarcity of digital skills among both students and teachers, and the limited access to "smart" digital devices posed additional challenges.[48] The provision of training in practical skills was disrupted when training centers were closed and the focus of instruction shifted to theoretical coursework. Work-based learning opportunities were also widely affected by the closure of enterprises during pandemic-induced lockdowns.[49] These disruptions in learning can lead to permanent disengagement from further education and training.

In the midst of this adversity emerged examples of rapid adoption of technological innovations in TVET delivery as well as impressive innovations in other areas. Modular approaches to training and certification were accelerated. Many countries launched new, short-term professional training to address skills shortages and redeploy workers to support the pandemic response.[50] In the process, important partnerships were established between TVET institutions, telecommunication operators, technology companies, and government counterparts. However, despite these successes, coordination was in general difficult in TVET systems in low- and middle-income countries characterized by a large number of small firms and microenterprises, many of them informal.[51]

Three limitations of government responses to the pandemic

Although understandable—governments were facing an unprecedented combination of a health emergency and a deep recession—the policies that low- and middle-income countries implemented had three main shortcomings in efforts to protect the human capital of young people.

The first limitation was their focus on overall employment, whereas *governments paid little specific attention to youth employment*. That said, some countries did implement policies to protect youth employment. Argentina enlarged its More and Better Jobs for Youth program, which provides young people with training, cash transfers, and intermediation support, such as facilitating job search and matching. The Malaysian government established a fund of RM 2 billion (US$487 million) to reskill and upskill 200,000 unemployed young workers. And the government of Indonesia introduced a Pre-Employment Card Program aimed at upskilling 2 million young workers. Nevertheless, such youth-specific policies were the exception. By and large, countries adopted universal "broad brush" policies to support entire populations. As a result, the specific needs of vulnerable groups, such as young people, were often overlooked. This made sense in the first months after the pandemic hit, but less so as countries entered a recovery phase in the labor market.

The second limitation was that *schools, universities, and other post-secondary institutions were closed for too long*. As discussed, it does not appear that enrollment declined steeply among young people in most countries where data are available. However, many countries simply promoted young people to the next grade or lowered the requirements for university admission. These practices mean that a substantial proportion of young people will have less human capital even if, on paper, they have completed the same years of schooling they would have completed in the absence of the pandemic.

The third limitation was that *governments did not deal effectively with disengagement and idle time among youth or with the effects of the pandemic on other aspects of well-being such as mental health*. Programs to avoid declines in mental health generally consisted of over-the-phone counseling interventions.[52] For example, in Bangladesh this type of intervention aimed at mitigating the mental health impact of the COVID-19 crisis among women had a significant positive impact not only on mental health but also on other outcomes, including food security and time invested in children.[53] Programs to address adverse effects on other dimensions beyond the labor market, including early pregnancy and impediments to the development of executive functions, were relatively rare and small in scale. Programs to address violence within the household mostly consisted of helplines and assistance at health centers and shelters. By and large, these efforts were not specific to youth.

WHAT SHOULD GOVERNMENTS DO NOW?

In all countries, policies should recognize that youth are a diverse group and that skills are the best insurance against a crisis. In settings where school-age youth have suffered large learning losses or have dropped out of school, policies should be put in place to encourage young people to return to school and make up for the lost skills. Dropouts may be a particular concern in some low- and lower-middle-income countries, as discussed earlier and in chapter 3.

For younger youth (ages 15–18) who may have dropped out of school, conditional cash transfers and information campaigns can be effective in encouraging them to return to school and in making up for lost skills, particularly for disadvantaged youth. Targeted learning recovery and retention programs for secondary school students who have been affected by pandemic-related school closures may also be needed to ensure they complete their basic education. The end of secondary schooling typically happens at or around age 18. The assessment of changes in employment for youth younger than 18 and young adults older than 18 is likely to differ substantially. For older youth (ages 19–24), key steps include making post-secondary education relevant and engaging; partnering with service providers to offer short-term, practical credentials; and providing information, transparency, and accountability. Governments can lower the barriers for youth to gain market-relevant skills by making tertiary education systems more flexible and accessible and offering bridging opportunities (short, stackable courses and microcredentials on in-demand topics), reenrollment campaigns, and scholarships.

It is also important to facilitate the insertion of young people into jobs to limit the extent of labor market scarring. How best to do this will vary by country, depending on the institutional setting. As discussed earlier in the chapter, the magnitude of the initial employment shock and the extent to which youth employment has recovered vary considerably across countries. In fact, the extent to which the employment of adults ages 25–64 has recovered also varies considerably across countries. Comparing the evolution of adult and youth employment can give countries some guidance on appropriate policies moving forward.

The results in this chapter indicate that the countries analyzed fall into three distinct groups, depending on the extent to which both adult and youth employment have recovered. This implies different policy responses as described in the sections that follow.

1. In countries where neither youth nor adult employment recovered, spur the economy to start hiring again

In some countries, neither adult nor youth employment has recovered from the pandemic. Figure 4.6, panel a, tracks the evolution of employment in one such country, South Africa, from the second quarter of 2011 to the fourth quarter of 2021. It shows a sharp reduction in employment of both adults and youth just after the onset of the pandemic and no evidence of a recovery thereafter. Panel b zeroes in on the period after the beginning of the pandemic and includes two other countries in which the pattern is similar, Bulgaria and Vietnam. In all three countries, the employment levels of both adults and youth at the end of 2021 were substantially below their pre-pandemic levels.

Countries where neither adult nor youth employment has recovered face a lack of labor demand that will be solved only if and when firms start hiring again. These countries should prioritize broad macroeconomic demand-side actions. Examples of these policies are general countercyclical policies through accommodative fiscal and monetary policy; support for formal firms through policies such as access to credit, wage subsidies, and exemptions from various taxes subject to fiscal space and monitoring of outcomes; and support for informal firms (such as in Bangladesh and Brazil), although this is generally hard to do. Without such efforts, even if supply-side skill and labor policies are well designed and expanded significantly, sizable benefits are unlikely to materialize.

Many countries in which labor demand has not recovered suffered from secular downward trends in employment before the pandemic. In these countries, jump-starting job recovery by supporting vigorous job creation will require tackling structural issues, including the sectoral and spatial dimensions underlying poor labor market adjustments, such as low geographic mobility among workers. Competition policies, regional development policies, tax reforms, and reforms of labor regulations may be needed. If countries do not address these fundamental issues, sluggish job creation is likely to continue.

FIGURE 4.6 In some countries, both youth and adult employment have not recovered from the pandemic

a. South Africa, 2011:Q2–2021:Q4

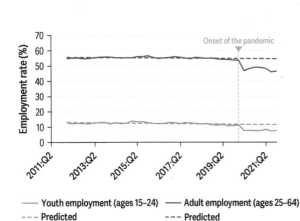

b. Bulgaria, South Africa, and Vietnam, 2020:Q2–2021:Q4

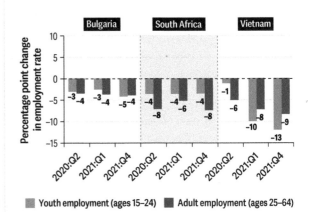

Source: Original calculations.

Note: Panel a shows the evolution of the employment to population ratio for South Africa from the second quarter (Q2) of 2011 through the second quarter of 2021 for youth (ages 15–24) and adults (ages 25–64). Panel b presents estimates of the impacts of the pandemic on youth employment in Bulgaria, South Africa, and Vietnam, given by the estimated employment losses at three points in time: the second quarter of 2020 (shortly after the onset of the pandemic), the first quarter (Q1) of 2021, and the fourth quarter (Q4) of 2021 (the last point in time in which data are available for most countries). Each bar corresponds to the difference between the observed and predicted employment rate in that period. All values in the figure refer to percentage point changes in employment relative to pre-pandemic employment levels. The predicted value extrapolates the pre-pandemic trend to the period after the onset of the pandemic. Seasonal effects were removed.

2. In countries where only adult employment has recovered but youth still lag behind, promote training, job intermediation, entrepreneurship programs, and new workforce-oriented initiatives adapted for youth

In this group of countries, adult employment has recovered, but youth employment has not. Jordan is one such country (figure 4.7, panel a). Eighteen months after the onset of the pandemic, there was no evidence of a recovery in youth employment, while adult employment almost fully returned to its pre-pandemic level. Other countries face similar, albeit less dramatic, patterns (figure 4.7, panel b). In India, there has been a full recovery of adult employment but only a partial recovery of youth employment. In the Philippines, the recovery of employment has also been larger among adults than youth.

In countries like those in figure 4.7, there is urgent need for actions specifically geared to help youth get back on track and avoid deep labor market scarring. This may not be a one-off intervention but rather a series of steps that should be sustained over time.

What specific types of programs can be implemented, and what effects can be expected? The main types of employment programs targeted at youth are *adapted* active labor market policies (ALMPs), including new forms of youth-focused training and skills certification programs, assistance with job search and matching through public employment services, entrepreneurship support programs, and new workforce-oriented initiatives for youth.

In general, the evidence on ALMPs is mixed, especially at scale. Successful programs cannot be built quickly. They succeed when they involve the private sector, and they need to target skill mismatches, ascertaining what jobs are available for young people and where there are labor shortages.

According to recent reviews, training programs can increase employment by as much as 10 percent, but many programs have no effects at all.[54] Program design and implementation are critical. Successful interventions are geared toward local employers' needs; they entail close cooperation with employers,

FIGURE 4.7 **In some countries, adult employment has recovered from the pandemic, but youth employment has not or has recovered less**

a. Jordan, 2011:Q2–2021:Q2

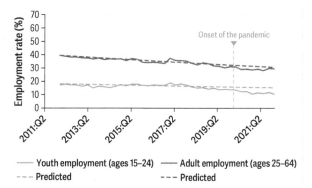

b. India, Jordan, and the Philippines, 2020:Q2–2021:Q1

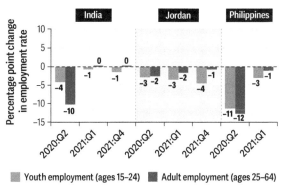

Source: Original calculations.
Note: Panel a shows the evolution of the employment to population ratio for Jordan from the second quarter (Q2) of 2011 through the second quarter of 2021 for youth (ages 15–24) and adults (ages 25–64). Panel b presents estimates of the impacts of the pandemic on youth employment in India, Jordan, and the Philippines, given by the estimated employment losses at three points in time: the second quarter of 2020 (shortly after the onset of the pandemic), the first quarter (Q1) of 2021, and the fourth quarter (Q4) of 2021 (the last point in time in which data are available for most countries). Each bar corresponds to the difference between the observed and predicted employment rate in that period. All values in the figure refer to percentage point changes in employment relative to pre-pandemic employment levels. The predicted value extrapolates the pre-pandemic trend to the period after the onset of the pandemic. Seasonal effects were removed. Data for 2021 (Q4) are not available for the Philippines.

including on curriculum design; they offer specific training, including for social-emotional skills; they track people after they are employed; and they are run by community organizations or private agencies.[55]

Intermediation programs usually cost less, but their benefits are also not guaranteed. They are more effective when there is a strong demand for particular kinds of workers, and there are mismatches that can be addressed by better job searches and knowledge of the labor market. Complementary services that have increased program success include transportation subsidies and certification of soft skills. To work for young people, these programs require adaptation and strong outreach to youth. Evidence about the importance of incentive systems for providers of job intermediation services is more mixed.

Successful entrepreneurship programs have had, on average, greater impacts than intermediation or training programs. This does not imply, however, that these programs should be strictly preferred to others. Effects depend on the needs of beneficiaries and how the services are delivered. In general, the literature suggests that programs that integrate multiple interventions are more likely to succeed.[56] Yet designing and implementing these programs take time. As a result, their scope could be smaller in an emergency in countries where a strong program does not yet exist.

In this context, how can countries reach youth through effective ALMPs? This requires program adaptation, which means different things for different sets of programs:

- Adapting training programs for youth means making content engaging for this age group and offering practical curricula, flexible schedules, and instruction methods that are less formal. For youth transitioning to work, it means linking with work experience—which youth are lacking—and promoting pathways to a job.
- Adapting intermediation services for youth means capturing vacancies and postings that are attractive to youth.
- Adapting entrepreneurship programs for youth means reaching out to business and labor associations (including those representing the informal economy); engaging and gaining support from families and communities, including through skills training and mentorships; and considering financial products and models tailored to the needs of youth.
- Adapting ALMPs for disadvantaged youth means addressing their participation constraints by offering a package of support services, including literacy, remedial education, vocational and job-readiness training, transportation subsidies, and career guidance and counseling.

However, even ALMPs successfully adapted for youth may not be sufficient. New workforce-oriented initiatives for youth may be needed. These consist of tuition incentives, paid apprenticeships, boot camps, and hiring subsidies for youth. Programs like these are geared toward work-based learning, creating an important opportunity to acquire valuable work experience (something that young people lack) and firm-specific human capital. Hiring subsidies, direct employment support, short-term job retention schemes, and start-up subsidies for youth can also have a role. These initiatives should build on changes in the demand for skills (favoring analytical and technical skills) and the fact that work modes have shifted toward virtual rather than in-person work, creating new opportunities that can be leveraged.

3. In countries where employment has fully recovered, monitor employment over time and act accordingly

In the third group of countries, both adult and youth employment have recovered to their pre-pandemic levels. Türkiye is one such country (figure 4.8, panel a). Similar patterns are observed in Brazil and Mexico (figure 4.8, panel b) and, to a lesser extent, in Morocco. These countries are no longer faced with an employment emergency but should monitor developments in the labor market (employment and wages by occupation, geography, age, gender) to ensure that progress has been shared by all groups.

In addition, policy makers in these countries should seek answers to three questions: (1) Is recovery occurring mainly for high-wage, high-education workers, with vulnerable workers being left behind?

FIGURE 4.8 In some countries, both youth and adult employment have recovered from the pandemic

a. Türkiye, 2011:Q2–2021:Q2

b. Brazil, Mexico, Morocco, and Türkiye, 2020:Q2–2021:Q4

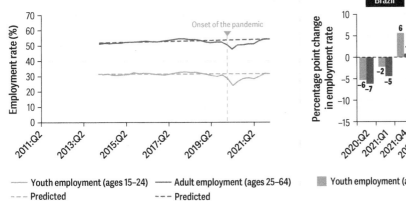

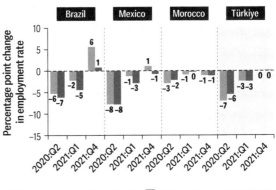

— Youth employment (ages 15–24) — Adult employment (ages 25–64)
--- Predicted   --- Predicted

■ Youth employment (ages 15–24) ■ Adult employment (ages 25–64)

Source: Original calculations.
Note: Panel a shows the evolution of the employment to population ratio for Türkiye from the second quarter (Q2) of 2011 through the second quarter of 2021 for youth (ages 15–24) and adults (ages 25–64). Panel b presents estimates of the impacts of the pandemic on youth employment in Brazil, Mexico, Morocco, and Türkiye, given by the estimated employment losses at three points in time: the second quarter of 2020 (shortly after the onset of the pandemic), in the first quarter (Q1) of 2021, and in the fourth quarter (Q4) of 2021 (the last point in time where data are available for most countries). Each bar corresponds to the difference between the observed and predicted employment rate in that period. All values in the figure refer to percentage point changes in employment relative to pre-pandemic employment levels. The predicted value extrapolates the pre-pandemic trend to the period after the beginning of the pandemic. Seasonal effects were removed.

(2) Are many jobs being left unfilled? (3) Are there big skill mismatches? If the answer to all these questions is "No," then the best course of action may simply be no action. If the answer is "Yes," then programs that increase the supply of skills (such as training) or decrease skill mismatches (such as job search assistance) may be needed. To answer these questions, countries need detailed employment data, including from labor force surveys, and a strategy for monitoring employment over time.[57]

Beyond employment and school enrollment: Addressing other aspects of youth well-being

Because of the negative impacts of the pandemic on mental health, executive functions, teenage pregnancy, and violence within the household, policies may be needed to avoid the potentially large associated losses of human capital. These initiatives are particularly important for disadvantaged youth.

Addressing any financial barriers to finishing secondary school and pursuing higher education will be key but are not sufficient. Evidence is still limited but suggestive. In the United States, for example, adolescents at risk of dropping out who participated in a mentoring program (with some of them randomized into mentoring and mindfulness) saw lower declines in mental health or executive functions than similar nonparticipants.[58] A study in China demonstrated that mindfulness training enhanced the well-being of adolescents who had low levels of resilience during the pandemic.[59] In another study, cognitive behavioral therapy improved behavior regulation for rural adolescents.[60] Yet a recent review of the literature highlights that very little is known about how to effectively build skills such as teamwork and problem-solving, especially at scale.[61] The complex design of policies to improve higher-order skills and executive functions may render them less adequate for short-term responses to crises. Where these programs exist, however, expanding them might be an important complement to schooling and labor policies for youth.

PUTTING IT ALL TOGETHER

In summary, the pandemic dealt a severe blow to the human capital of youth. Many young people have missed critical investments in education and skills development, including on-the-job learning. This finding raises important concerns about long-term consequences through scarring. By and large, countries responded to the employment shock with general countercyclical measures, policies to sustain firms, and policies to maintain employment within firms. The latter largely targeted formal firms, and in many countries young workers were left out. In addition, many governments expanded the coverage and generosity of cash transfers. Although these policies helped maintain income, they are unlikely to have resulted in substantial reductions in unemployment or inactivity among youth. Countries also shut down secondary schools, universities, and TVET institutions. Going forward, policies will be different for countries where adult employment has recovered and youth employment has not and for countries where neither has recovered. The latter should focus on spurring firms to start hiring again. In the former, promoting *adapted* ALMPs for youth should be a priority. Where these programs exist, their focus could expand to cover other aspects of youth well-being.

ANNEX 4A. METHODOLOGY TO CALCULATE CHANGES IN EMPLOYMENT (AND OTHER OUTCOMES) THAT CAN BE ATTRIBUTED TO THE PANDEMIC

The methodology used in this chapter to calculate changes in employment (and other outcomes) that can be attributed to the pandemic is similar to that used to calculate changes in enrollment in preschool and school in chapters 2 and 3, respectively. The estimation approach follows three steps. First, a regression using pre-pandemic data (generally available on a quarterly basis from the first quarter of 2012 onward) is used to estimate time trends and seasonal (quarterly) effects on employment. Next, the coefficients from this regression are used to predict what employment would have been in each quarter in 2020 and 2021. Finally, observed employment is subtracted from predicted employment to arrive at an estimate of the effect of the pandemic on employment for a given subgroup (for example, youth or adults) in a given country.[62]

Figure 4A.1 shows why removing trends and seasonal effects is important. It focuses on the evolution of youth employment in the Philippines. Panel a plots *observed* employment by quarter (solid blue line), estimates of the trend (dashed brown line) and seasonal effects (dotted blue line), and estimates of predicted employment after the trends and seasonal effects have been removed (solid orange line).

Panel b then uses these estimates to calculate the effect of the pandemic on youth employment in three ways. First, a "naïve" estimate (scenario 1) simply compares employment after the onset of the pandemic with employment just before the pandemic in the fourth quarter of 2019. A second estimate removes the time trend but not the seasonal effects (scenario 2). Finally, the preferred estimate removes both the trend and seasonal effects (scenario 3).

The bars in panel b show that because youth employment in the Philippines generally spikes in the second quarter of the year, estimates that do not account for seasonal effects underestimate employment losses in the second quarter of 2020 (a decline of 31 percent in the naïve estimate, compared with a decline of 33 percent in the preferred estimate). On the other hand, because of the sharp downward trend in youth employment in the Philippines, estimates that do not take into account the trend overestimate the effects of the pandemic on youth employment in the second quarter of 2021 (a decline of 14 percent in the naïve estimate, compared with a decline of 9 percent in the preferred estimate). In summary, figure 4A.1 underlines the importance of correctly estimating "counterfactual" employment—the employment levels most likely observed in the absence of the pandemic.

FIGURE 4A.1 The importance of removing trends and seasonal effects for the estimation of the effects of the pandemic on employment and other outcomes

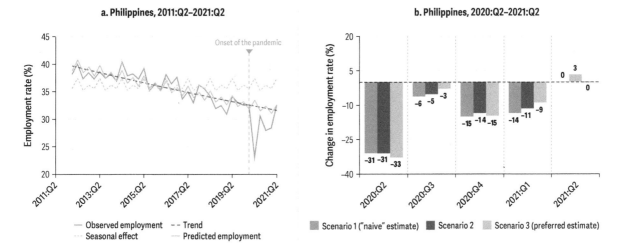

a. Philippines, 2011:Q2–2021:Q2

b. Philippines, 2020:Q2–2021:Q2

Legend:
— Observed employment - - Trend
··· Seasonal effect — Predicted employment

■ Scenario 1 ("naive" estimate) ■ Scenario 2 ▪ Scenario 3 (preferred estimate)

Source: Original calculations using labor force survey data.
Note: Panel a shows the evolution of the ratio of employment to population for the Philippines from the second quarter (Q2) of 2011 through the second quarter of 2021 for youth (ages 15–24). Panel b presents the percentage changes of the employment rate employing three scenarios: (1) comparing employment with the last pre-pandemic period (2019:Q4); (2) removing the trend but not the seasonal effects; and (3) removing trends and seasonal effects.

NOTES

1. The chapter uses the terms *youth* and *young people* interchangeably.
2. See, for example, Jacobson, LaLonde, and Sullivan (1993); Pritadrajati, Kusuma, and Saxena (2021). For a survey of the literature on the persistent effects of initial labor market conditions on young adults and their sources, see Von Wachter (2020). For recent evidence, see Rothstein (2021).
3. Bell and Blanchflower (2011).
4. See, for example, Altonji, Kahn, and Speer (2016); Kahn (2010); Oreopoulos, Von Wachter, and Heisz (2012).
5. Silva et al. (2021).
6. This chapter considers the overall effects of the pandemic, which include the effect of the health shock and the associated policy responses. Some differences across countries could, therefore, reflect differences in the intensity of countries' responses.
7. These estimates are based largely on employment data from national accounts, covering 88 developing countries and 75 percent of the global population. The data cover 76.3 percent of the population of high-income countries, 85.6 percent of upper-middle-income countries, and 74.3 percent of lower-middle-income countries. Low-income countries are not included because data coverage is low, representing only 15.2 percent of the population of this group and including only three countries: Mozambique, Rwanda, and Uganda.
8. The data span the 2012–21 period in most countries and are generally available on a quarterly basis. One of the countries analyzed (Ethiopia) is a low-income country; three (Pakistan, the Philippines, and Vietnam) are lower-middle-income countries; and the other eight are upper-middle-income countries. In addition to regional representation, the availability of quarterly microdata for 2011–21 determined the choice of countries.

9. Ferreira and Schady (2009).
10. FAWE Uganda Chapter (2021).
11. Zulaika et al. (2022).
12. Baird et al. (2022).
13. Kaestner and Yarnoff (2011); Maclean (2015).
14. See Blakemore and Choudhury (2006); Crone (2009); Duflo (2012); Lloyd and Young (2009); Thomas, Knowland, and Rogers (2020).
15. Ji, Saylor, and Earle (2021).
16. Chang, Tomaso, and Nelson (2021).
17. Lavigne-Cerván et al. (2021).
18. Appelhans et al. (2021).
19. Brodeur, Grigoryeva, and Kattan (2021); Silverio-Murillo et al. (2021).
20. Chang, Tomaso, and Nelson (2021).
21. Asanov et al. (2021).
22. Torres et al. (2017).
23. Kenya, Presidential Policy and Strategy Unit and Population Council (2021).
24. Biddlecom et al. (2008); Jukes, Simmons, and Bundy (2008).
25. For evidence on Sierra Leone, see Bandiera et al. (2019a, 2019b, 2020). For evidence on Sierra Leone, Guinea, and Liberia, see Elston et al. (2017) and UNDP (2015).
26. Elston et al. (2017).
27. Zulaika et al. (2022).
28. Jones et al. (2021).
29. Baird et al. (2022).
30. Buso et al. (2020); Terrier, Chen, and Sutter (2021).
31. Jones et al. (2022).
32. The percentages reported refer to the forgone revenue and additional spending in the form of macro-economic support as a percentage of GDP during 2020 in response to the COVID-19 pandemic using International Monetary Fund (IMF) data (IMF Fiscal Affairs Department, "Fiscal Monitor Database of Country Fiscal Measures in Response to the COVID-19 Pandemic," October 2021).
33. Unemployment benefits payable to workers subject to job losses were used by 43 percent of the countries covered. These benefits mainly consisted of changes in severance payments, dismissal procedures, hiring flexibility, working conditions, leave policy, and labor inspections. In some cases, they were extended to informal and self-employed workers who were not previously eligible, either because of their type of work or because they did not satisfy the contribution requirements to qualify. Countries with a more formal workforce and existing unemployment benefits systems were more likely to reform unemployment benefits and labor regulations in response to the pandemic.
34. Authors' calculations using Asenjo and Pignatti (2019).
35. This inventory covered 217 countries (88 high-income countries, 58 upper-middle-income countries, 46 lower-middle-income countries, and 25 low-income countries), as well as 819 policies or programs on income support, 287 on active labor market policies, 405 on labor regulations, and 1,670 on firm liquidity support. See Gentilini et al. (2020) for a review of social protection programs expansion during the pandemic.
36. OECD (2020).
37. Aiyar and Dao (2021). See Neumark (2011) for an evaluation of the effects of employment subsidies and other employment policies implemented during the 2008–09 global financial crisis in the United States; Cahuc, Kramarz, and Nevoux (2021) for a review of short-time work compensation schemes; and Bruhn (2020) for evidence on Mexico.
38. Bishop and Day (2020). In Switzerland, Kopp and Siegenthaler (2021) find that short-time job retention schemes prevented a large number of dismissals and significantly reduced the incidence of long-term unemployment. Interestingly, results indicate that employment effects were mostly driven by a reduction in dismissals among firms that would otherwise have experienced mass layoffs. In France, the

short-term job retention scheme was evaluated using the proximity of a firm to other firms that had used a similar type of program during the Great Recession. In this setting, Cahuc, Kramarz, and Nevoux (2021) find large and significant employment effects of these types of programs. In Italy, a study exploiting plausibly exogenous variation in program eligibility rules based on the interaction between industry and firm size finds that supported firms experienced a 40 percent reduction in hours worked per employee, which was met by an increase of similar magnitude in the number of headcount employees (Giupponi and Landais 2018). For a review of evidence on the effects of job retention schemes in high-income countries, see Giupponi, Landais, and Lapeyre (2022) and OECD (2021).

39. Ando et al. (2022). During the design of these programs, several trade-offs appeared. Should the programs cover all workers or only some? How should the programs select those who are supported, and how long should the support last? Should the support be directed to unemployment rather than to employment—that is, should it protect the job or the worker (independently of the job)? Do the programs lead to long-term effects on firms (that paid a part of the wage subsidy)? How large should the firm contribution be? Did programs that lasted after lockdowns reduce growth prospects by hindering resource allocation toward expanding firms and sectors?

40. World Bank (2022b).

41. Guerrero-Amezaga et al. (2022).

42. Bonomo, Brito, and Martins (2014).

43. Carranza et al. (2020).

44. World Bank, Social Protection and Jobs Responses to COVID-19 Tracker, https://openknowledge.worldbank .org/handle/10986/33635.

45. World Bank, Social Protection and Jobs Responses to COVID-19 Tracker, https://openknowledge.worldbank .org/handle/10986/33635.

46. Carranza et al. (2020).

47. Contreras et al. (2022).

48. ILO, World Bank, and UNESCO (2021).

49. ILO, World Bank, and UNESCO (2021).

50. Hoftijzer et al. (2020); World Bank, ILO, and UNESCO (forthcoming). TVET centers developed new courses to train workers or volunteers to support health care professionals; raise awareness about protective and preventive measures, health and safety regulations, hygiene, and infection control; and generate trained workers for the production, repair, and maintenance of medical equipment or for care services (as in China, Ecuador, Haiti, India, Nepal, Trinidad and Tobago, Uruguay, and Vietnam). Many countries reported measures to tackle the pandemic-related shortage of workers in information and communications technology (ICT) and related services (as in Moldova and Sri Lanka) or to train workers necessary to produce personal protective equipment or call center operators for health support services (as in Indonesia).

51. World Bank, ILO, and UNESCO (forthcoming).

52. A review conducted before the pandemic of 39 mental health trials in low- and middle-income countries captured 238 effect estimates on various economic outcomes (related to income, employment, education, and many others). It found that over half were positive and statistically significant. The trials typically included some combination of a psychosocial and pharmacological intervention (Lund et al. 2020).

53. Vlassopoulos et al. (2021).

54. See Kluve et al. (2016); McKenzie (2017).

55. Card, Kluve, and Weber (2018).

56. Card, Kluve, and Weber (2018).

57. A key argument made in this chapter is that a setback for young people in their employment experience carries long-term effects (scarring, no accumulation of social skills on the job, and so on). Thus even when youth and adult employment rate developments converge (recovery or nonrecovery), there could be a role for youth-focused policies to address potential long-term effects in the affected cohorts. This possibility implies that, in addition to focusing on promoting general demand-side policies, countries could also promote policies or dimensions of policies that favor youth employment. This should apply to all three categories of countries.

58. Miller et al. (2021).
59. Yuan (2021).
60. Carr and Stewart (2019).
61. Deming (2022).
62. For further details on this methodology, see Isaacs et al. (forthcoming).

REFERENCES

Aaronson, D. 1998. "Using Sibling Data to Estimate the Impact of Neighborhoods on Children's Educational Outcomes." *Journal of Human Resources* 33 (4): 915–46.

Aiyar, M. S., and M. C. Dao. 2021. *The Effectiveness of Job-Retention Schemes: COVID-19 Evidence from the German States.* Washington, DC: International Monetary Fund.

Altonji, J. G., L. B. Kahn, and J. D. Speer. 2016. "Cashier or Consultant? Entry Labor Market Conditions, Field of Study, and Career Success." *Journal of Labor Economics* 34 (S1): S361–401.

Ando, S., R. Balakrishnan, B. Gruss, J. J. Hallaert, L. B. F. Jirasavetakul, K. Kirabaeva, N. Klein, et al. 2022. "European Labor Markets and the COVID-19 Pandemic: Fallout and the Path Ahead." Departmental Paper No. 2022/004, European Department, International Monetary Fund, Washington, DC.

Appelhans, B. M., A. S. Thomas, G. I. Roisman, C. Booth-LaForce, and M. E. Bleil. 2021. "Preexisting Executive Function Deficits and Change in Health Behaviors during the COVID-19 Pandemic." *International Journal of Behavioral Medicine* 28 (6): 813–19.

Asanov, I., F. Flores, D. McKenzie, M. Mensmann, and M. Schulte. 2021. "Remote-Learning, Time-Use, and Mental Health of Ecuadorian High-School Students during the COVID-19 Quarantine." *World Development* 138: 105225.

Asenjo, A., and C. Pignatti. 2019. "Unemployment Insurance Schemes around the World: Evidence and Policy Options." International Labour Office, Geneva.

Baird, S., M. Murphy, J. Seager, N. Jones, A. Malhotra, S. Alheiwidi, G. Emirie, et al. 2022. "Intersecting Disadvantages for Married Adolescents: Life after Marriage Pre– and Post–COVID-19 in Contexts of Displacement." *Journal of Adolescent Health* 70 (3): S86–S96.

Bandiera, O., N. Buehren, M. Goldstein, I. Rasul, and A. Smurra. 2019a. "Empowering Adolescent Girls in a Crisis Context: Lessons from Sierra Leone in the Time of Ebola." Gender Innovation Lab Policy Brief No. 34, World Bank, Washington, DC.

Bandiera, O., N. Buehren, M. Goldstein, I. Rasul, and A. Smurra. 2019b. "The Economic Lives of Young Women in the Time of Ebola: Lessons from an Empowerment Program." Policy Research Working Paper 8760, World Bank, Washington, DC.

Bandiera, O., N. Buehren, M. Goldstein, I. Rasul, and A. Smurra. 2020. "Do School Closures during an Epidemic Have Persistent Effects? Evidence from Sierra Leone in the Time of Ebola." J-PAL Working Paper, Abdul Latif Jameel Poverty Action Lab, Cambridge, MA.

Bell, D. N., and D. G. Blanchflower. 2011. "Young People and the Great Recession." *Oxford Review of Economic Policy* 27 (2): 241–67.

Biddlecom, A., R. Gregory, C. B. Lloyd, and B. S. Mensch. 2008. "Associations between Premarital Sex and Leaving School in Four Sub-Saharan African Countries." *Studies in Family Planning* 39 (4): 337–50.

Bishop, J., and I. Day. 2020. "How Many Jobs Did JobKeeper Keep?" Research Discussion Paper 2020-07, Reserve Bank of Australia, Sydney.

Blakemore, S. J., and S. Choudhury. 2006. "Development of the Adolescent Brain: Implications for Executive Function and Social Cognition." *Journal of Child Psychology and Psychiatry* 47 (3-4): 296–312.

Bonomo, M. A., R. D. Brito, and B. S. Martins. 2014. "Macroeconomic and Financial Consequences of the After-Crisis Government-Driven Credit Expansion in Brazil." Working Paper 378, Banco Central do Brasil, Rio de Janeiro.

Brodeur, A., I. Grigoryeva, and L. Kattan. 2021. "Stay-at-Home Orders, Social Distancing, and Trust." *Journal of Population Economics* 34 (4): 1321–54.

Bruhn, M. 2020. "Can Wage Subsidies Boost Employment in the Wake of an Economic Crisis? Evidence from Mexico." *Journal of Development Studies* 56 (8): 1558–77.

Buso, I. M., S. De Caprariis, D. Di Cagno, L. Ferrari, V. Larocca, F. Marazzi, L. Panaccione, et al. 2020. "The Effects of COVID-19 Lockdown on Fairness and Cooperation: Evidence from a Lablike Experiment." *Economics Letters* 196 (C): 109577.

Cahuc, P., F. Kramarz, and S. Nevoux. 2021. "The Heterogeneous Impact of Short-Time Work: From Saved Jobs to Windfall Effects." CEPR Discussion Paper 16168, Center for Economic and Policy Research, Washington, DC.

Card, D., J. Kluve, and A. Weber. 2018. "What Works? A Meta Analysis of Recent Active Labor Market Program Evaluations." *Journal of the European Economic Association* 16 (3): 894–931.

Carr, K. L., and M. W. Stewart. 2019. "Effectiveness of School-Based Health Center Delivery of a Cognitive Skills Building Intervention in Young, Rural Adolescents: Potential Applications for Addiction and Mood." *Journal of Pediatric Nursing* 47: 23–29.

Carranza, E., T. Farole, U. Gentilini, M. Morgandi, T. Packard, I. Santos, and M. Weber. 2020. "Managing the Employment Impacts of the COVID-19 Crisis: Policy Options for Relief and Restructuring." Jobs Working Paper No. 49, World Bank, Washington, DC.

Chang, O., C. Tomaso, and T. Nelson. 2021. "Components of Executive Function as Predictors of Youth Mental Health during COVID-19." Media Hub, University of Nebraska-Lincoln. https://mediahub.unl.edu/media/17408.

Contreras, S., M. D. Delis, A. Ghosh, and I. Hasan. 2022. "Bank Failures, Local Business Dynamics, and Government Policy." *Small Business Economics* 58 (4): 1823–51.

Crone, E. A. 2009. "Executive Functions in Adolescence: Inferences from Brain and Behavior." *Developmental Science* 12 (6): 825–30.

Deming, D. J. 2022. "Four Facts about Human Capital." *Journal of Economic Perspectives* 36 (3): 75–102.

Duflo, E. 2012. "Women Empowerment and Economic Development." *Journal of Economic Literature* 50 (4): 1051–79.

Elston, J. W., C. Cartwright, P. Ndumbi, and J. Wright. 2017. "The Health Impact of the 2014–15 Ebola Outbreak." *Public Health* 143: 60–70.

FAWE (Forum for African Women Educationalists) Uganda Chapter. 2021. "Research Findings on the Situation of, and Impact of, COVID-19 on School Going Girls and Young Women in Uganda." FAWE Uganda Chapter, Kampala.

Ferreira, F. H., and N. Schady. 2009. "Aggregate Economic Shocks, Child Schooling, and Child Health." *World Bank Research Observer* 24 (2): 147–81.

Gentilini, U., M. Almenfi, I. Orton, and P. Dale. 2020. "Social Protection and Jobs Responses to COVID-19: A Real-Time Review of Country Measures." World Bank, Washington, DC.

Giupponi, G., and C. Landais. 2018. "Subsidizing Labor Hoarding in Recessions: The Employment and Welfare Effects of Short-Term Work." CEP Discussion Paper 1580, Centre for Economic Performance, London School of Economics and Political Science.

Giupponi, G., C. Landais, and A. Lapeyre. 2022. "Should We Insure Workers or Jobs during Recessions?" *Journal of Economic Perspectives* 36 (2): 29–54.

Guerrero-Amezaga, M. E., J. E. Humphries, C. A. Neilson, N. Shimberg, and G. Ulyssea. 2022. "Small Firms and the Pandemic: Evidence from Latin America." *Journal of Development Economics* 155: 102775.

Hoftijzer, M., V. Levin, I. Santos, and M. Weber. 2020. "TVET Systems' Response to COVID-19: Challenges and Opportunities." Policy Note, World Bank, Washington, DC.

ILO (International Labour Organization), World Bank, and UNESCO (United Nations Educational, Scientific, and Cultural Organization). 2021. *Skills Development in the Time of COVID-19: Taking Stock of the Initial Responses in Technical and Vocational Education and Training.* Geneva: ILO and World Bank.

Isaacs, M., D. Parra, N. Schady, and J. Silva. Forthcoming. "The Impact of COVID-19 on Labor Markets in Developing Countries." World Bank, Washington, DC.

Jacobson, L. S., R. J. LaLonde, and D. G. Sullivan. 1993. "Earnings Losses of Displaced Workers." *American Economic Review* 83 (4): 685–709.

Ji, X., J. Saylor, and F. S. Earle. 2021. "Sufficient Sleep Attenuates COVID-19 Pandemic-Related Executive Dysfunction in Late Adolescents and Young Adults." *Sleep Medicine* 85: 21–24.

Jones, N., S. Baird, B. Abu Hamad, Z. A. Bhutta, E. Oakley, M. Shah, J. Sadji, et al. 2022. "Compounding Inequalities: Adolescent Psychosocial Wellbeing and Resilience among Refugee and Host Communities in Jordan during the COVID-19 Pandemic." *PLoS ONE* 17 (2): e0261773.

Jones, N., G. Guglielmi, A. Małachowska, B. Abu Hamad, and W. Yadete, with S. Abu Hamad, E. Abu Hamra, F. Alam, S. Alheiwidi, T. Alabbadi, N. Al-Redaisy, W. Amaireh, et al. 2021. *"Some Got Married, Others Don't Want to Attend School as They Are Involved in Income-Generation": Adolescent Experiences following COVID-19 Lockdowns in Low- and Middle-Income Countries.* London: GAGE (Gender and Adolescence: Global Evidence).

Jukes, M., S. Simmons, and D. Bundy. 2008. "Education and Vulnerability: The Role of Schools in Protecting Young Women and Girls from HIV in Southern Africa." *AIDS* 22 (Suppl. 4): S41–S56.

Kaestner, R., and B. Yarnoff. 2011. "Long-Term Effects of Minimum Legal Drinking Age Laws on Adult Alcohol Use and Driving Fatalities." *Journal of Law and Economics* 54 (2): 325–63.

Kahn, L. B. 2010. "The Long-Term Labor Market Consequences of Graduating from College in a Bad Economy." *Labour Economics* 17 (2): 303–16.

Kenya, Presidential Policy and Strategy Unit, and Population Council. 2021. *Promises to Keep: Impact of COVID-19 on Adolescents in Kenya.* Nairobi: Presidential Policy and Strategy Unit (Kenya) and Population Council.

Kluve, J., S. Puerto, D. A. Robalino, J. Romero, F. Rother, J. Stöterau, F. Weidenkaff, et al. 2016. "Do Youth Employment Programs Improve Labor Market Outcomes? A Systematic Review." IZA Discussion Paper 10263, Institute of Labor Economics (IZA), Bonn.

Kopp, D., and M. Siegenthaler. 2021. "Short-Time Work and Unemployment in and after the Great Recession." *Journal of the European Economic Association* 19 (4): 2283–321.

Krugman, P. 2009. "Free to Lose." *New York Times*, November 12, 2009, A31.

Lavigne-Cerván, R., B. Costa-López, R. Juárez-Ruiz de Mier, M. Real-Fernández, M. Sánchez-Muñoz de León, and I. Navarro-Soria. 2021. "Consequences of COVID-19 Confinement on Anxiety, Sleep and Executive Functions of Children and Adolescents in Spain." *Frontiers in Psychology* 12: 565516.

Lloyd, C., and J. Young. 2009. *New Lessons: The Power of Educating Adolescent Girls—A Girls Count Report on Adolescent Girls.* New York: Population Council.

Lund, C., K. Orkin, M. Witte, T. Davies, J. Haushofer, J. Bass, and V. Patel. 2020. "Economic Impacts of Mental Health Interventions in Low- and Middle-Income Countries: A Systematic Review and Meta-analysis." https://custom.cvent.com/4E741122FD8B4A1B97E483EC8BB51CC4/files/05fc213973d84c45b58741a9a137b574.pdf.

Maclean, J. C. 2015. "The Lasting Effects of Leaving School in an Economic Downturn on Alcohol Use." *ILR Review* 68 (1): 120–52.

McKenzie, D. 2017. "How Effective Are Active Labor Market Policies in Developing Countries? A Critical Review of Recent Evidence." *World Bank Research Observer* 32 (2): 127–54.

Miller, R. L., M. Moran, L. B. Shomaker, N. Seiter, N. Sanchez, M. Verros, S. Rayburn, et al. 2021. "Health Effects of COVID-19 for Vulnerable Adolescents in a Randomized Controlled Trial." *School Psychology* 36 (5): 293.

Neumark, D. 2011. *Spurring Job Creation in Response to Severe Recessions: Reconsidering Hiring Credits* (No. w16866). Cambridge, MA: National Bureau of Economic Research.

OECD (Organisation for Economic Co-operation and Development). 2020. "Job Retention Schemes during the COVID-19 Lockdown and Beyond." Background document prepared for chapter 1 of *OECD Employment Outlook 2020: COVID-19: From a Health to a Jobs Crisis.* Paris: OECD Publishing.

OECD (Organisation for Economic Co-operation and Development). 2021. *OECD Employment Outlook 2021: Navigating the COVID-19 Crisis and Recovery.* Paris: OECD Publishing.

Oreopoulos, P., T. Von Wachter, and A. Heisz. 2012. "The Short- and Long-Term Career Effects of Graduating in a Recession." *American Economic Journal: Applied Economics* 4 (1): 1–29.

Pritadrajati, D. S., A. C. Kusuma, and S. C. Saxena. 2021. "Scarred for Life: Lasting Consequences of Unemployment and Informal Self-Employment: An Empirical Evidence from Indonesia." *Economic Analysis and Policy* 70: 206–19.

Rothstein, J. 2021. "The Lost Generation? Labor Market Outcomes for Post Great Recession Entrants." *Journal of Human Resources,* June 9. doi: 10.3368/jhr.58.5.092011206R1.

Silva, J., L. D. Sousa, T. G. Packard, and R. Robertson. 2021. *Employment in Crisis: The Path to Better Jobs in a Post–COVID-19 Latin America*. World Bank Latin America and Caribbean Studies. Washington, DC: World Bank.

Silverio-Murillo, A., L. Hoehn-Velasco, A. R. Tirado, and J. R. B. de la Miyar. 2021. "COVID-19 Blues: Lockdowns and Mental Health–Related Google Searches in Latin America." *Social Science and Medicine* 281: 114040.

Terrier, C., D. L. Chen, and M. Sutter. 2021. "COVID-19 within Families Amplifies the Prosociality Gap between Adolescents of High and Low Socioeconomic Status." *Proceedings of the National Academy of Sciences* 118 (46): e2110891118.

Thomas, M. S., V. C. Knowland, and C. Rogers. 2020. "The Science of Adult Literacy." Social Protection and Jobs Discussion Paper No. 2001, World Bank, Washington, DC.

Torres, C., P. Otero, B. Bustamante, V. Blanco, O. Díaz, and F. L. Vázquez. 2017. "Mental Health Problems and Related Factors in Ecuadorian College Students." *International Journal of Environmental Research and Public Health* 14 (5): 530.

UNDP (United Nations Development Programme). 2015. "Confronting the Gender Impact of Ebola Virus Disease in Guinea, Liberia and Sierra Leone." UNDP Africa Policy Note, Vol. 2, No. 1, January 30, UNDP, New York.

Vlassopoulos, M., A. Siddique, T. Rahman, D. Pakrashi, A. Islam, and F. Ahmed. 2021. "Improving Women's Mental Health during a Pandemic." IZA Discussion Paper No. 14786, Institute of Labor Economics (IZA), Bonn.

Von Wachter, T. 2020. "The Persistent Effects of Initial Labor Market Conditions for Young Adults and Their Sources." *Journal of Economic Perspectives* 34 (4): 168–94.

World Bank. 2022a. "Brazil: Income Support for the Poor Affected by Recent Economic Crises (P179365)." Project Appraisal Document, World Bank, Washington, DC.

World Bank. 2022b. *New Approaches to Closing the Fiscal Gap.* LAC Semiannual Update, October 2022. World Bank, Washington, DC.

World Bank, ILO (International Labour Organization), and UNESCO (United Nations Educational, Scientific, and Cultural Organization). Forthcoming. "Building Better TVET Systems: Principles and Practice in Low- and Middle-Income Countries." World Bank, ILO, and UNESCO, Washington, DC, Geneva, and Paris.

Yuan, Y. 2021. "Mindfulness Training on the Resilience of Adolescents under the COVID-19 Epidemic: A Latent Growth Curve Analysis." *Personality and Individual Differences* 172: 110560.

Zulaika, G., M. Bulbarelli, E. Nyothach, A. van Eijk, L. Mason, E. Fwaya, D. Obor, et al. 2022. "Impact of COVID-19 Lockdowns on Adolescent Pregnancy and School Dropout among Secondary Schoolgirls in Kenya." *BMJ Global Health* 7 (1): e007666.

5

RECOVERY AND RESILIENCE

From Human Development Programs to Systems

Ritika D'Souza, Shwetlena Sabarwal, Norbert Schady,
Joana Silva, and Andres Yi Chang

ABSTRACT
This chapter advocates moving away from program-by-program, sector-by-sector efforts and toward a systemwide approach to respond to future shocks to human development (HD). This more comprehensive approach considers responses that cut across health, education, labor, and social protection and puts in place mechanisms that allow policies to adapt to evolving needs quickly and effectively in order to improve human development outcomes at scale. The discussion highlights why having HD systems matters during shocks. It provides examples of what worked in response to the pandemic. And it describes how to create agile, resilient, and adaptive HD systems that can endure, adjust, and respond better to future crises over the medium to long term. Key steps include (1) improving the ability of programs to contract and expand quickly, (2) promoting effective coordination across sectors, (3) using data and technology more effectively, and (4) strengthening the capacity to adapt proven solutions to local conditions. This chapter provides concrete examples of these features at work. While comprehensive HD systems that encompass all sectors and all actors may be aspirational for some countries, the COVID-19 pandemic has shown that taking even small steps toward a more systemic approach to human development will improve the effectiveness of future responses.

A MOMENT OF REFLECTION

It is time to reset. As we build a strong recovery, we must seize the opportunity for change.

—António Guterres, United Nations Secretary-General
Remarks, United Nations General Assembly Special Session[1]

❝

The COVID-19 pandemic eroded multiple dimensions of human capital at critical periods in the life cycle. Young children suffered declines in motor, language, cognitive, and social-emotional development. Unprecedentedly long school closures led to hundreds of millions of children missing at least one year of schooling, an increase in dropouts in some lower-income contexts, and little learning, if any at all, while schools were closed. Many young people either were denied access to the job market or entered it with diminished skills and limited prospects. Unless these losses are addressed, many cohorts that experienced the pandemic will have accumulated much less human capital than they would have otherwise, with repercussions that could last well into adulthood.

Previous chapters have highlighted the policies and programs needed urgently to minimize these COVID-induced losses. For young children, this effort involves prioritizing transfers to households whose income has not recovered, catch-up campaigns for vaccination and nutrition, parenting programs to encourage more cognitive and social-emotional stimulation in the home, efforts to restore and expand coverage of preprimary education, and mental health counseling programs for parents. To reverse learning losses in school-age children, countries should keep schools open to the extent possible and increase instructional time, assess learning, match instruction to students' learning level, promote catch-up campaigns for students who have fallen furthest behind, and streamline the curriculum to focus on foundational learning. To minimize dropouts, governments should track students at risk of dropping out and alleviate financial constraints to school attendance. For youth, appropriate policies will vary according to the extent to which both adult and youth employment have recovered. In countries where neither adult nor youth employment has recovered, policies should include efforts to encourage firms to start hiring again. In countries where adult employment has recovered but youth employment has not, support for training, job intermediation, entrepreneurship, and workforce development programs adapted to youth is key. Implementing these corrective measures is no small task and will require strong political commitment and institutional capacity. But the cost of inaction could be catastrophic. Countries risk losing several generations of children and young people—the workforce of tomorrow.

At the same time, reversing the immediate consequences of the pandemic is only part of the battle. The response to COVID-19 has thrown into sharp relief long-standing fissures in human development (HD) systems and service delivery. And as new crises loom—including the war in Ukraine, other conflicts, and climate shocks—countries must reflect on lessons from the pandemic to reimagine and rebuild systems that do a better job of nurturing and protecting human development in the future. Only by addressing systemic constraints can countries break out of the constant cycle of shocks and recovery to make meaningful progress. In this case, an ounce of prevention is truly worth a pound of cure.

A central lesson reinforced during the pandemic is that human development involves multiple dimensions that build on and complement one another: HD systems that recognize and exploit these connections will fare better than a set of individual programs that cannot make these links. The COVID-19 crisis provided a powerful illustration of how a health shock can have ripple effects across dimensions as diverse as cognitive development, learning, livelihoods, and mental health. And responses that focused entirely on containing the spread of the disease were likely to come at the cost of other important outcomes. Given the multidimensional, sequential, and cumulative nature of human capital accumulation, multisectoral and cohesive HD can be more effective at supporting human capital formation during "normal times," but also can do a better job of protecting human capital more comprehensively during the next inevitable crisis, whether it is another pandemic or some other aggregate shock.

Complementing previous chapters, this chapter adds a medium- to long-term agenda for the policy response to the pandemic. It makes the case for countries to invest in cohesive and multisectoral HD systems that are agile, resilient, and adaptative in response to shocks. Countries already have in place a menu of policies in health, social protection, labor, and education. Going beyond these sector-specific programs and implementing some of the interventions recommended in previous chapters requires coordination across sectors (such as putting in place targeted support for youth not working and not in school and targeted parenting and nutrition supplementation support for families with young children) (see figure 5.1). These interventions can play a critical role in addressing the multidimensional effects of the pandemic on human capital. Strong health, social protection, labor, and education systems, complemented by integrated HD systems that coordinate policies and activities across sectors, can serve as key enablers in implementing cross-sectoral interventions at scale.

The key attributes of the type of systems described in this chapter—coordinating across sectors, using data effectively, leveraging technology, and tailoring solutions to local contexts—are desirable even in the absence of crisis, but they also can make critical contributions to protecting human capital during shocks.

FIGURE 5.1 Human development systems that integrate policies and activities across social sectors are more impactful

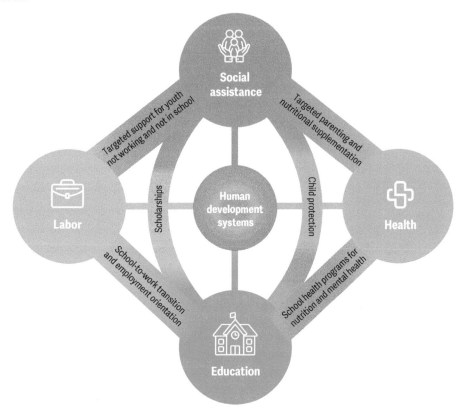

Source: Original figure for this publication.

In the short term, as countries continue to recover from the COVID-19 crisis, HD systems can serve to integrate and implement programs from the menu of responses highlighted in chapters 2 to 4. In the longer term, these systems can better support individuals to reach their human development potential, even in the face of crises.

WHAT ARE THE CRITICAL COMPONENTS OF AN HD SYSTEM THAT CAN RESPOND TO SYSTEMIC SHOCKS?

When building a bridge, the quality of different parts of the bridge matter, but how the different parts are put together also matters. To understand why HD systems are particularly important for the formation and protection of human capital, it is useful to return to three central ideas from chapter 1. First, *the construction of human capital is a cumulative process*. Investments today will have higher returns if they are followed by investments tomorrow. Conversely, disinvestments at any point in the life cycle—as occurred during the pandemic—can affect people over their entire lives. Second, *human capital is multidimensional*. As such, the actions to build and protect human capital fall outside the mandate of any single sector or ministry (education, health, social protection, and labor, at a minimum). Moreover, the returns to investments in one dimension—say, a program to improve teacher quality—may be limited if other dimensions are not taken into account—for example, if children in school are hungry. Third, *many actors are involved in building human capital*—families, different levels of government, the private sector, nongovernmental organizations (NGOs), and civil society organizations, to name a few. These three characteristics of human capital accumulation mean that it is important to coordinate the interventions of different actors. This coordination is particularly critical and difficult when a systemic shock affects multiple dimensions of well-being, as was the case during the pandemic.

An HD system builds on existing sectoral systems and individual programs.[2] It then takes a broader look at how investments in human capital should be coordinated and complementarities exploited. To achieve this coordination, these systems should have some features that are important in the absence of a crisis but that can be especially important in responding to an unexpected shock.

HD systems should be agile, resilient, and adaptive. Systemic shocks—whether a pandemic, a natural disaster, or a macroeconomic crisis—are by their very nature largely unpredictable. The only certainty is that they will happen. An HD system needs to be agile—to be able to jump into action as soon as a shock strikes. It should be resilient—that is, critical services should not be interrupted when a shock hits (although the mechanisms by which critical services are delivered may have to change temporarily). HD systems should also be adaptive. During a crisis, circumstances change quickly. A well-functioning HD system should be able to adapt accordingly—for example, using new information to see who has been hardest hit and whether they are receiving the services that are indispensable to them.

HD systems should coordinate efficiently across sectors. Services are generally provided by individual sectors or programs. Thus, in "normal" times, the education ministry (or a local authority charged with this function) provides in-service training to teachers, distributes textbooks, monitors school enrollment, and may implement nationwide tests to assess student learning. Interactions with other sectors—for example, to monitor students' school attendance if families are receiving conditional cash transfers—may exist, but they tend to be limited and are not central to the function of the ministry in question. Much the same occurs in other sectors such as health and social protection.

During a crisis, however, coordination across sectors is indispensable, and there needs to be a way to consider and deal with trade-offs. Consider, for example, the closing of schools during the pandemic. Looked at strictly from the point of view of health, very long school closures probably appeared to be a reasonable policy option. However, this perspective did not take account of the deep losses of learning. In this case, there was a need to consider *both* the mortality risks from opening schools *and* the loss of human capital that school closures implied and how to assess these competing risks.

HD systems should use data and technology effectively. Data and technology are important for the delivery of services—and never more so than during a systemic shock. Data systems should be interoperable, so that—ideally—one could establish not only whether a household is receiving income transfers, but also whether children in that household are attending school and whether mothers of young children are receiving postnatal checkups and their children have received vaccinations. New data should be fed into the system regularly and automatically.

There should be smart use of technology—whether to make payments to households or transfer resources to frontline providers. The pandemic showed that investments in technology can help governments deliver at least some services when in-person delivery is not possible. However, technology by itself is no panacea, as made clear by the limitations of remote schooling, especially in countries that had not invested in technology before the pandemic struck, but even in those that had.

HD systems should tailor proven solutions to local conditions. In addressing gaps in human capital accumulation, governments can look to programs that have worked in other countries. However, evidence that an intervention was successful in one context does not ensure that it will work if replicated in a different setting. Adapting policies and programs to the local context is essential for their success. National, regional, and local governments should tailor policies to address the specific needs and challenges of their constituents and consider the overarching context—including HD programs in other sectors—in which these policies are to be implemented. Doing so may mean adapting delivery mechanisms (such as reaching people via phone or text messages rather than in person) or ensuring that important actors are aligned (such as workers' unions and the private sector). Moreover, adapting proven solutions to local contexts requires iterative learning. No silver bullets can be imported to solve problems. Trial and error with a view to improving program design will be part of the process.

What do HD systems look like in practice? The final section of this chapter describes design features that are the foundation for well-functioning HD systems, capable of responding effectively when there is a sudden, unexpected shock. Before discussing how to build up such systems moving forward, however, the chapter first turns to how well systems responded during the pandemic.

HOW DID HD SYSTEMS FARE DURING THE PANDEMIC?

During this pandemic, the most vulnerable have been the hardest hit … We must increase our resilience. We must work together and take an integrated approach to the health, hunger, education, climate, and equity crises—no one is safe from COVID-19 until everyone is safe.

—Volkan Bozkir, President of the UN General Assembly
Remarks, UN General Assembly, 2021[3]

❝

In the wake of the COVID-19 pandemic, policy makers were faced with the herculean task of containing the spread of the disease while addressing the many disruptions and challenges it engendered. All of this had to happen in an environment where the understanding of the COVID-19 virus itself—and of the ripple effects of lockdowns and other restrictions—was rapidly evolving.

Countries responded to the pandemic in different ways. Some countries quickly expanded existing programs that operated independently and had minimal coordination with other programs. The agility of these responses varied, depending, for example, on the existence of registries that included income and demographic information on current beneficiaries and vulnerable nonbeneficiaries or the presence of digital payment systems. Few of the responses, however, coordinated with other programs, and fewer still were adaptive. Some countries were able to reconfigure programs substantially or create temporary programs that coordinated actions within a specific sector. For new programs, scaling down once urgent needs were met was often challenging due to the lack of institutionalized mechanisms and established rules. Moreover, because they were new, some programs had not been stress-tested and had difficulty operating effectively at scale. Finally, a limited number of countries were able to take a more coordinated cross-sectoral approach to human development. This coordination was challenging at times. But when successful, it led to more adequate support for hard-hit groups with multiple needs. Overall, countries that had made prior investments in strengthening institutions, promoting the effective use of data, creating evidence-based HD programs, and fostering resilient and adaptive systems were the best positioned to confront the challenges brought about by the pandemic (see box 5.1). The discussion that follows provides examples for each set of responses.[4]

BOX 5.1 Relying on prior investments to confront future crises better

As countries look to the future with the certainty that the COVID-19 pandemic will not be the last global shock they experience, it is worth underscoring that countries that make deliberate investments in resilient systems will be best placed to face crises. For instance, countries like Argentina, Brazil, Colombia, Ghana, and Morocco, all of which introduced new social assistance measures during the pandemic, relied on prior investments by using social registries to identify vulnerable households at different income thresholds for eligibility. Indonesia relied on its single hospital-claims-processing system to engage the private sector in the public health response to COVID-19. And, over a decade, Uruguay's remote-learning program had developed technological infrastructure and built capacity that allowed for a rapid pivot to online learning during pandemic lockdowns.

Countries that had made prior investments in collecting reliable health and population data were also well served by these data systems during the pandemic. In Guinea, for example, a health monitoring system developed to address low vaccination rates during a measles epidemic in 2019 was instrumental in detecting the first cases of COVID-19 in 2020. During the measles outbreak, a multidisciplinary team (composed mainly of epidemiologists and anthropologists) identified gaps between vaccination targets reported in the health information system and those identified in the field. In response, the government set up teams to visit households in high-risk prefectures to provide information and vaccinations and to strengthen daily reporting to the National Health Security Agency. In addition to limiting the spread of COVID-19, the system also played a significant role in quickly containing the 2021 Ebola outbreak in Guinea.

Coverage of existing individual programs was expanded quickly to provide critical support to at-risk populations

The COVID-19 crisis exacerbated long-standing inequalities within countries. While some sections of society were able to comply with lockdown restrictions and prevent COVID infection, for others, the threat of infection was coupled with a loss of livelihood, food insecurity, lack of stable and affordable housing, and lack of access to health care. Governments needed to identify and provide support rapidly to vulnerable populations—a number that grew steadily during the pandemic.

Many countries *expanded existing programs developed for normal times* to extend coverage to individuals or households that had been badly affected by the pandemic but that would not have met the traditional criteria to be included as beneficiaries (see box 5.2). For instance, Argentina relied on expansions to Programa Sumar—the successor to Plan Nacer, first launched in 2004—to ensure access to health care for the unemployed. Programa Sumar provides universal health coverage for the uninsured and relies on regular cross-checks of social security databases and active outreach to ensure continuity of coverage for persons who lose their job. During the COVID-19 pandemic and after initial disruptions of the provision of essential services due to lockdowns, Programa Sumar's effective coverage—measured by the number of people who received at least one priority health service over the previous 12 months—increased by about 20 percent.

BOX 5.2 How countries expanded their social protection programs during the COVID-19 pandemic

Starting in March 2020 when lockdowns began, social protection rapidly became a fundamental component of countries' COVID-19 response. This expansion included around 3,900 social protection and labor measures in 223 jurisdictions globally (figure B5.2.1).[a] This unprecedented expansion of social protection was built on underlying systems and existing infrastructure, which allowed some countries to respond better to the pandemic than others.

FIGURE B5.2.1 The number of social protection measures introduced and extended grew rapidly during the height of the COVID-19 pandemic in 2020 and 2021

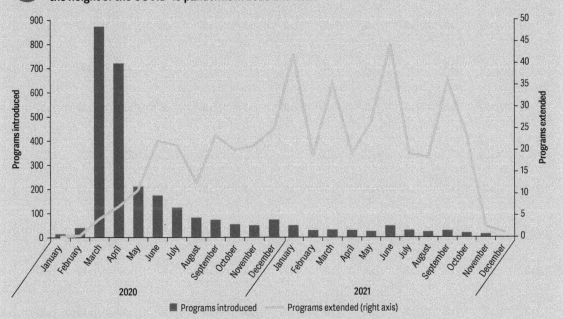

Source: Data from Gentilini et al. 2022.
Note: The figure covers 223 jurisdictions around the world.

The pandemic underscored the importance of adaptive systems, including adaptive social protection systems, that can deliver not only social protection programs but also other programs related to health, education, labor, and beyond. For example, existing social protection delivery systems were instrumental in massively scaling up social assistance interventions that reached nearly 1.4 billion people (17 percent of the world's population) in 2020–21. Having cross-sectoral social protection instruments in place (such as cash and in-kind transfers, fee waivers, and public works) helped people to meet their basic needs and access basic services. This support, in turn, helped to preserve human capital during the pandemic.

A review of more than 30 cross-country and country-specific studies finds that social protection interventions attenuated the adverse effects of the pandemic to varying degrees. Some offset all or most of the pandemic's negative impacts, and most partially mitigated these effects.[b] In Ethiopia, for instance, the Productive Safety Net Programme largely mitigated food insecurity,[c] while in Argentina assistance amounting to 1.48 percent of gross domestic product (GDP) helped to keep 1 million people from falling into poverty.[d] In Colombia, the income support program Ingreso Solidario mitigated more than half of the drop in food consumption for households whose member(s) lost a job or significant earnings,[e] and cash

(continued)

BOX 5.2 *(continued)*

transfers amounting to 0.87 percent of GDP kept an estimated 200,000 people out of poverty.[f] In Togo, assistance improved access to health care services for the most vulnerable households.[g]

To roll out large population-based assistance efforts, governments used a variety of methods to identify additional beneficiaries.[h] Social registries and registries of beneficiaries helped significantly and were used for 22 percent of programs (such as in Brazil, Ecuador, Mauritania, Pakistan, and Peru). Other administrative data and registries also played a large role and were tapped by 27 percent of programs. Their usefulness suggests the need for countries to step up efforts to integrate data sources across administrative units and to use social security and tax records. Other methods to identify beneficiaries included using the civil registry (7 percent) and databases of informal workers and the self-employed (6 percent). The remaining programs (35 percent) collected new data from applicants through open registration and enrollment campaigns. This practice, which is slower than using preexisting data, indicates the need for countries to improve their identification practices and prepare for future shocks.[i]

For example, Morocco, whose social registry covers 26 percent of the population, reached more than 5 million informal worker households (78 percent of the population) who were identified by leveraging the database for the RAMED health insurance waiver program. Guatemala relied on data about household electricity consumption. India used data on more than 200 million low-income women for whom bank accounts had been opened in a drive to increase financial inclusion. Togo used a recently generated voter database that covered 95 percent of adults and included information on occupation, which the government used to target workers in the informal sector. Namibia checked the civil registry against income tax records. Colombia leveraged the temporary Ingreso Solidario program to select an additional 3 million beneficiaries, which nearly doubled the number of people receiving social assistance compared to levels before the pandemic.[j] These examples from different countries and regions around the world exemplify the importance of having adaptive systems that can be expanded quickly during future shocks.

a. Gentilini et al. (2022).
b. Gentilini (2022).
c. Abay et al. (2020); Duchoslav and Hirvonen (2021).
d. Blofield, Giambruno, and Pribble (2021); Blofield, Hoffmann, and Llanos (2020); Blofield, Lustig, and Trasberg (2021); Lustig et al. (2020).
e. Gallego et al. (2021).
f. Blofield, Giambruno, and Pribble (2021); Blofield, Hoffmann, and Llanos (2020); Blofield, Lustig, and Trasberg (2021); Lustig et al. (2020).
g. Tossou (2021).
h. Hammad et al. (2021).
i. Gentilini et al. (2022).
j. UNDP (2020).

> *Temporary cash transfer programs that provided emergency support to households during the pandemic relied heavily on the databases and infrastructure of existing programs to identify beneficiaries rapidly and deliver support.*

Social protection programs, in particular, grew rapidly during the pandemic, reaching nearly 1.4 billion people (17 percent of the world's population) over 2020–21. These programs were at the core of the pandemic response to support the most vulnerable people in most low- and middle-income countries. This response was possible because, before the pandemic, about half of the global population was included in social protection systems or registries. Even though these registries varied in their coverage of the poor and vulnerable and the type of household information collected, countries that used social registries expanded the coverage of social assistance programs three times faster than countries that used identification mechanisms based on other databases, new enrollment, and combinations thereof.[5]

Countries that had made *prior investments in technology were able to expand social assistance coverage more quickly.* During lockdowns, countries relied on technology of varying degrees of sophistication both to identify and to deliver benefits to new beneficiaries. In the Arab Republic of Egypt, two cash transfer programs—Karama and Takaful—that expanded coverage during the pandemic distributed mobile SIM cards and Meeza debit cards to eligible beneficiaries to streamline the delivery of key messages and program benefits. Jordan's cash transfer program, launched in 2019, included a state-of-the-art delivery platform, which allowed automated processes for online registration, data verification, selection of households for field verification, and digital payments. The program made use of an automated data exchange platform that includes more than 30 government entities. The platform was key to delivering emergency cash transfers to nearly 400,000 new households that relied on informal sources of income and had fallen into poverty as a result of the pandemic.

In some countries, *programs built during other shocks were redirected or reactivated* to respond to the needs of the pandemic. Sierra Leone adapted the social safety net systems it had originally set up to respond to Ebola, flooding, and landslides to roll out cash transfers and provide additional types of support during the pandemic. Similarly, Somalia leveraged the Baxnaano social safety net program first introduced by the federal government to provide support to households facing chronic poverty aggravated by climate shocks. In the first three years of the program's implementation, more than 1 million people (about 9 percent of the population) received unconditional cash transfers (US$20 a month per beneficiary household for a three-year cycle). During the pandemic, Baxnaano's built-in shock-responsive features extended this support to more than 2 million people (inclusive of the long-term safety net beneficiaries) who received emergency top-ups.

Existing programs were substantially adapted or temporary programs were created in coordination with other efforts within the same sector

In the face of the pandemic, many countries found existing delivery systems inadequate to meet the increased demand for services and support. Some countries responded with *new temporary measures to support individuals during the pandemic*. In Colombia, for instance, the government introduced the temporary Ingreso Solidario program, supporting an additional 3 million households that would not have been included in permanent social protection schemes due to budgetary restrictions (Colombia Mayor, Familias en Acción, and Jóvenes en Acción programs) or because they would not have been eligible under existing social protection interventions (including low-income households without children or elderly members).

In some cases, countries were able to engage providers beyond the traditional public sector to deliver services. The Indian state of Kerala, for example, contracted more than 300 additional private hospitals under the publicly funded insurance scheme to sustain service delivery during the pandemic. This expansion more than doubled the number of private hospitals in the scheme.

Partnering with local actors was equally important. In Senegal, an exceptional cash transfer program covering 1 million households (around 55 percent of the population) relied on an established network of local NGOs covering the entire country to deliver direct services (see box 5.3 for details).[6]

In some countries, *programs changed the modality of service delivery* in the face of lockdowns and mobility restrictions. Many school feeding programs shifted (or diversified) modalities during school closures from on-site provision to take-home meals or rations, or even vouchers or cash to continue supporting children at risk of malnutrition. Public works programs, which traditionally support physical and manual labor, were extended to new types of work demanded during the pandemic, including raising community awareness of COVID-19 and hygiene, contact tracing, disinfection of public facilities, and vaccination campaigns. Schooling was adapted. Remote learning was implemented in many countries, with various degrees of success in service provision.

A good example is Uruguay, which was able to move from in-person instruction to online learning during pandemic-related school closures. The country began investing in a functional remote-learning program, Plan Ceibal, in 2007. Over the past decade, this program has helped to ensure access to free laptops for students and teachers, has provided them with internet connections, and, critically, has trained teachers in remote instruction.[7] When schools in Uruguay were shut down due to the pandemic in April 2020, the education system had mechanisms in place to reach and help students immediately with remote learning

Engaging providers beyond the traditional public sector was an effective strategy for many countries to ensure the continuity of service delivery during the pandemic. For example, the Indian state of Kerala built on years of previous engagement of the private sector with the state government to contract additional private hospitals during the pandemic. Similarly, India's national insurance program, Ayushman Bharat Pradhan Mantri Jan Arogya Yojana, increased private laboratory testing by covering costs.

Existing contracts and systems between the government of Indonesia and private hospitals also contributed significantly to the country's rapid response to the pandemic. The national health insurance scheme (JKN) contracts both public and private hospitals and had put in place a single hospital-claims-processing system that serviced all contracted hospitals. This system made it easier to use the full capacity of the health system to treat seriously ill patients at no cost to the patient, enabling seamless claims processing for services provided in both public and private hospitals. In Nigeria, the Private Sector Health Alliance partnered with the government to develop the Alliance for Emergency Preparedness and Response (A4EPR) to strengthen preparedness and response capacity for disease outbreaks. During the pandemic, Nigeria quickly scaled up engagement with the private sector by forming the Coalition against COVID-19, which provided additional support to the Nigeria Center for Disease Control and other parts of the government. Partnership with the private sector also enabled adaptiveness, affordability, and scale-up of interventions for surge response.

Collaboration with local stakeholders was also crucial. In Senegal, an exceptional cash transfer program covering 1 million households (around 55 percent of the population) relied on an established network of local nongovernmental organizations covering the entire country to deliver direct services, mobilizing 6,000 community-based agents for direct outreach to beneficiaries. Given the penetration of mobile phones, the program also engaged digital service providers to facilitate digital cash transfers. Experience with the provision of cash transfers digitally in response to drought-related food insecurity, floods, and fires in 2017, 2020, and 2022 was used to inform the design of a program that encompassed different sectors and engaged different actors to deliver services in crises.

as a complement to many other measures. Further, the country recognized that remote learning was not a perfect substitute for in-person instruction and reopened schools after only three months—despite having an established remote-learning platform.

Finally, some countries *combined programs and services within a sector*. For example, Mexico combined income support with training and social security coverage for youths. The country increased income support for participants of a preexisting social assistance program and expanded its Youth Building the Future Program, providing 18- to 29-year-olds who were Not in Education, Employment, or Training with 12 months of workplace training, combined with a monthly allowance and social security coverage. Brazil protected low-wage formal workers by expanding unemployment insurance and providing wage subsidies. In addition, the country protected informal workers at risk of poverty by expanding its Bolsa Familia cash transfer program and providing a new emergency cash transfer.

A cross-sectoral HD systems approach was less common

Truly cross-sectoral responses were rare. When they happened, they mostly took the form of cash assistance. Moreover, most government responses to the pandemic that occurred across sectors were limited to information sharing (not coordinated initiatives) and included few sectors.

Yet there are some examples of successful cross-sectoral coordination. Various countries leveraged their existing school feeding programs to deliver (conditional) cash transfers as well as to continue delivering nutrition assistance as schools closed due to the pandemic. In Tunisia, cash-based transfers were used to assist households with children who were not receiving school meals due to school closures. In Trinidad and Tobago, the government provided children enrolled in the national school feeding program with a temporary food support card, particularly those not covered by another national food support program. In Bangladesh, eligibility for food subsidies, scholarships, and other programs implemented during the COVID-19 pandemic was authenticated with help from civil registration and vital statistics data, highlighting the importance of cross-sectoral platforms.

> *Some countries used existing structures of health, education, and social protection to deliver benefits to other sectors.*

Another successful example of cross-sectoral coordination is Türkiye's Integrated Social Assistance Information System (ISAS) under the Ministry of Family and Social Services. The ISAS builds on a strong e-governance structure and a well-functioning electronic identification system that allows for dynamic entry and exit. Beyond that, it is integrated with more than 25 databases, including databases from the Ministry of Education monitoring education conditionalities and databases concerning the country's universal health insurance scheme. During the pandemic, the government of Türkiye leveraged ISAS to deploy cash transfers to existing beneficiary households and subsequently expanded them to include additional beneficiaries.

Cross-sectoral coordination was one of the biggest challenges to developing a systemic approach to human development programs. Some countries prioritized the formation of cross-sectoral steering committees or developed comprehensive cross-sectoral strategies with some success. For instance, in Moldova, the Commission for Exceptional Situations and the Extraordinary National Commission for Public Health played an essential role in coordinating and planning intersectoral measures to respond to the pandemic at the national level. Likewise, China created a whole-of-government strategy and established a Joint Prevention and Control Mechanism linking 32 ministries for communication, collaboration, and resource mobilization. Mozambique also leveraged a whole-of-government approach to integrate its health and disaster response to COVID-19. However, some of these responses did not include key sectors or coordinate the lockdown measures effectively with economic and income support measures or did not have enough power to balance political pressures. Other risks and challenges with these strategies included diluted responsibilities, lengthy decision-making, and often limited capacity to address complex technical issues.

Generally, programs implemented in response to the pandemic did not look at human development outcomes as a whole and did not consider challenges outside their sector. When the pandemic hit, infection and mortality were most salient. Most countries focused their energies on preventing the spread of the disease and providing treatment. While this focus was critical in the early stages of the pandemic, many countries did not have the tools or systems in place to track the situation as it evolved and adapt their responses to protect human capital more comprehensively. For example, many countries instated lockdowns and restricted mobility to limit the spread of COVID-19, but were slower to put in place support for households that were suddenly deprived of income from work. The lack of a comprehensive approach that also considered the impact of lockdowns on other dimensions of human capital resulted in school closures that were much too long in many countries, given the health risks.

BUILDING AGILE, RESILIENT, AND ADAPTIVE HD SYSTEMS

Intelligence is the ability to adapt to change.

—Stephen Hawking, *A Briefer History of Time*
(Hawking and Mlodinow 2005)

❝

The COVID-19 pandemic has reinforced the importance of building systems that prepare for and prevent global crises and also protect populations when they do occur. With new research documenting a greater probability of novel disease outbreaks,[8] building robust pandemic preparedness and response systems has taken center stage (see box 5.4). At the same time, the pandemic has highlighted the need to move from a host of individual programs to HD systems that can protect people and their human capital during a crisis. These HD systems must be agile (respond quickly), resilient (withstand shocks to continue service delivery), and adaptive (modify program modalities over the duration of the shock and as the shock fades). As noted in the previous section, while the human development policy response to the pandemic was unprecedented, responses that spanned sectors and engaged different actors were rare. So, how can such HD systems be built in the future?

Agile, resilient, and adaptive systems are challenging to build and require considerable political commitment. That said, the review of policy responses during the pandemic can help to identify important characteristics and features that can inform countries as they restructure systems found to be lacking during the COVID-19 crisis. The discussion that follows describes key steps toward building agile, resilient, and adaptive HD systems. These characteristics are beneficial even in the absence of a crisis, but they can be particularly important in mounting a comprehensive HD response during a crisis. They include (1) improving the ability to expand and contract quickly and stress-testing it; (2) promoting interoperability and the capacity of local actors to make decisions in response to changing conditions, along with ensuring effective coordination (mandate and authority) that engages actors at all levels across sectors; (3) using data and technology more effectively; and (4) strengthening the capacity to adapt proven solutions to local conditions.

Improving the ability to expand and contract quickly and stress-testing it

As countries continue to experience the effects of shocks, they will need systems that can reach more people rapidly, provide additional support, or both. At the same time, to conserve scarce resources, systems should be able to cut back this temporary expansion in an orderly way as the situation improves. For instance, as different COVID-19 waves hit, some countries were able to expand and contract social assistance programs quickly as needed. They were able to do so using unified social registries. Likewise, health systems that had preexisting relationships, contractual arrangements, and a level of trust with the private sector were better able to tap into private sector capacities to meet surges in demand and resolve supply constraints than systems that did not have these links in place.

The empowerment of frontline facilities with fungible resources to make critical just-in-time decisions is key to fostering this ability to expand and contract quickly. Empowerment can include allowing facilities a degree of autonomy to spend resources without cumbersome approvals in public financial management (PFM) systems. In the area of health care, there is a large agenda regarding the flexibility of PFM systems,[9] involving the reallocation of resources according to unexpected needs and procurement. This agenda is important to resolve supply chain issues for crisis response (money should move quickly for products to move quickly), but also to mitigate disruptions in service delivery for routine care and enable an agile response to local-ized conditions. As an example, during the pandemic, advance payments to hospitals by the Philippines' national insurance agency and Thailand's hospital revenue accounts gave hospitals flexibility in executing their budgets to support their pandemic response.[10]

The existence of digital communication, payment, and service delivery platforms is also critical for the system's ability to expand support quickly. Having the capacity to deliver services in specific domains before a shock occurs can also help to reach vulnerable populations more effectively and rapidly when a crisis hits. For example, some countries had almost no programs to address mental health or gender-based violence before the spike in demand for these services during the COVID-19 pandemic, and they could not effectively launch new programs in the midst of a crisis. Other countries already had established programs and platforms and were able to expand their services when the pandemic hit. Similarly, some countries had previous experi-ence with distance learning systems and were able to understand their benefits and limitations better and to deploy them rapidly and efficiently as schools closed.

Systems that can expand and contract as needed should be "stress-tested" beforehand to ensure that they are prepared. In general, the objective of stress-testing before a crisis is to identify potential weaknesses or vulnerabilities in a system, so that precautionary steps can be taken to address these weaknesses in a way that ensures the system's continuity during an emergency. It is challenging to build or improve systems to deliver at scale during a crisis. The COVID-19 pandemic demonstrated the importance of having tested systems in place. The crisis showed how the existence, efficiency, and adaptability of systems can determine how well countries are able to respond to a major shock when it strikes.

Promoting interoperability, the capacity of local actors, and effective coordination across sectors

A systemwide, holistic human development response to shocks and crises recognizes that the whole (the system) is greater than the sum of its parts (a collection of programs working in isolation). A key objective for decision-makers should be establishing interconnectedness and interoperability across sectors. On the one hand, programs and policies that are designed as if they operate in a vacuum are doomed to fail, more often than not. On the other hand, systems that recognize the myriad actors and interdependencies involved and how to leverage them are more likely to have the positive impact they intend. This interoperability is even more critical in crises, when policy makers must make quick decisions involving many competing needs, often in a constrained fiscal environment.

HD systems that are agile, adaptive, and resilient during shocks and crises should connect at various levels:

- *Across human development sectors*, to develop holistic solutions. For instance, if food availability has not been constrained, cash transfers can be used to support nutrition among the poor in a crisis. Income support can be complemented with interventions that increase employability (through connections with jobs, training, and productive inclusion programs).[11] Relatedly, social assistance can be enhanced to have a broader impact on key dimensions of well-being, including health, education, food security, poverty, and inequality.

- *Across different levels of the government*, so that the link between the front lines and center is strong. In some countries, government bureaucracies are large and complex. Aligning high-level politicians with technocrats and frontline employees during a shock or a crisis is essential for systems to deliver an effective response. Each level should understand its role and have the resources, capabilities, and management to perform this role to the best of its abilities. Moreover, levels should communicate with one another and provide constant actionable feedback. Strengthening case management to refer people to the complementary services and programs they need is also key.

- *Across household needs*, so that families can make decisions that protect the human capital of all members. Households are important actors and are most often the ultimate beneficiaries of human development policies. To support a family effectively, it is important to understand its needs and the types of income support and services it is receiving. It is also important to understand family members' motivations and preferences and to predict how households will respond to the benefits or information provided to them in order to ensure that policies have their intended effect. For instance, a household could spend the additional income it receives through a program in many ways: protecting education for all the children, concentrating its spending on the older daughter or son, filling nutrition gaps, or acquiring more durable goods, among others.

This connectedness can be stimulated through cross-sectoral steering committees that include representatives from key sectors with enough power to balance political pressures. Cross-sectoral committees can coordinate joint strategies to respond to the human capital crisis and manage common databases that multiple programs can use to identify and target affected populations rapidly with a package of programs.

Shared data platforms and technology can also bolster coordination across different stakeholders and agencies and facilitate joint decision-making. In Cambodia, for instance, an online information management system set up to deliver the government's cash transfer programs shares real-time data from beneficiaries on the ground with stakeholders including the local commune administration and the Ministry of Social Affairs, Veterans, and Youth.

Systems also need to consider the specific circumstances of their beneficiaries, particularly those who might have challenges accessing the services provided. Systems that did not do so were more likely to fail to accomplish their objectives during the pandemic. For instance, when education systems deployed remote learning, many did not consider or could not do much about the lower take-up among disadvantaged groups that lacked access to reliable internet service, digital devices, or both. Around the world, about 1.3 billion children lack internet access at home.[12] In the best-case scenario, these children relied on television or radio lessons; in the worst, they had no access to remote lessons at all. The low quality and lack of interactivity of these remote lessons was also a major obstacle for children learning from home, as discussed in chapter 3.

HD system responses to a shock or crisis should work for everyone and not just for a few. By design, they should aim to benefit everyone, emphasizing that the needs of certain vulnerable groups must be prioritized. This ability to foster inclusion and a participatory spirit is a key ingredient of adaptability and resilience.

Using data and technology more effectively

Data and technology are critical to the identification and tracking of individuals both before and during a crisis and to the functioning of payment and delivery systems. They are also essential to the design and adjustment of effective policies. Investing in data collection and information systems allows countries to provide

BOX 5.5 Togo's use of technology to extend support to vulnerable populations during the COVID-19 pandemic

The government of Togo provides an outstanding example of the use of technology to extend support to vulnerable populations. The government launched the Novissi program in April 2020, just eight days after the country's president proclaimed a health emergency. Cash disbursements were almost instantaneous once someone qualified, with people receiving disbursements on their mobile money accounts in less than two minutes. Novissi used low-tech mobile technology so that customers could enroll and receive money without needing an internet connection. Individuals with basic 2G phones and no internet could register just by dialing a code on their mobile device to access a specific menu. In addition, the program improved the targeting of beneficiaries by using machine learning, satellite imaging, cell phone records, and artificial intelligence.

Using mobile technologies, unconventional data sources, and machine learning, Togo was able to distribute US$34 million in cash assistance to 25 percent of the adult population—more than 920,000 vulnerable people—while many other countries struggled to identify, register, and pay millions in need because of social distancing policies. The program was also able to incorporate gender-sensitive design elements. Women—as the primary managers of the household—received around 15 percent more money than men.

targeted support when required. Leveraging technology, countries can build cross-sectoral beneficiary registries, platforms, and payment systems that allow them to deliver cross-sectoral benefits and services. The use of digital technologies was key in the provision and delivery of services during the pandemic (see box 5.5 for an example).

During the pandemic, the use of data and technology for service delivery went from luxury to necessity. Even across countries that spent similar shares of GDP on policy responses to the pandemic, the effectiveness of these responses varied considerably (as documented in previous chapters). Thus, similar spending on human development yielded very different outcomes across countries. In some cases, these differences were driven by underlying conditions that enabled (or did not enable) the effective use of data and technology.

Identifying and tracking individuals, both before and during a crisis

Supporting people who are the most vulnerable, have the greatest needs, or are suffering the most is a priority during a crisis. It is important to have adaptive systems that can target vulnerable populations before, during, and after a shock, as needed. The ability to target and reach people who need help the most is closely interlinked with the timeliness and accuracy of available population data. Developing better databases with wider coverage and updated information is essential to better identify and target populations in need.

Leveraging data for targeting can also provide more policy options in confronting future shocks and pandemics. For instance, the government of Bangladesh, supported by a group of researchers, developed and implemented models to predict floods and affected households. Using these data and models, it may be possible to provide cash transfers *before* floods hit, which could help households to mitigate the effects of the shock as soon as flooding begins.[13]

As discussed earlier in this chapter, data-driven policies allow for quicker and more targeted responses. For instance, social protection systems that have invested in administrative systems to identify people in need of support—such

> *Data and technology can be used more effectively to (1) identify and track individuals, both before and during a crisis; (2) design effective programs; and (3) make payment and delivery systems more agile and interoperable.*

as social registries or efficient on-demand programs—can identify and enroll new beneficiaries who meet certain conditions more quickly. In Ukraine, for example, an automated application system allowed for the enrollment verification process to be completed within five minutes. Armenia and Georgia were able to leverage data from their existing fiscal systems to identify and enroll new beneficiaries swiftly. Other countries, where unemployment insurance programs were already established and thus had a governance structure, were able to expand their support rapidly to formal workers and businesses.[14]

Designing effective programs

Government policies and programs should be based on the best available evidence on what works and what does not work in different contexts—including the policies and programs that were put in place to respond to the COVID-19 pandemic. Unfortunately, the evidence was often limited or not taken into account. As discussed in this report, in many instances, this mistake was costly—and should not be repeated in the future.

Systems not only should be constructed based on evidence, but also should generate their own data and use the information to improve their functioning. Efficient evidence-based systems should recognize that evidence is dynamic, changes constantly, and needs to be updated often. Effective data generation and use are of the utmost importance.[15] The pandemic highlighted how many systems were unprepared and had to fly blind without having data (or without knowing how to use data) to guide their mitigation and recovery efforts. Data-driven systems not only should allow governments to identify who is getting what and set up what is needed, but also should allow them to foresee what a successful alternative looks like. Beyond that, efficient data-driven systems allow governments to monitor policies and change course in the short term and, at the same time, to evaluate and inform future programs in the medium and long term.

Various examples highlight the data challenges that countries faced during the COVID-19 pandemic. For instance, it was impossible for many countries to know whether students were using remote-learning systems or which groups were having difficulty accessing them. Likewise, many countries were unable to count COVID-19 cases and gauge mortality with any degree of accuracy. In contrast, some countries (such as Peru) made the data on mortality publicly available at a high level of disaggregation (at the level of the municipality). This availability, in turn, made it possible to estimate excess deaths and their distribution credibly. Most other countries, including in Latin America, did not make such data available. These examples highlight that, with regard to data and digital capabilities, it was both the best of times (as the world realized the need for data capabilities) and the worst of times (as countries found themselves without any reliable data source to inform their actions).

Improving payment and delivery systems

The pandemic pushed governments, the private sector, and civil society to develop new payment and delivery systems. In the context of HD systems, delivering packages of services using digital technologies can be particularly challenging, but critical.

So far, the pandemic has yielded some positive examples and more policy options for the future. For instance, various countries had successful experiences with digital outreach, onboarding, payments, and digital processes—such as text message–based surveys and telephone surveys—to get information back from end users. Although not all of these techniques were developed during the pandemic, they were greatly improved and played a more prominent and important role than in the past in delivering a larger set of services.

Action is needed now to be ready for future shocks and achieve greater impact.

Some human development sectors were better prepared to leverage technology in a broader way than others. For instance, in the health sector, the shock spurred collaboration and many successful innovations, such as the rapid development of vaccines. In contrast, in the field of education, technology and distance learning largely failed. In this regard, it is important to note that technology and innovation are complements to and not substitutes for in-person service delivery in human development sectors. One of the reasons why distance learning did not have the expected results is that it could not replace teachers. In the area of health care, at least in some contexts, telemedicine was not able to replace doctor visits, either.

Many innovative remedial policies were rapidly launched during the pandemic. For instance, the Democratic Republic of Congo and Togo used novel approaches such as machine learning to build cash transfer systems from scratch. These systems need to be assessed to see how well they targeted the population groups they intended to reach. Similarly, in some higher-income countries, e-prescription platforms allowed prescriptions to be filled remotely, thus maintaining continuity in treatment despite constraints in service delivery on both the supply side (such as overwhelmed health providers) and on the demand side (such as patients fearing infection through direct contact with pharmacies). However, whether these systems will remain relevant or need to be adjusted in the future remains uncertain.

Strengthening the capacity to adapt proven solutions to local conditions

Adaptive systems can tailor proven solutions to local conditions. For instance, in Nepal, local governments adapted a phone-based tutoring model that was highly effective in Botswana to teach foundational math to elementary school students.[16] Within four months of implementation, this intervention had increased foundational numeracy among students in grades 3–5 by 30 percent.[17]

Similarly, in Guanajuato, Mexico, the government developed monitoring systems capable of tracking learning outcomes before the pandemic. The continuation and adaptation of these tools as schools reopened enabled an early and rigorous measurement of learning losses.[18] To reverse these learning losses and address other pandemic-related challenges, the government worked with a broader team and an NGO to put in place a remote tutoring program. The government is also designing an early detection system for dropouts, based on artificial intelligence, and inspired by other countries' successful experiences. This system will alert headmasters when a child is likely to drop out, so that preventive measures can be put in place.

THE PATH FORWARD

The world as we have created it is a process of our thinking. It cannot be changed without changing our thinking.

—Albert Einstein, theoretical physicist and Nobel Prize winner
Quoted in Calaprice (2005)

Action is needed now to be ready for future shocks. The world will continue to contend with global crises and long-term development challenges. The latent probability of a disease outbreak worse than the 1918 flu has increased by four to five times.[19] Already, in the months following the economic rebound from the COVID-19 pandemic, sluggish supply chains have struggled to keep up with increasing demand for food and energy, leading to capacity constraints, supply bottlenecks, and rising prices. The war in Ukraine has further restricted trade, leading to major price spikes and concerns about energy and food security. One certainty is that countries will face at least one major shock, if not many more, in the near future. If governments do not start taking steps to prepare, better results are unlikely.

Human development involves multiple dimensions that build on and complement one another. Systems that recognize and exploit these connections will fare better than a set of sectoral programs that cannot make these links. Further, HD systems that can build coalitions across sectors, use data effectively, and leverage technology are more likely to be adaptable and show resilience in crises.

While comprehensive HD systems that encompass all sectors and all actors may be aspirational for some countries, the COVID-19 pandemic has shown that—as perfection can be the enemy of progress—even small steps toward a more systemic approach to human development will improve the effectiveness of future responses. In addition to the immediate policy actions that strengthen individual sectors outlined in previous chapters, countries should start thinking about these longer-term challenges and take the necessary steps to build integrated HD systems that are better able to confront future shocks. Only by constantly trying, learning, and adjusting will collections of policies and programs start to resemble an ideal HD system that can foster human capital formation during normal times and protect it during the next shock.

NOTES

1. See https://www.un.org/fr/desa/covid-19-recovery-focus-un-general-assembly-special-session.
2. Consider social protection systems as an example. These systems are designed to help vulnerable groups to cope with shocks and crises and make critical investments in their human capital. While specific services and benefits may vary, virtually all programs are implemented using a similar delivery chain. This chain involves four phases. The first phase is *providing access*, which includes outreach, intake, and registration of potential beneficiaries and an assessment of their characteristics, needs, and conditions. The second phase is *enrolling beneficiaries*, including the selection, notification, and onboarding of project beneficiaries. The third phase is *providing the intervention* to enrolled beneficiaries. The fourth phase is *managing data* on beneficiaries to ensure that their information is accurate and up-to-date and that they comply with any shared responsibilities, grievances, and appeals as well as to track reassessments or beneficiaries exiting the program(s) (Lindert et al. 2020). While these delivery chains may look slightly different in the case of health and education, most sectoral systems rely on a similar approach of identifying a target population for a service, enrolling participants or beneficiaries, delivering the intervention, and maintaining data on both beneficiaries and the effectiveness of the service.
3. See https://twitter.com/glblctznimpact/status/1364254945550102540.
4. A comprehensive stocktaking and assessment of the many ways in which governments responded to this crisis is beyond the scope of this chapter, not least because new and pertinent data on the effects of these actions are still coming to light. Nonetheless, applying the lens of agile, resilient, and adaptative HD systems to government responses is helpful in identifying the approaches that were implemented to protect people's human capital during this period in low- and middle-income countries.
5. Gentilini et al. (2022).
6. World Bank (2022).
7. UNICEF and ITU (2020). Several studies have shown limited impacts of providing free laptops on learning outcomes in the short term. This example shows that, while those investments may not have paid off in the short term, they did so in the context of this crisis—but only when they were coupled with effective training for teachers.
8. Marani et al. (2021).
9. PFM uses a web-based online software application to track funds released and report on expenditures at all levels of program implementation in real time.
10. Sachdev et al. (2022).
11. Productive inclusion programs provide an integrated package of services, such as grants and training, to promote self-employment and wage employment among the poor. See Rigolini (2016).
12. UNICEF and ITU (2020).
13. Pople et al. (2021).
14. World Bank (forthcoming).
15. World Bank (2021).
16. Angrist, Bergman, and Matsheng (2022).
17. Radhakrishnan et al. (2021).
18. Alasino et al. (forthcoming).
19. Marani et al. (2021).

REFERENCES

Abay, K., G. Berhane, J. Hoddinott, and K. Tafere. 2020. "COVID-19 and Food Security in Ethiopia: Do Social Protection Programs Protect?" Policy Research Working Paper 9475, World Bank, Washington, DC.

Alasino, E., D. Luna, M. Romero, N. Schady, and A. Yi Chang. Forthcoming. "COVID-19 School Closures and Learning Losses in Mexico." World Bank: Washington DC.

Angrist, N., P. Bergman, and M. Matsheng. 2022. "Experimental Evidence on Learning Using Low-Tech When School Is Out." *Nature Human Behaviour* 6 (7): 941–50.

Blofield, M., C. Giambruno, and J. Pribble. 2021. "Breadth and Sufficiency of Cash Transfer Responses in Ten Latin American Countries during the First 12 Months of the COVID-19 Pandemic." Commitment to Equity (CEQ) Working Paper 114, Department of Economics, Tulane University, New Orleans, LA.

Blofield, M., B. Hoffmann, and M. Llanos. 2020. "Assessing the Political and Social Impact of the COVID-19 Crisis in Latin America." GIGA Focus Lateinamerika 3, GIGA (German Institute of Global and Area Studies), Leibniz-Institut für Globale und Regionale Studien, Institut für Lateinamerika-Studien, Hamburg. https://nbn-resolving.org/urn:nbn:de:0168-ssoar-67260-7.

Blofield, M., M. Lustig, and M. Trasberg. 2021. "Social Protection during the Pandemic: Argentina, Brazil, Colombia, and Mexico." Commitment to Equity (CEQ) Working Paper 104, Department of Economics, Tulane University, New Orleans, LA.

Calaprice, A., ed. 2005. *The New Quotable Einstein.* Princeton, NJ: Princeton University Press.

CGD (Center for Global Development). 2021. "What's Next? Predicting the Frequency and Scale of Future Pandemics." Center for Global Development, Washington, DC.

Duchoslav, J., and K. Hirvonen. 2021. "Delivery of Social Protection Programs to Combat COVID-19 in Africa." In *Building Resilient African Food Systems after COVID-19*, edited by John M. Ulimwengu, Mark A. Constas, and Éliane Ubalijoro. ReSAKSS 2021 Annual Trends and Outlook Report. Kigali, Rwanda, and Washington, DC: Akademia 2063 and International Food Policy Research Institute (IFPRI).

Gallego, J., B. Hoffmann, P. Ibarrarán, M. P. Medina, C. Pecha, O. Romero, M. Stampini, D. Vargas, and D. A. Vera-Cossio. 2021. "Impactos del programa Ingreso Solidario frente a la crisis del COVID-19 en Colombia." Technical Note IDB-TN-2162, Inter-American Development Bank, Washington, DC.

Gentilini, U. 2022. *Cash Transfers in Pandemic Times: Evidence, Practices, and Implications from the Largest Scale Up in History.* Washington, DC: World Bank.

Gentilini, U., M. Almenfi, H. T. M. M. Iyengar, Y. Okamura, J. A. Downes, P. Dale, M. Weber, et al. 2022. "Social Protection and Jobs Responses to COVID-19: A Real-Time Review of Country Measures." Living Paper Version 16, February 2, 2022, World Bank, Washington, DC.

Hammad, M., P. Pławiak, K. Wang, and U. R. Acharya. 2021. "ResNet-Attention Model for Human Authentication Using ECG Signals." *Expert Systems* 38 (6): e12547.

Hawking, S., and L. Mlodinow. 2005. *A Briefer History of Time.* New York: Bantam.

Kyobe Bosa, H. 2022. "Uganda's Ebola Outbreak Is a Test of What We've Learned from Covid." Opinion Guest Essay. *New York Times*, November 3, 2022. https://www.nytimes.com/2022/11/03/opinion/uganda-ebola-trust.html.

Lindert, K., T. G. Karippacheril, I. Rodriguez Caillava, and K. Nishikawa Chavez. 2020. *Sourcebook on the Foundations of Social Protection Delivery Systems.* Washington, DC: World Bank.

Lustig, N., V. M. Pabon, F. Sanz, and S. D. Younger. 2020. "The Impact of COVID-19 Lockdowns and Expanded Social Assistance on Inequality, Poverty and Mobility in Argentina, Brazil, Colombia, and Mexico." Working Paper 558, Center for Global Development, Washington, DC.

Marani, M., G. G. Katul, W. K. Pan, and A. J. Parolari. 2021. "Intensity and Frequency of Extreme Novel Epidemics." *Proceedings of the National Academy of Sciences* 118 (35): e2105482118.

Pople, A., R. Hill, S. Dercon, and B. Brunckhorst. 2021. "Anticipatory Cash Transfers in Climate Disaster Response." CSAE Working Paper, Centre for the Study of African Economies, University of Oxford.

Radhakrishnan, K., N. Angrist, P. Bergman, C. Cullen, M. Matsheng, A. Ramakrishnan, S. Sabarwal, and U. Sharma. 2021. "Learning in the Time of COVID-19: Insights from Nepal." World Bank, Washington, DC.

Rigolini, J. 2016. "What Can Be Expected from Productive Inclusion Programs?" *IZA World of Labor 2016*: 301. doi: 10.15185/izawol.301.

Sachdev, S., S. Viriyathorn, S. Chotchoungchatchai, W. Patcharanarumol, and V. Tangcharoensathien. 2022. "Thailand's COVID-19: How Public Financial Management Facilitated Effective and Accountable Health Sector Responses." *International Journal of Health Planning and Management* 37 (4): 1894–906.

Tossou, Y. 2021. "Effect of COVID-19 on Demand for Healthcare in Togo." *Health Economics Review* 11 (1): 1–12.

UNDP (United Nations Development Programme). 2020. "Expanding Social Protection during COVID-19." UNDP, New York. https://sdgintegration.undp.org/countries/colombia.

UNICEF (United Nations Children's Fund) and ITU (International Telecommunication Union). 2020. *How Many Children and Young People Have Internet Access at Home? Estimating Digital Connectivity during the COVID-19 Pandemic*. New York: UNICEF.

WHO (World Health Organization) and World Bank. 2022. "Analysis of Pandemic Preparedness and Response (PPR) Architecture, Needs, Gaps, and Mechanisms." Prepared for the G-20 Joint Finance and Financial Health Task Force, G-20 Indonesia 2022, March 22, 2022. https://thedocs.worldbank .org/en/doc/5760109c4db174ff90a8dfa7d025644a-0290032022/original/G20-Gaps-in-PPR-Financing -Mechanisms-WHO-and-WB-pdf.pdf.

World Bank. 2021. *World Development Report 2021: Data for Better Lives*. Washington, DC: World Bank.

World Bank. 2022. "Project Appraisal Document on a Proposed Credit in the Amount of EUR 90.2 Million (US$100 Million Equivalent) to the Republic of Senegal for an Adaptive Safety Net Project." World Bank, Washington, DC. https://documents1.worldbank.org/curated/en/362331655308211699/pdf/Senegal -Adaptive-Safety-Net-Project.pdf.

World Bank. Forthcoming. *Protecting Human Capital through Shocks and Crises: Learning from the COVID-19 Response to Build Better and More Resilient Delivery Systems*. Washington, DC: World Bank.

6

HUMAN CAPITAL
RECOVERY

What Will It Take?

Alaka Holla and Joana Silva

ABSTRACT

Although economic recovery following the COVID-19 pandemic continues around the world, the long-term outlook remains uncertain because an important driver of growth—human capital accumulation—declined significantly during the pandemic. This chapter summarizes the impacts of the pandemic on young children, school-age children, and youth, as well as this report's policy recommendations for recovering losses in human capital following the pandemic and future aggregate shocks more generally. Acknowledging that countries operate under ever-shrinking fiscal space and face multiple crises that may compete for attention, this chapter proposes an approach to prioritize policy options to transform a collapse of human capital into a recovery. First, countries should focus on transition periods in the life cycle—early childhood to school age, school age to youth, and youth to adulthood—because these defining moments can create skill deficits that interfere with the entire subsequent trajectory of human capital accumulation. Second, countries should consider not just the fiscal cost of a policy but also its implementation complexity and the political commitment required. For each policy recommended in previous chapters, this chapter rates how costly each policy is in terms of required fiscal space, implementation complexity, and political commitment.

LOSSES IN HUMAN CAPITAL HAVE BEEN DEEP AND PERVASIVE

With estimates of excess mortality for 2020 and 2021 as high as 14.8 million, the COVID-19 pandemic was a global health emergency. It generated economic contractions and a global recession that pushed an additional 70 million people into extreme poverty.[1] The consequences of the pandemic, however, have not been limited to its effects on mortality, economic activity, or poverty. This report presents evidence and original research to demonstrate that the pandemic also triggered a collapse in human capital accumulation at three critical stages of the life cycle: early childhood (0–5 years), the school-age period (6–14 years), and youth (15–24 years).

The youngest children (below age 6) faced more stressful home environments during the pandemic (see chapter 2). In some countries, domestic violence increased, and the mental health of parents declined.[2] Children also benefited from fewer services, even before they were born, because institutional deliveries declined in many low-income contexts.[3] Moreover, the more limited coverage of essential childhood vaccines erased 10 years of global progress.[4] Preschool-age children in low- and middle-income countries lost, on average, more than half a year of instructional time in the first year of the pandemic.[5] Data analyzed for this report suggest that preschool attendance has still not recovered to pre-pandemic levels.

This deterioration in care and services has already translated into large declines in child development. Toddlers observed in rural Bangladesh in 2022, for example, show marked deficits in cognitive and motor skills, compared with toddlers observed in 2019.[6] These pandemic-induced setbacks were severer among children of less-educated mothers. After the pandemic, children were also more anxious and withdrawn. Preschool-age children in several countries (Brazil, Chile, Rwanda, and Uruguay) have learned 30–50 percent less than pre-pandemic cohorts.[7]

School-age children suffered considerably from school closures (see chapter 3). Overall, 1.3 billion children in low- and middle-income countries missed at least half a year of school, 960 million missed at least a full year, and 711 million missed a year and a half or more. Despite widespread efforts in remote learning, children failed to learn when not in school: on average, one month of school closures led to one month of lost learning. Children exhibited not only *forgone* learning; in some countries, learning was also *forgotten*—that is, children lost skills they had already mastered before schools closed. School closures translated into larger learning losses in countries with lower gross domestic product (GDP) per capita.

The reopening of schools can only partially stem this substantial deterioration of skills. Although student dropouts did not increase notably in upper-middle-income countries, analysis for this report shows they did in lower- and lower-middle-income countries. Declines in enrollment were similar for boys and girls, but were substantially larger for children in low-education households.

Adolescents and young adults experienced significant employment losses or difficulties finding a job (see chapter 4). Data from national accounts reveal that the pandemic led globally to a sharp reduction and an uneven recovery in employment. Although employment has recovered in high- and upper-middle-income countries, in lower-middle-income countries 40 million people who would have had a job in the absence of the pandemic did not have one at the end of 2021. In several low- and middle-income countries, there was little sign of a recovery even 18 months after the onset of the pandemic. Youth employment and wages fell sharply—during the pandemic, youth earnings contracted by 15 percent in 2020 and 12 percent in 2021 in a sample of developing countries for which data were available.

Exits from or delays in joining the labor force do not necessarily lead to labor market scarring. Youth could choose to continue their education. In countries where school enrollment increased during the pandemic, however, the increases were smaller than the corresponding declines in employment, implying that more young people were neither studying nor working than would have been the case in the absence of the pandemic. A sample of low- and middle-income countries with available data (Brazil, Ethiopia, Mexico, Pakistan, South Africa, and Vietnam) reveals that in 2021 about one-quarter of all young people were not working or studying—an increase of 3.2 million idle youth in these countries alone.

On top of these declines in education, employment, and earnings among youth, the pandemic also damaged other aspects of human capital. Some countries experienced surges in teenage pregnancy, impairments in mental health, and diminished development of key social-emotional skills and executive functions.[8]

Thus despite an economic recovery following the COVID-19 pandemic, today the long-term outlook remains uncertain because an important driver of growth—human capital accumulation—declined significantly during the pandemic.

THE PANDEMIC REVEALED SYSTEMIC WEAKNESSES IN PROVIDING INTEGRATED SOLUTIONS

The pandemic revealed systemic weaknesses relevant not just to the pandemic but also to the array of aggregate shocks facing countries today, such as conflicts, rising food prices, and climate change.

Most countries implemented separate menus of sector-specific programs in response to the pandemic. Yet these programs only partially addressed its immediate consequences (see chapter 5). Because human capital accumulates over time, it requires sustained investments along multiple dimensions across the life cycle that build on and complement one another. Countries able to integrate programs across sectors and exploit complementarities fared better in protecting human capital during the pandemic than countries that implemented a set of individual unlinked programs. For example, several countries leveraged existing school feeding programs to deliver both cash transfers and nutrition assistance directly to households during school closures. Others relied on data from civil registration and vital statistics to authenticate eligibility for food subsidies, scholarships, and other programs implemented during the pandemic. Such cross-sectoral responses often relied on prior investments that had strengthened institutions, promoted the use of data, and fostered resilient and adaptive systems.

Most countries were able to expand existing programs during the pandemic. This expansion occurred in all sectors, but especially in health and social protection. Social protection programs grew rapidly during the pandemic, reaching nearly 1.4 billion people (17 percent of the world's population) over 2020–21.[9]

Few countries, however, were able to mount truly cross-sectoral and adaptive responses to the pandemic. Although some countries expanded existing programs to provide services and support, few coordinated programs across sectors. Some countries were able to reconfigure programs substantially or create temporary programs that coordinated actions *within* a specific sector. For example, countries in Latin America introduced temporary social protection schemes to support households that would not have been included in permanent social protection schemes due to budgetary restrictions or would not have been eligible under existing social protection interventions. However, for many new programs introduced during the pandemic, operating at scale, or scaling down once urgent needs were met, proved to be challenging.

HUMAN CAPITAL LOSSES FROM THE PANDEMIC THREATEN THE PRODUCTIVITY OF MULTIPLE GENERATIONS

Although pandemic-related lockdowns have largely ended worldwide, it would be a mistake to ignore the consequences of the declines in human capital observed today among the youngest children, school-age cohorts, adolescents, and young adults. Evidence from past shocks suggests that the total ramifications of early deficits in human capital will be evident only later, when children and youth reach adulthood. The declines observed in cognitive development among toddlers today, for example, could translate into a 17 percent decline in earnings when these children enter the labor market in 20 years and a 25 percent decline when they reach prime working age. Likewise, when the cumulative nature of learning losses is taken into account, the estimated long-term cost of pandemic-related learning losses is staggeringly high: US$23,514–$31,800 in lost earnings over a typical student's lifetime, with a present value of US$21 trillion—or 17 percent of current GDP.[10] For young workers joining the workforce during economic crises, more than 10 years may be needed to recover. During this first decade after entering the labor market, the depressed earnings and employment among youth during the pandemic could translate into a 9 percent reduction in the present discounted value of earnings, with up to a 13 percent reduction among labor market entrants with lower education.[11]

The future costs of the pandemic, however, will not be limited to individuals' forgone earnings. Human capital losses today will also deepen the fiscal liabilities of governments in the future. Lost earnings translate into lower tax revenue. Setbacks in cognitive and social-emotional skills, mental health, and school progression will increase future reliance on social assistance, as well as necessitate additional public spending to address crime and poor physical and mental health.[12]

> *People under the age of 25 today—that is, those most affected by the erosion of human capital—will make up more than 90 percent of the prime-age workforce in 2050. Thus these cohorts will represent not just a lost generation but rather multiple lost generations.*

People under the age of 25 today—that is, those most affected by the erosion of human capital—will make up more than 90 percent of the prime-age workforce in 2050. Thus these cohorts will represent not just a lost generation but rather *multiple* lost generations. Moreover, their exposure to crises did not end with lockdowns. Pushing against recovery efforts are other, more recent aggregate shocks such as the war in Ukraine and high inflation. These other crises can both reduce the funding allocated to efforts to recover human capital and directly impede the accumulation of human capital.

RECOVERY AND RESILIENCE REQUIRE IMMEDIATE INVESTMENT—THEY ARE NOT AUTOMATIC

Because setbacks in human capital have been less immediately visible, and because services in health, education, and social protection have generally reached near pre-pandemic levels, it may be tempting to conclude that children, adolescents, and young adults will soon recover from any pandemic-induced losses and that systems have learned to cope with crises. However, the evidence does not support this assumption of automatic recovery and resilience. Recent findings suggest that children's skills still lag far behind where they were before the pandemic. Numerous studies from a range of disciplines find that early adversity tends to persist without explicit remediation.

Recovery of human capital losses will require substantial, sustained efforts. Figure 6.1 summarizes the priority areas of intervention for each stage of the life cycle where past evidence has demonstrated impacts commensurate with the size of pandemic-induced losses.

Young children. For infants and toddlers (ages 0–3), targeted nutritional supplementation could recover the nutritional status of the youngest children. Significant declines in cognitive, motor, and social-emotional skills could be addressed by increasing the coverage of parenting programs that seek to improve the quality of parent-child interactions through social-emotional support and early stimulation. For children ages 4–5, fully reopening preschools, where they are still closed, and expanding the coverage of pre-primary education would be a cost-effective way to ensure that children have the basic level of skills needed to start their primary education ready to learn. Because these children are far behind the skill levels of earlier cohorts, pre-primary schools will need to adjust curricula and pedagogy so that children's transition to primary school is smoother.

Adults also suffered substantial setbacks in mental health, which can interfere with the care they provide their children. Low-dose mental health counseling delivered by paraprofessionals could be scaled through existing platforms in health and social protection systems.

School-age children. Four strategies for reversing learning losses and accelerating learning gains should receive priority. First, instructional time should be increased. Second, education systems should assess students and equip teachers to match instruction to students' levels of learning. For example, a *teach-at-the-right-level* approach divides children into instructional groups for some part of the day based on learning needs instead of age or grade; dedicates more time to teaching literacy and numeracy; and regularly assesses student learning to guide teaching. Another, perhaps quicker, strategy is remedial (catch-up) education for

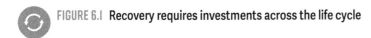

FIGURE 6.1 Recovery requires investments across the life cycle

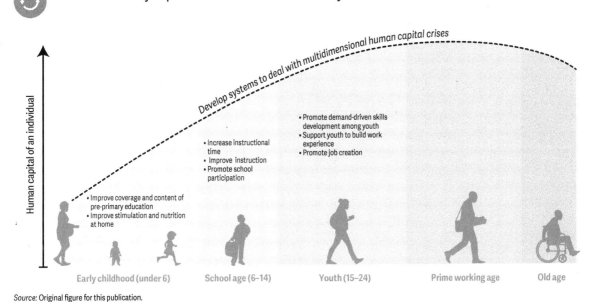

Source: Original figure for this publication.

children who have fallen behind, using programs such as within- or after-school tutoring. Third, curricula should be streamlined to focus on foundational skills. And, fourth, governments should work to create a national political commitment to learning recovery. Addressing the learning crisis should be a national priority. In doing so, transparent, up-to-date learning assessments and data disaggregated by gender and socioeconomic status are essential.

In countries where dropouts increased, governments also need to implement policies that bring children and young people back to school. They could, for example, provide financial incentives (stipends or scholarships) or nonfinancial incentives (such as school feeding) and put in place systems that track students at risk of soon dropping out. Even where dropouts did not increase immediately after lockdowns, countries should monitor students because large learning losses may reduce children's ability and willingness to stay in school as they struggle to keep up with curricula.

Youth. For countries where neither adult nor youth employment has recovered, policies should primarily be geared toward motivating firms to start hiring again. Such policies might include general countercyclical policies through accommodative fiscal and monetary policy or those that provide formal and informal firms with support. For countries where adult employment has recovered but youth employment has not, training, intermediation, entrepreneurship programs adapted for youth, and new workforce-oriented initiatives for youth that help them build work-based experience are particularly important. Adapted training and intermediation services need to develop curricula and identify opportunities that are attractive to this age group, while paying attention to the constraints that disadvantaged youth might face in accessing these programs. New workforce-oriented initiatives such as tuition incentives, paid apprenticeships, and hiring subsidies should align with the skills demanded in the job market.

For younger youth (ages 15–18) who have dropped out of school, conditional cash transfers and information campaigns can be effective in encouraging them to return, particularly for disadvantaged youth. For older youth (ages 19–24), governments should prioritize making post-secondary education relevant and engaging and partnering with service providers to offer short-term, practical credentials.

Human development (HD) systems. Multisectoral, cohesive HD systems can be more effective than isolated programs at supporting human capital formation during "normal times." But they can also protect human capital more comprehensively during crises, as discussed in chapter 5. To build agile, resilient, and adaptive HD systems, countries should invest in data collection (including household and labor force surveys) and information systems that link information from health, social protection, and education administrative systems to provide targeted support when required. Investments in the right technology would enable this kind of integration. During the pandemic, innovations in service delivery (such as remote parenting advice or telemedicine) demonstrated how digital technology can complement, and sometimes partially substitute for, services. Some countries also connected separate information systems to support more multidimensional and coordinated crisis responses. For example, Türkiye's Integrated Social Assistance Information System under the Ministry of Family and Social Services contains 25 databases (including ones from other ministries), such as a database for monitoring the education conditionalities of a conditional cash transfer program and a database of the country's universal health insurance scheme. During the pandemic, the government used the integrated information system to deploy support more efficiently.

Investments in cross-sectoral coordination are also critical, including establishing joint committees with representation from all ministries that deal with aspects of human development. Countries that had in place coordination mechanisms with a mandate for different sectors to work together were better able to implement cross-sectoral responses. Finally, countries should invest in flexible payment systems and contractual mechanisms that allow for the rapid reallocation of resources in response to evolving crises, including cross-sectoral public financial management systems and contractual relationships with the private sector to meet surges in demand.

HOW CAN COUNTRIES PRIORITIZE RECOVERY STRATEGIES WHEN FISCAL SPACE IS TIGHT?

The menu of policies to recover human capital presented in chapters 2 through 5 of this volume is long, and subsequent crises have further eroded fiscal space. Most countries are unlikely to have the budget, bandwidth, or political support to implement all interventions with documented evidence of impacts. Moreover, countries that already had low levels of human capital before the pandemic inevitably face a double burden of recovering losses and addressing long-standing barriers. In fact, in 2018—two years before the onset of COVID-19 and its associated school closures—the World Bank declared there was a global learning crisis.[13] This means that already poorly performing countries (for example, with lower skills across the life cycle, high youth unemployment, or worse mental health outcomes) need to do more than high-performing countries.

This report proposes an approach to prioritizing policy recommendations based on two criteria: (1) the critical transition periods in the life cycle; and (2) the constraints arising from a program's fiscal costs, the complexities of implementation, and the political commitment required to implement some reforms.

Policy prioritization should be based not only on the stages of the life cycle, but also on the transitions between them

Chapters 2, 3, and 4 of this report diagnosed, respectively, the pandemic-related damage and proposed recovery policies for three stages of the life cycle—early childhood, school age, and youth. However, the effect of the pandemic during the transitions *between* stages—from early childhood to school age, from school age to youth, and from youth to adulthood—is equally important (box 6.1). First, a minimum level of skill and development is typically assumed at the start of each phase, and entire processes are built around this starting assumption. For example, when a child starts primary school, the curriculum and prescribed pedagogy, as well as the training received by her teacher, assume that the child can separate easily from her caregiver at drop-off, verbally express herself and understand instructions from the teacher, and remain focused and on task for short stretches of time. If an entire cohort lacks this preparation and the primary

BOX 6.1 Transitions between stages of the life cycle are critical moments

Critical decisions tend to be made during the transition from one stage of the life cycle to the next, and typically these decisions are difficult to reverse. Before children are school age, parents decide whether to enroll them in pre-primary education or whether their formal schooling will begin in primary school. When youth reach the age at which they complete their compulsory education and pursue formal employment, they decide to either continue their education or enter the labor force.

In general, evidence suggests that children are most likely to drop out of school when they are moving across levels of education. In Brazil, for example, 39 percent of individuals ages 25–34 have completed exactly 12 years of schooling (finished upper-secondary school), while only 4 percent have completed 11 years of schooling (dropped out of school one year before high school graduation), and only 3 percent have completed 13 years of schooling (that is, completed one year of post-secondary education)—see figure B6.1.1. In other countries, similar "bunching" occurs at grades that correspond to completion of different education cycles. In Mexico, for example, 10 percent of all individuals ages 25–34 have completed six years of schooling (graduated from elementary school); 29 percent have completed nine years of schooling (graduated from lower-secondary school); and 20 percent have completed 12 years of schooling (graduated from upper-secondary school). In Brazil, Colombia,

FIGURE B6.1.1 Dropouts are much more likely to occur at the end of a schooling cycle
Share of population ages 25–34

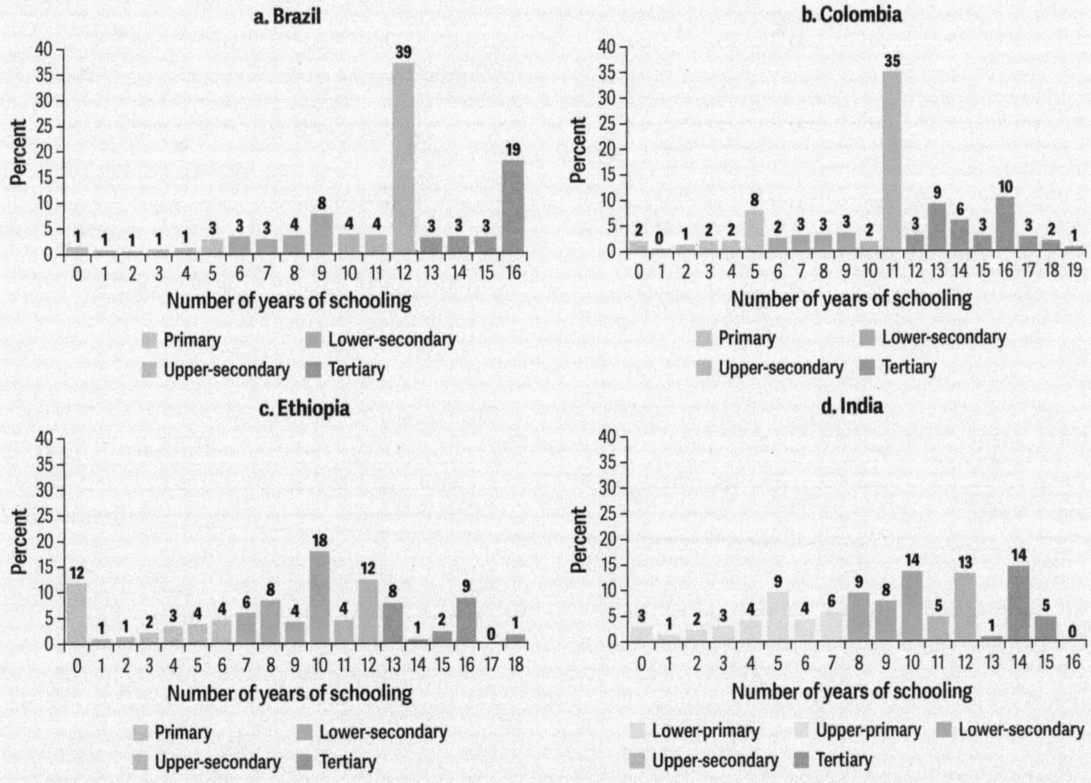

(figure continued)

(continued)

BOX 6.1 *(continued)*

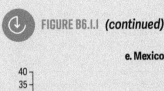

FIGURE B6.1.1 *(continued)*

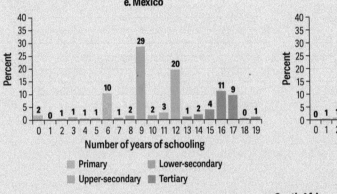

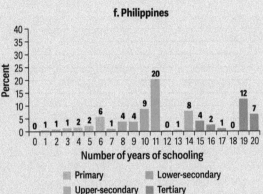

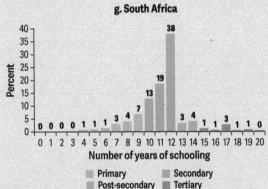

Source: Original calculations for this publication using labor force survey data, 2016–19.
Note: The bars represent the average shares of the population ages 25–34 by number of years of schooling completed. These shares are computed for each pre-pandemic cohort using data for 2016–19. In each year, the share is computed. The bars represent the average share for the 2016–19 period.

and the Philippines, this pattern of bunching at the terminal year of an education level is similarly pronounced. In South Africa, most individuals make the transition to secondary school, but very few pursue further education. In other countries, such as Ethiopia and India, dropouts do occur more often as children transition to the next education level, but they are also more evenly spread across all years of education compared with other countries.

Why does this bunching of completed years of schooling occur right before the transition to the next education cycle? One reason is inertia—once enrolled in a particular level, a large proportion of students complete all grades at that level. Another is that costs tend to be associated with transitions. In many countries, moving to the next education level involves going to a different school (which may be less convenient for many families), may require passing a particular exam, and may involve an increase in direct costs (for tuition fees, transportation, or boarding). Finally, there are what economists have described as "sheepskin effects"—nonlinearities in the returns to schooling. For example, the increase in wages resulting from completing 11 versus 10 years of schooling may be small, while the increase in wages from completing year 12 of schooling, corresponding to high school graduation,

(continued)

BOX 6.I *(continued)*

is generally large.[a] In the Philippines, for example, the increase in wages corresponding to the last grade of the secondary school cycle has been reported to be more than 10 times as large as those corresponding to any other grade in secondary school.[b] Under these circumstances, it makes a great deal of economic sense for individuals to complete an education cycle, whereas it may make less sense to move on to the next stage unless they are reasonably confident they can complete it. Conversely, dropouts are more likely to occur during transitions.

There is also evidence that children's education is particularly vulnerable to positive and negative shocks during these transitions. In a well-studied conditional cash transfer program in Mexico, for example, the largest impacts on enrollment occurred during the transition between primary and secondary school.[c] Also in Mexico, the opening of foreign-owned factories generated an influx of new export manufacturing jobs. These new employment opportunities reduced educational attainment among children who were at the age they would have been starting high school. For every 25 new jobs created, one student dropped out at grade 9 instead of finishing high school.[d]

As for effects of the pandemic, it is likely too early to tell whether dropouts are larger in transition grades. Chapter 2 presents evidence that in many countries preschool enrollment has substantially declined following the pandemic. For older school-age children, however, dropping out can occur with a lag and may not emerge until children are in a position to transition to a new level of education. As chapter 3 reports, losses in learning have been massive among school-age children. If curricula and pedagogy are not adjusted to help them recover their losses and get back on track, these children will struggle throughout the rest of their schooling and may eventually drop out earlier than they would have in the absence of the pandemic.

a. Hungerford and Solon (1987); Jaeger and Page (1996).
b. Schady (2001).
c. Behrman, Sengupta, and Todd (2005); de Janvry and Sadoulet (2006); Schultz (2004).
d. Atkin (2016).

school curriculum and pedagogy do not adjust accordingly, these children will be behind for a long time—perhaps always—and governments will earn a lower return on their investments in primary and secondary education. Thus recovering losses either just before children transition to primary school or just afterward would reduce the total potential losses that children accumulate as they progress through school. Likewise, firms' tasks and processes may be based on the expectation that workers possess a minimum level of skills. Because firms are generally not set up to train young workers in the skills they should have acquired in high school or university, any lost learning among youth would not be addressed once they exit school and would likely generate a skills mismatch that could lead to a prolonged churn of workers.

Second, when making a transition to a subsequent stage in the life cycle, children tend to pass into the purview of another sector. For example, the ministry of social development may be responsible for pre-primary education, while the ministry of education handles primary education. When youth transition into employment, they may no longer be the concern of the ministry of education but rather the ministry of labor. Without an explicit mechanism for the two sectors to coordinate (as described in chapter 5), successful transitions may not happen.

Adjustments within a life-cycle stage, on the other hand, may be easier to facilitate. For example, because grade-specific curricula tend to build on what was taught in the previous grade, it may be easier to address skill deficits by importing material from one grade to another. Moreover, children in school routinely come to a common setting, which can thus be used as a hub for providing other services—such as mental health counseling or nutritious school meals—that can address other setbacks in human capital. However, it may be more difficult to reach younger children or youth not attending school, who would need to be targeted as individuals or through services that target households.

If a complete menu of recovery policies is prohibitively expensive, countries could prioritize addressing human capital losses that occur as individuals transition—or fail to do so—from one stage to the next, as discussed in box 6.1. In other words, recovery policies should focus on children who either are about to transition or just transitioned to a subsequent stage in the life cycle.

Current and future fiscal trade-offs

A poor global economic outlook, with record-high levels of debt, rising interest rates, and a medium-term outlook of poor growth and high inflation, has implications for any proposed policy agenda and for the trade-offs facing governments today, which may still be in crisis rather than recovery mode. A large body of evidence, however, has shown that public investments in the human capital of young people eventually pay for themselves and may actually save governments money in the long term through the higher tax revenue, reductions in social assistance, and declines in criminal activity that accompany increases in individual earnings.[14] These investments also have a large impact on growth, inequality, and poverty decades later.[15]

Even though future returns may be high, the policy priorities recommended in this report vary in terms of their up-front fiscal efforts, depending on the reach of the program (such as generosity and coverage) and the investments required for implementation. Key aspects include whether policies involve working within existing programs (expansion on the intensive margin) or creation of new programs (expansion on the extensive margin); whether they require heavy investments in data and systems; and whether complementary interventions are needed for programs to be effective.

Table 6.1 presents the menu of policies proposed in this report and uses existing evidence to classify each intervention. Because relative prices differ dramatically across countries, the first column makes a relative assessment of whether the immediate fiscal outlays required for implementation would be low, medium, or high. Modifying pre-primary curricula, for example, requires very little funding, although a review of the evidence suggests the impacts could be sizable.[16] Supporting firms during and after a crisis, however, entails a substantial up-front investment.

Nonfiscal constraints

As table 6.1 shows, however, not all constraints are fiscal. For some of the proposed policies, surmounting implementation complexity and obtaining political commitment may be even harder. Table 6.1 rates the implementation complexity of each of the main policy recommendations presented in chapters 2 to 5, building on the work of Bhagavan and Virgin, as well as Domorenok, Graziano, and Polverari.[17] Complexity increases if implementation requires (1) the development of new infrastructure, policies, or platforms instead of use of existing ones; (2) specialized training and technical capacity; and (3) cross-sectoral or federal and local coordination for policy formulation and implementation. When programs are assessed with these criteria, data information systems and preparing preschool children for the transition to primary school have low fiscal costs but high institutional complexity.

Table 6.1 also rates policies based on the degree of political commitment needed for implementation, measured by whether (1) civil society lacks awareness that the reform will improve outcomes or should be a priority; (2) groups or vested interests stand to lose from implementation; and (3) the reform goes beyond the implied social contract. For example, in countries where children attend only a half-day of school, the public may not be aware of the benefits associated with increases in instructional time. Teachers and organizations advocating for teacher welfare may worry about increases in working hours. A full day of school may not be expected to be part of a minimum services package provided by the government. Similarly, hiring subsidies for youth would require a high degree of political commitment, according to these criteria.

TABLE 6.1 Policies vary in their fiscal costs, implementation complexity, and required political commitment

Policy	Fiscal costs	Implementation complexity	Political commitment
Improve coverage and content of pre-primary education			
• Reopen schools and subsidize private providers to reopen	●●	●	●●
• Scale current provision with existing facilities and nonspecialized workforce	●●	●●	●
• Insert social-emotional skills into curricula and prepare for transition to primary school	●	●	●
Improve stimulation and nutrition at home			
• Expand coverage of parenting programs	●●	●●	●
• Implement targeted nutritional supplementation	●	●	
• Expand cash transfers	●●●	●●	●●
Increase instructional time			
• Lengthen school day or school year	●●●	●●	●●●
• Limit school closures			●●●
Improve instruction			
• Assess learning	●	●●	●
• Match instruction to students' level	●●	●●●	●●
• Implement catch-up and remediation policies for students with largest learning deficits	●●●	●●	●●
• Focus on foundations and streamline the curriculum	●●	●●●	●●●
Promote school participation			
• Monitor students at risk of dropping out	●	●●	●
• Alleviate financial constraints and provide incentives for youth to attend school	●●●	●●	●●
Promote demand-driven skills development among youth			
• Training and skills certification programs adapted for youth	●●	●●	●
• Employment services adapted for youth	●	●	●
• Entrepreneurship support programs adapted for youth	●	●●	●
Support youth to build work experience			
• Paid apprenticeships and boot camps	●●	●●	●
• Hiring subsidies	●●	●●	●●●
Promote job creation			
• General countercyclical policies	●●●	●	●●●
• Support for formal and informal firms and their workforce	●●●	●●●	●●●
Develop systems to deal with multidimensional human capital crises			
• Data collection and information systems	●	●●●	●
• Cross-sectoral beneficiary registries, platforms, and payment systems	●	●●●	●●
• Cross-sectoral coordination mechanisms	●	●	●●
• Cross-sectoral public finance management systems and contracts with the private sector to meet surges in demand	●	●●●	●●

Source: Original table for this publication.
Note: Policies are rated low (one circle), medium (two circles), or high (three circles) for each category. No circles indicates that there are zero costs.

THE PATH TO RECOVERY

The COVID-19 pandemic has been an extraordinary global shock. Amplifying the shock, human capital has eroded at critical points in the life cycle. To recover these losses, governments will have to implement an ambitious policy agenda and overcome constraints imposed by fiscal space, implementation complexity, and political commitment. Moreover, to return to or exceed the pre-pandemic path, the rate of human capital accumulation will have to be higher than it was before the pandemic. Otherwise, the stock of human capital will be permanently lower, which will, in turn, lower aggregate productivity and growth.

But reversing the short-term consequences of the pandemic is only part of the battle. To break out of the constant cycle of shocks and recovery that inhibits meaningful progress, countries must also address the systemic constraints that often are at the heart of the problem. This crisis has thrown into relief long-standing weaknesses in, and sometimes a total absence of, service delivery systems and the inadequacy of their coverage and support of the most vulnerable. These lessons should be used to reimagine and build systems that are agile, resilient, and adaptive and that can protect human capital during the next inevitable crisis. The pandemic may have led to a clear collapse in human capital, but what it takes to get on the path to recovery is equally clear. Transforming the collapse into a recovery should start now.

NOTES

1. Msemburi et al. (2023); World Bank (2022).
2. Bau et al. (2022); Bullinger et al. (2021); Moya et al. (2021).
3. Ahmed et al. (2021).
4. WHO and UNICEF (2021).
5. McCoy et al. (2021).
6. Hamadani et al. (2022).
7. Abufhele et al. (2022, Chile); Bartholo et al. (2022, Brazil); González et al. (2022, Uruguay); Holla et al. (2022, Rwanda).
8. Brodeur, Grigoryeva, and Kattan (2021); Ji, Saylor, and Earle (2021); Silverio-Murillo et al. (2021); Zulaika et al. (2022).
9. Gentilini et al. (2022).
10. World Bank et al. (2022).
11. Von Wachter (2020).
12. Anders, Barr, and Smith (2023); Hendren and Sprung-Keyser (2020).
13. World Bank (2018).
14. Hendren and Sprung-Keyser (2020).
15. World Bank (2022).
16. Holla (2021).
17. Bhagavan and Virgin (2004); Domorenok, Graziano, and Polverari (2021).

REFERENCES

Abufhele, A., D. Bravo, F. López Bóo, and P. Soto-Ramirez. 2022. "Developmental Losses in Young Children from Pre-primary Program Closures during the COVID-19 Pandemic." Technical Note 2385, Inter-American Development Bank, Washington, DC.

Ahmed, T., T. Roberton, J. P. Alfred, M. L. Baye, M. Diabate, H. Kiarie, P. Mbaka, et al. 2021. "Indirect Effects on Maternal and Child Mortality from the COVID-19 Pandemic: Evidence from Disruptions in Healthcare Utilization in 18 Low- and Middle-Income Countries." Johns Hopkins Center for Humanitarian Health, Baltimore, MD.

Anders, J., A. C. Barr, and A. A. Smith. 2023. "The Effect of Early Childhood Education on Adult Criminality: Evidence from the 1960s through 1990s. *American Economic Journal: Economic Policy* 15 (1): 37–69. https://pubs.aeaweb.org/doi/pdfplus/10.1257/pol.20200660.

Atkin, D. 2016. "Endogenous Skill Acquisition and Export Manufacturing in Mexico." *American Economic Review* 106 (8): 2046–85.

Bartholo, T., M. Koslinski, P. Tymms, and D. Lopes de Castro. 2022. "Learning Loss and Learning Inequality during the Covid-19 Pandemic." https://dro.dur.ac.uk/36314/.

Bau, N., G. Khanna, C. Low, M. Shah, S. Sharmin, and A. Voena. 2022. "Women's Well-Being during a Pandemic and Its Containment." *Journal of Development Economics* 156: 102839.

Behrman, J. R., P. Sengupta, and P. Todd. 2005. "Progressing through PROGRESA: An Impact Assessment of a School Subsidy Experiment in Rural Mexico." *Economic Development and Cultural Change* 54 (1): 237–75.

Bhagavan, M. R., and I. Virgin. 2004. *Generic Aspects of Institutional Capacity Development in Developing Countries*. Stockholm: Stockholm Environment Institute.

Brodeur, A., I. Grigoryeva, and L. Kattan. 2021. "Stay-at-Home Orders, Social Distancing, and Trust." *Journal of Population Economics* 34 (4): 1321–54.

Bullinger, L. R., A. Boy, S. Messner, and S. Self-Brown. 2021. "Pediatric Emergency Department Visits due to Child Abuse and Neglect following COVID-19 Public Health Emergency Declaration in the Southeastern United States." *BMC Pediatrics* 21 (401): 1–9.

de Janvry, A., and E. Sadoulet. 2006. "Making Conditional Cash Transfer Programs More Efficient: Designing for Maximum Effect of the Conditionality." *World Bank Economic Review* 20 (1): 1–29. https://doi.org/10.1093/wber/lhj002.

Domorenok, E., P. Graziano, and L. Polverari. 2021. "Introduction: Policy Integration and Institutional Capacity: Theoretical, Conceptual and Empirical Challenges." *Policy and Society* 40 (1): 1–18.

Gentilini, U., M. Almenfi, H. T. M. M. Iyengar, Y. Okamura, J. A. Downes, P. Dale, M. Weber, et al. 2022. "Social Protection and Jobs Responses to COVID-19: A Real-Time Review of Country Measures." "Living Paper" Version 16 (February 2, 2022), World Bank, Washington, DC.

González, M., T. Loose, M. Liz, M. Pérez, J. I. Rodríguez-Vinçon, C. Tomás-Llerena, and A. Vásquez-Echeverría. 2022. "School Readiness Losses during the COVID-19 Outbreak: A Comparison of Two Cohorts of Young Children." *Child Development* 93 (4): 910–24.

Hamadani, J., M. Imrul, S. Grantham-McGregor, S. Alam, M. Tipu, D. Parra Alvarez, S. Shiraji, et al. 2022. "The Effect of the COVID-19 Pandemic on Children's Development and Nutritional Status at Age 20 Months in Rural Bangladesh." Unpublished manuscript.

Hendren, N., and B. Sprung-Keyser. 2020. "A Unified Welfare Analysis of Government Policies." *Quarterly Journal of Economics* 135 (3): 1209–1318.

Holla, A., M. Bendini, L. Dinarte, and I. Trako. 2021. "Is Investment in Preprimary Education Too Low? Lessons from (Quasi) Experimental Evidence across Countries." Policy Research Working Paper 9723, World Bank, Washington, DC.

Holla, A., L. B. Luna, M. M. Isaacs Prieto, C. Dusabe, M. Abimpaye, N. Kabarungi, and N. Schady. 2022. "The Impacts of the COVID-19 Pandemic on Skill Development in Preschool: Evidence from Rwanda." Unpublished manuscript.

Hungerford, T., and G. Solon. 1987. "Sheepskin Effects in the Returns to Education." *Review of Economics and Statistics* 69 (1): 175–77.

Jaeger, D., and M. Page. 1996. "Degrees Matter: New Evidence on Sheepskin Effects on the Returns to Education." *Review of Economics and Statistics* 78 (4): 733–40.

Ji, X., J. Saylor, and F. S. Earle. 2021. "Sufficient Sleep Attenuates COVID-19 Pandemic-Related Executive Dysfunction in Late Adolescents and Young Adults." *Sleep Medicine* 85: 21–24.

McCoy, D. C., J. Cuartas, J. Behrman, C. Cappa, J. Heymann, F. López Bóo, C. Lu, et al. 2021. "Global Estimates of the Implications of COVID-19–Related Preprimary School Closures for Children's Instructional Access, Development, Learning, and Economic Wellbeing." *Child Development* 92 (5): e883–e899.

Moya, A., P. Serneels, A. Desrosiers, V. Reyes, M. J. Torres, and A. Lieberman. 2021. "The COVID-19 Pandemic and Maternal Mental Health in a Fragile and Conflict-Affected Setting in Tumaco, Colombia: A Cohort Study." *The Lancet Global Health* 9 (8): e1068–e1076.

Msemburi, W., A. Karlinsky, V. Knutson, S. Aleshin-Ghendel, S. Chatterji, and J. Wakefield. 2023. "The WHO Estimates of Excess Mortality Associated with the COVID-19 Pandemic." *Nature* 613: 130–37.

Schady, N. 2001. "Convexity and Sheepskin Effects in the Human Capital Earnings Function: Recent Evidence for Filipino Men." *Oxford Bulletin of Economics and Statistics* 65 (2): 171–96.

Schultz, T. P. 2004. "School Subsidies for the Poor: Evaluating the Mexican Progresa Poverty Program." *Journal of Development Economics* 74 (1): 199–250.

Silverio-Murillo, A., L. Hoehn-Velasco, A. R. Tirado, and J. R. B. de la Miyar. 2021. "COVID-19 Blues: Lockdowns and Mental Health-Related Google Searches in Latin America." *Social Science and Medicine* 281: 114040.

Von Wachter, T. 2020. "The Persistent Effects of Initial Labor Market Conditions for Young Adults and Their Sources." *Journal of Economic Perspectives* 34 (4): 168–94.

WHO (World Health Organization) and UNICEF (United Nations Children's Fund). 2021. "Progress and Challenges with Sustaining and Advancing Immunization Coverage during the COVID-19 Pandemic: 2021 WHO/UNICEF Estimates of National Immunization Coverage (WUENIC)." WHO and UNICEF, Geneva and New York.

World Bank. 2018. *World Development Report 2018: Learning to Realize Education's Promise.* Washington, DC: World Bank.

World Bank. 2022. *Poverty and Shared Prosperity 2022: Correcting Course.* Washington, DC: World Bank.

World Bank, UIS (United Nations Educational, Scientific, and Cultural Organization–UNESCO Institute for Statistics), UNICEF (United Nations Children's Fund), FCDO (Foreign Commonwealth and Development Office, Government of the United Kingdom), USAID (United States Agency for International Development), Bill and Melinda Gates Foundation, and UNESCO (United Nations Educational, Scientific, and Cultural Organization). 2022. *The State of Global Learning Poverty: 2022 Update.* Washington, DC: World Bank.

Zulaika, G., M. Bulbarelli, E. Nyothach, A. van Eijk, L. Mason, E. Fwaya, D. Obor, et al. 2022. "Impact of COVID-19 Lockdowns on Adolescent Pregnancy and School Dropout among Secondary Schoolgirls in Kenya." *BMJ Global Health* 7 (1): e007666.